Sawyer
November,
2003

In Search of

ROBINSON
CRUSOE

Robinson Crusoe, shipwrecked, clings desperately to a rock.

IN SEARCH OF
ROBINSON CRUSOE

Tim Severin

BASIC
BOOKS

A Member of the Perseus Books Group

Published by Basic Books,
A Member of the Perseus Books Group.

A CIP catalog record for this book
is available from the Library of Congress.
ISBN 0-465-07698-X

Design by Janice Tapia
FIRST EDITION

02 03 04 05 / 10 9 8 7 6 5 4 3 2 1

CONTENTS

IN SEARCH OF

ROBINSON CRUSOE

Crusoe builds a bonfire as a signal to a vessel.

Chapter I

MAROON

He stands alone on the shoreline. He is such a savage sight that the six oarsmen in the approaching ship's boat take quick glances over their shoulders as they row closer. His legs and callused feet are bare, and the hairy pelts of animals cover his upper thighs and body. He has stitched the skins together into an uncouth jacket, using rawhide thongs. A clumsy, rough cap of the same material protects his head. The coarse animal hair on the pelts merges with the overflow of his long beard and his wild mat of hair so that he resembles a shaggy animal, excited and reared up on two legs.

The two officers in the boat, Captain Thomas Dover and Second Mate Robert Frye, scan the stony beach, trying to judge the best place to land, and the hairy creature waves to them urgently, pointing to a suitable spot. He then rushes forward to greet them as they splash ashore. The visitors are too astonished to speak as the apparition, choking with emotion, throws his arms around the new arrivals and hugs them. The hirsute man has not been able to tan the skins he wears. They reek as when they clothed their original owners, the wild goats of the island. The man stinks.

The *Duke*'s yawl finds him. Three weeks earlier Captain Woodes Rogers had steered his thirty-gun "private ship of war" around Cape Horn after a difficult four-month passage from Cork in Ireland, and slipped furtively into the Pacific. He and Captain Stephen Courtney of the accompanying twenty-six-gun *Duchess* then lay course for an uninhabited island nearly 400 miles off the coast of Chile. This is poachers' thinking. The remote island is well away from the usual shipping lanes and will be a temporary base where the crews, more than three hundred men packed in the two cramped, damp ships, can go ashore to stretch their legs and recuperate from their grueling voyage. Then they will launch a surprise attack on the coast of Chile.

The two captains carry licenses to justify this predatory behavior. Their "letters of marque and reprisal," written in florid legal language by government clerks in London, give them leave to harry the enemies of the king of Great Britain. In the year 1709 the King's enemies include all subjects and allies of the Spanish crown. In return the Spanish regard such raiders as pirates, and use that blunt word to describe them. They also suspect, rightly, that some of the sailors aboard the raiding vessels are ex-buccaneers who have conducted previous hit-and-run raids along the coast of what is modern-day Chile and Peru. If the Spanish authorities can catch them, the luckier ones may be exchanged for ransom, but most will spend the rest of their lives in prison or as slave labor. A few, positively identified for their crimes, will face execution.

So it is a shock when the ships' lookouts spot a light burning on the heights of the island. The two vessels first glimpse the distant outline of land at seven o'clock on the morning of 31 January. The island lies to the west of their track, and they immediately turn toward it. But the new course is upwind and neither vessel is a swift sailer. They make such slow progress that by noon the following day they are wallowing through the swell and are still some four leagues from their landfall. Aboard the *Duke* Dr. Thomas Dover impetuously asks for the pinnace to be lowered and manned so that he can be rowed ashore. His wish is granted because he is one of the English shareholders who invested the substantial sum of fourteen thousand pounds to arm and victual the two ships, and he holds the rank of "second captain." Later he will become famous for creating a patent medicine based on opium resin. Dover's Powder will be a stock item of ships' medicine chests for the next two hundred years, prescribed for colds, coughs, insomnia, rheumatism, and dysentery. But its headstrong inventor is no mariner. The distance to the island is too far to row. When darkness falls, the doctor's boat has still some way to go and the watchers aboard the ships become alarmed. It is obvious that the pinnace will have to turn back and in the darkness may miss the ships altogether. The *Duke* and *Duchess* sling lanterns in the rigging to guide home the strays and fire off muskets and a gun on the quarterdeck to help them get their bearings. The lookouts peer into the darkness for signs of the returning boat. This is when they distinctly see a point of light. They think at first that it is a lantern aboard the pinnace, but soon realize that the flare must come from a bonfire on land.

This is very ominous. It had been presumed that there was no one living on the island. A bonfire means human presence. Dr. Dover could not have lit the fire because the pinnace reappears out of the darkness at midnight, and her crew report that they failed to set foot ashore. The obvious explanation for the light is that the Spaniards have garrisoned the island. If so, the privateers risk a fiasco. The garrison could already have sent word to the mainland, warning about the arrival of foreign vessels, and the raiders would have lost the all-important element of surprise. But the Spaniards are not the first foe who spring to mind: England is at war with France, and Woodes Rogers and his officers fear that a hostile French squadron has entered the Pacific ahead of them and taken possession of the strategic island. "We are all convinced the light is on the shore, and design to make our ships ready to engage, believing them to be *French* Ships at anchor," Woodes Rogers writes in his account of the voyage published three years later.

But he also notes that his own ship and the *Duchess* have "a great many Men down with the Cold, and some with Scurvy," and as overall commander of the privateering enterprise he knows that some invalids will die if they are not gotten ashore for treatment. So he has little choice but to proceed with the original plan of landing on Juan Fernandez.

He orders the two ships to prepare to fight any enemy and slowly keeps his course, timing his approach so as to arrive in full daylight. As the sun rises on the morning of February 2, the lookouts grow more puzzled by the hour. There is no sign of human activity on shore. The steep green hills of the island seem utterly deserted.

The *Duke* edges round the island, cautiously leading the way. Her pilot, William Dampier, is an ex-buccaneer and he was here four years earlier on a similar raid. He is aware that the best place to moor the vessels is in a shallow bay on the northeast shore. When the anchorage comes into view, there is still nothing to be seen. Not a ship in the bay, no boat drawn up on the beach, not even a hut or a wisp of smoke rising from the thick vegetation which clothes the slopes that rise in a steep bowl from the small area of flat ground close to the water's edge. The place looks as though no living soul has set foot there since the beginning of time. The ships are still tacking slowly into the anchorage, making sluggish headway against the fluky and unpredictable wind that blows in sudden gusts from the high ground, when the impatient second captain, Dr. Dover, again decides to lead a reconnaissance. Dover takes the *Duke*'s yawl, six oarsmen, and the second mate, and heads off for the beach even before the ships have dropped anchor.

The man in goatskins sighted them the previous evening. Months earlier he had cut a supply of firewood and stacked it ready for use. Last night he stayed up tending the blaze so that it would serve as a beacon, unaware that the bright point of light risked scaring away his rescuers. He has also cooked some goat's meat, knowing the sea-weary crews would relish it. Now he offers to show his visitors the secret hut where he lives. It is scarcely a mile away but the undergrowth is so thick, and the path so difficult, that only Robert Frye, the second mate, accompanies the hairy islander as he pushes his way through the brushwood, protected by his goatskin jacket. Frye arrives at a modest shelter made of branches and thatched with local grass. The interior has been lined with more goatskins. The only furnishings are a sea chest, a cooking pot, and some worn bedding, together with a musket that lacks gunpowder and a makeshift knife fashioned by rubbing down an iron hoop into a blade. Significantly, there are also some navigation instruments and a basic library comprising several books of navigational tables, as well as some devotional texts, and a Bible. Nearby is a second, smaller hut which the man uses as his kitchen. He says he has been living there for four years and four months, on his own.

Aboard the *Duke,* Captain Woodes Rogers is becoming anxious to know what is keeping the yawl so long. He sends the pinnace to investigate, and the boat returns almost immediately, carrying the wild-looking stranger and a scrabbling, clattering cargo of large bright pink crayfish, which the men in the yawl have found crawling in great numbers in the shallows. Rogers hospitably offers the newcomer a drink, but he declines. He has not touched a drop of alcohol since he has been on the island, he says, and he no longer has the habit. It is difficult to understand what he is saying. He speaks slowly, dragging out his words and dividing them into halves as though he has been losing the power of speech during his long period of isolation. Curiously, the same phenomenon will later be noticed of dogs abandoned on the island. It will be claimed that they temporarily lose the ability to bark, and only regain their voices when they are returned to the company of other dogs.

The newcomer identifies himself. He is Alexander Selkirk, born in Scotland and a mariner by profession. He is now thirty- three years old and last saw a friendly face when he was twenty-nine. He has kept track of his time on the island by carving marks into a tree to record the months and days. During his four years of solitary existence he has seen several ships pass by. But they were always Spanish vessels, and he was too frightened to attract their attention for fear of what might happen to him. Usually the Spanish ships maintained their course and steered past the island, but on one occasion two ships came right into the bay, dropped anchor, and put men ashore. They caught a glimpse of him, fired shots, and chased after him. Dodging back into the bushes, he ran off and scrambled up a tree to hide. His hunters paused right underneath him while one of them urinated against the tree trunk, but they did not glance above their heads and failed to notice him. The Spaniards shot several goats for their larder, then abandoned their human chase and sailed away, confident that they were leaving the fugitive to harmless solitude.

The Scotsman also volunteers the surprising information that he is not a castaway, but had chosen to be on the island by himself, at least at the beginning. He had come ashore from the privateer galley *Cinque Ports*, where he was sailing master, after quarreling with her captain, Thomas Stradling. The galley had been in need of an overhaul after a series of mismanaged raids on the mainland, and Stradling had decided to bring his leaky vessel to the island to make repairs. Selkirk detested his captain so heartily that when the galley was ready to leave, Selkirk refused to sail with her. The vessel was still unfit for sea, in his opinion, and he would rather stay behind on the island. Clearly, Stradling was sick of his cantankerous crewman and swiftly granted his request. He set Selkirk ashore with his personal baggage, a pound of gunpowder and some shot for his musket, a small quantity of tobacco, and a little food. It will later be claimed that Selkirk suffered a change of heart at the last minute. As the ship's boat began to row away, he ran down into the water and shouted out to departing boat, begging to be taken back aboard. Stradling is alleged to have called back, mocking him and telling him that he was glad to be rid of him. Technically, therefore, Alexander Selkirk is a maroon, someone purposely left ashore on a deserted island or coast to fend for himself.

Unexpectedly, the *Duke's* pilot vouches for Selkirk. He recognizes the Scotsman as a former shipmate and says that he was the best man aboard the *Cinque Ports*. Rogers realizes that finding Selkirk is a stroke of good fortune for his own enterprise. The navigation instruments kept in the Scotsman's hut indicate that he knows how to find his way at sea, and clearly he has firsthand knowledge of the poorly charted South American coast. So Woodes Rogers loses no time in offering Selkirk a post as mate aboard the *Duke;* when the Scotsman accepts, Rogers dispatches him back to the beach to assist the shore parties.

Selkirk guides Dr. Dover and his assistants to the places where they can gather wild turnips, watercress, and native greenstuffs. These will help to cure the ships' scurvy-stricken invalids, who are brought ashore and housed in tents made of sails stretched between the trees. In the following days Selkirk also leads shore parties on goat hunting expeditions and astonishes them with his technique. After years of living on the mountainous island, he is so fit and agile that he does not shoot the goats. He simply runs after them until he overtakes them, then grabs one. The only time a goat can outpace him is when it is running downhill. He catches up with a wild goat in the space of a few minutes and comes back with the bleating animal draped across his shoulders. On one occasion he returns with two goats in his clutch. When the hunters bring a dog ashore from the *Duke* to help them, Selkirk outruns that animal too. It is a bulldog, a breed not known for its speed, and the Scotsman leaves it far behind. Selkirk explains to his visitors that he learned to catch goats by hand after he had used up the pound of gunpowder that the begrudging Captain Stradling had allowed him. In the end he became so deft that he had turned the chase into a sport. Catching a goat, he would mark the animal by slitting its ears, and let it go. He calculates that his total catch over the years is four hundred animals. The sailors soon take to calling him the Governor in amused reference to his mastery of the little island kingdom he has made his home for so long.

Only two of the scurvy victims die—a very light toll in the opinion of Woodes Rogers—and within ten days the other convalescents have recovered their health enough for the privateers to make ready to leave the island. Barrels of fresh water are taken aboard, and eighty casks of oil the sailors have boiled down from the blubber of the sea lions and seals who breed in huge colonies along the shore. The roaring and groaning of these animals fill the air for miles around, so much so that Selkirk says that noise frightened him when he first came ashore. The sailors from the *Duke* and *Duchess* must carry sticks to beat a path through the cumbersome animals as they lounge on the beach. Their blubber oil provides fuel for lamps and grease for cooking, and some of the sailors develop a taste for seal meat, though most prefer goat flesh. Three days before departure Rogers sends two boats with Selkirk and a gang of hunters to take a batch of wild goats from the western end of the island. According to Selkirk, it is home to very large numbers of the animals, though he has never been able to get there because access is too steep and rocky. On arrival, the hunters find that once again the Governor is correct. They count more than a thousand goats, but bungle the roundup. Most of the animals escape over a cliff, and the hunters bring back only nineteen for the expedition larder.

As the two ships sail for their surprise attack on the mainland coast, Woodes Rogers observes in his journal that Selkirk needs time to adapt to normal shipboard life. His feet swell up and hurt when he tries to wear shoes, and he has difficulty eating the ship's food. There was no salt on Selkirk's island—a reason why he could not cure his goatskins properly—and for a long time he finds it hard to digest the ship's rations, which are heavily salted for preservation. His diet for four years has been based on fresh goat meat, fresh vegetables, and wild plants. In the beginning he also ate many crayfish "as big as lobsters" because they were so easy to catch in the shallows. But eventually he got so tired of the taste of crayfish, whether boiled or roasted, that he could eat them only "as jellies," a seafarer's term for shipboard food that was neither solid nor salted. Fishing was also very easy, but for some reason the fish he caught gave him diarrhea, so he stopped catching them. Woodes Rogers notes also that Selkirk remains taciturn and withdrawn. But this may be the Scotsman's natural character, because his restrained manner does not detract from the performance of his duties. Selkirk has now joined a much more successful enterprise than his venture with the odious Captain Stradling. Selkirk will learn, probably with grim satisfaction, that his former commander met his just deserts after the marooning. His patched-up ship foundered on the mainland coast, and several of the crew drowned. The others, including Stradling, managed to get away from the wreck on rafts. The Spaniards captured them and threw them into prison.

Woodes Rogers, by contrast, now has a run of good luck. His force intercepts one small ship after another and robs their passengers at swordpoint. The marauders hold to ransom several coastal towns, and steadily amass a treasure in pieces of eight, gold necklaces and chains, and silver sword handles and plate. The only real disappointment is their failure to capture the larger of the two Manila Galleons bringing this year's shipment of treasure from the Philippines to Acapulco. The smaller galleon strikes her flag after a stiff sea fight, during which a bullet hits Woodes Rogers in the upper left cheek and carries away part of the jaw, so that some of his teeth drop out on deck. With one treasure ship taken, Rogers then doggedly sets off to intercept the larger, richer galleon, but she proves to be too powerful, though Rogers presses home the attack with his usual determination, lying on the deck in a pool of blood after a flying splinter strikes his heel.

Selkirk behaves admirably throughout the expedition. He leads boat crews on raids along the rivers and is appointed to command one of the prizes. By the time the *Duke* and *Duchess* eventually drop anchor in London, having sailed right round the world to get there, Selkirk's share of the prize money is calculated to be worth £800. This is a very considerable reward at a time when a shopkeeper might expect to earn £45 a year, though just how much of the £800 he actually receives is uncertain because the division of the expedition's spoils will be contested through the courts for years to come. Selkirk himself has been away for eight years, one month, and three days.

The successful return of the privateers in October 1711 causes a sensation. There are excited reports that the original investors will make more than 500 percent profit. Dr. Dover, for example, eventually collects £2,755, including "storm money" (£100) and "plunder money" (£24). Tavern gossips savor the tales of desperate battles and the whiff of gunpowder. Educated society picks over the descriptions of strange lands, their plants and animals, and the hitherto unknown customs of their natives. Edward Cooke, second captain of the *Duchess,* quickly publishes a book about his experiences on the expedition, *A Voyage to the South Sea,* and soon afterward Woodes Rogers does the same; his volume is titled *A Cruising Voyage Round the World*. Both volumes describe the bizarre episode of picking up the solitary islander dressed in his goatskins, and

Selkirk becomes a celebrity. The essayist Richard Steele will claim in issue number 26 of his magazine *The Englishman,* published on 3 December 1713, that he met and interviewed Selkirk, though this may have been a journalistic fabrication. Steele writes that even if he had not known Selkirk's story before he met him, there was something about the Scotsman's demeanor that suggests that the man had been "much separated from Company." There was a "strong but cheerful seriousness in his Look, and a certain disregard for the ordinary things about him as if he had been sunk in thought." Steele makes the point that it must have been an extraordinary experience for a mariner like Selkirk who had spent his working life in the close company of sailors crammed aboard ship, suddenly to be left to live on his own. Steele also publishes the surprising assertion that Selkirk did not want to be rescued by the *Duke* and *Duchess.* All he wanted was to help the sailors with the gift of fresh supplies and send them on their way. According to Steele, now that the Scotsman was back in normal life, he felt he was worse off than when he was on the island. Steele quotes Selkirk as saying, "I am now worth 800 Pounds, but shall never be so happy" as when I was not worth a Farthing."

Steele has his own reasons for portraying "the Governor" as a disillusioned man. Steele is promoting the theory that a man is most content when he lives a simple life. According to Steele, Selkirk managed to survive cheerfully on his island with only rudimentary food and shelter and therefore "this plain man's story is a memorable example of that he is happiest who confines his Wants to natural necessities." Steele underlines his message by claiming that when he met Selkirk in the street some time later, the process had been reversed. Selkirk had readapted to society, just as he had grown accustomed to wearing shoes again. Day-to-day contact with people had removed all trace of loneliness, and Steele scarcely recognized him.

Alexander Selkirk should now have faded into the background. He was not the only mariner to be rescued from a lonely shore and to tell of his adventures, and the remainder of his life was away from the spotlight. He went to Scotland to visit his family and stayed there for about two years, presumably living off his prize money as it was dribbled out to former crew members by the shareholder consortium. By March 1717 he moved to London, where he entered into a "marriage"—whether formal or informal is not clear—with a Scottish girl, Sophia Bruce.

So he was probably in London when advertisements began to appear in the London newspapers announcing the publication of a romantic novel. The picture on the front page of the book bears a conspicuous resemblance to Selkirk himself. The engraving is the book's only illustration and shows a rather melancholy-looking man standing on the shore of an island, gazing inland. He is dressed in a goatskin coat belted at the waist over shaggy breeches, his feet and shins are bare, and he has a heavy beard. On his head is an odd-looking conical hat. The man carries a flintlock musket on each shoulder—one more gun than Selkirk possessed—and the barrel of a pistol can just be seen, tucked into his belt. A bowl-hilted sword hangs behind him and completes his armament. Even if Selkirk himself did not recognize the resemblance, others certainly did. As far as they were concerned, Alexander Selkirk, former sailing master of the *Cinque Ports,* was the true-life model for *The Life and Strange Surprizing Adventures of Robinson Crusoe . . . etc etc Written by Himself.*

In a drawer in a second-floor office in the Old Customs House in Edinburgh lies a small cup. Six inches high, it is shaped like a burgundy glass. But it is not made of glass. The bowl is fashioned from the thin shell of a nut. It has a warm sheen, the color of café au lait, and resembles a small hollow Easter egg with its top neatly sliced off. Someone has scratched a simple chevron pattern around the outside of the bowl with the point of a knife. The stem and base of the cup are of fine rosewood, turned and polished, and were clearly added much later to create the resemblance to a wine goblet. Riveted around the upper rim of the cup is a silver band. It bears the inscription THE CUP OF ALEX. SELKIRK WHILST IN JUAN FERNANDEZ 1704–07.

"I think it is genuine," said Dr. David Caulfield, curator of antiquities for the Royal Museum of Scotland. "The cup was purchased in the nineteenth century from Alexander Selkirk's family in Fife. It was bought by a local land owner, who donated it to the Museum of the Society of Antiquaries of Scotland. From there it passed to us." The Old Customs House serves as an outbuilding for the museum, and Dr. Caulfield had promptly agreed to my request to see the Selkirk relics. According to the Royal Museum's records, the cup was sold by a "poor widow" in the village of Largo, Selkirk's native place. She was seventy-eight years old and a direct descendant in the fourth generation of Alexander Selkirk, mariner. At the time of the sale the widow claimed that the nut-cup originally possessed a silver stem and base, but these had been removed by her father. "I believe that Sir Walter Scott paid for the silver band to be added to the rim, with its inscription," continued the curator. "I will show you our other piece of Selkirk memorabilia—his sea chest."

He led me down to the ground floor and into a bleak stockroom with bare walls and row upon row of what could have been bookcases. Instead of books they held anonymous packages wrapped in dusty plastic sheeting. Packages too big to find space on the shelves had been stacked on the bare cement floor. He pulled aside a plastic sheet. It covered a substantial oblong box, two feet deep, eighteen inches wide, and three feet long. It looked like a large version of the sturdy plywood boxes British children used to take to boarding school to hold their personal possessions, except that its lid was curved instead of flat, and it was made of dark red timber, perhaps mahogany or cedar. The letters A.S., about two inches high, were lightly carved on the front lefthand corner of the battered and scuffed lid. I unfastened the metal hasp and swung up the lid. The impression of a school box was reinforced by the presence of a little side compartment, the place where schoolchildren were required to stow their pens and pencils. There was a yellowing piece of notepaper stuck on the inside of the lid. Written in ink in a sloping hand were the words "The Sea Chest which belonged to Alexander Selkirk the prototype of Robinson Crusoe."

"I think the chest could also be genuine," said the curator. "It was acquired by the same collector, at the same time, and from the same source as the drinking cup. Somewhere—though we don't have it in the museum—there is also a musket said to be the same one Selkirk used on Juan Fernandez. It has the date 1705 carved on the stock. But the gun appears to have been manufactured at a later date, and so it is probably a fake. I seem to recall that there are at least two other "Selkirk muskets" in circulation. Both are supposed to have been the gun he brought back from his island, but they have never been authenticated."

I wondered about the sea chest. It seemed too big and bulky to have been toted aboard Woodes Rogers's ship when Selkirk was rescued from his island, and then to survive the round-the-world voyage. And how had it arrived in Largo intact? If the chest belonged to Selkirk, then it probably dated from his later days in the Royal Navy. There was a line of four broad arrow marks stamped along the rear edge of the lid. They could have been government stamps, or perhaps they were old museum marks. As for the curious drinking cup, I was puzzled. It was described in the catalogues as a "coconut shell." What sort of coconut tree could have provided a nut of that size—only three and a quarter inches deep and two and a half inches in diameter. Did dwarf coconuts grow on the island where Selkirk was marooned? Or was it something he had collected at another landfall on his round-the-world voyage?

I suspected that there was much more to be learned of Selkirk's life as a maroon than the testimony provided by one or two souvenirs he brought home with him. If I visited the island where he was stranded, would I find practical details that would throw more light on what really happened to him during those four lonely years? And if I did find those extra details, how many of them, I wondered, were really echoed in the story of Robinson Crusoe?

My visit to the Royal Museum of Scotland was the essential first step in a much larger quest. I wanted to examine the truth behind our universal image of the maroon, Robinson Crusoe. My curiosity, I knew, ought to question much more than the single tale of Alexander Selkirk. There were other maroons and castaways who lived through similar adventures at much the same time, men of Selkirk's period who were also shipwrecked, abandoned, or accidentally stranded in remote locations. Several had written graphic accounts of their escapades. They had described how they struggled to survive, and how they tried to escape their predicament. Their stories were less well known than Selkirk's, but they were central to my investigation because their narratives were autobiographical and not, like Selkirk's, based on secondhand observation. Such tales were yardsticks against which to compare the imaginary world of Robinson Crusoe and, by the same measure, judge Selkirk's particular experience. Already I had resolved to visit the scenes of their adventures and see those places in the context of being a maroon or a castaway in the early eighteenth century. A goblet made from a coconut and a mysterious dark-red sea chest were only the first clues along the trail.

Daniel Defoe neither denied nor confirmed that Selkirk was the model for his hero in *The Life and Strange Surprizing Adventures of Robinson Crusoe.* Defoe was a secretive man and was busy writing a sequel to cash in on his novel's stunning success. *Robinson Crusoe* was a publishing phenomenon. Readers scrambled to buy it. A second edition appeared within two weeks, and another less than a month later in two versions from two different printers. By mid-August the authorized publisher had churned out four editions and was farming out the printing to subcontractors in order to harvest maximum sales before imitators began to issue illegal copies. The literary hyenas were quick on the scent. There were at least four bogus versions on the market at year's end, and a popular journal brazenly began to serialize the novel for its readers in seventy-seven installments, without asking the author's permission. Daniel Defoe was soon identified as that author, but he chose not to put his name to the sequel, the *Farther Adventures of Robinson Crusoe,* which he dashed off in less than four months. By then the leading character has little resemblance to Selkirk. In the second volume Robinson Crusoe pays a short return visit to his island, which is now a prosperous colony, makes several trading trips in the East Indies, and—an old man—comes home by the overland route through China and Siberia. And there was no echo at all of Selkirk in the third and final volume to appear with Robinson Crusoe in its title, as Defoe wrung the last scrap of advantage from his original publishing triumph. *Serious Reflections during the Life and Surprizing Adventures of Robinson Crusoe* was a dull book of moralizing, and it sank without trace.

But *The Life and Strange Surprizing Adventures* continued to delight its readers. They relished the practical details of how Robinson Crusoe, the sole survivor of a shipwreck, manages to build himself a house, grow crops, and live quite comfortably by a mix of inventiveness and hard work. Defoe had a genius for describing his hero's thoughts and worries, and he made Crusoe so plausible that many of his readers empathized with him in his predicament. Friday appears conveniently on the scene just when the narrative might be getting tedious, and there follows plenty of action with battles against cannibals and the arrival of a European ship in the hands of piratical mutineers whom Crusoe outwits, and thus manages his escape from the island.

The book had gone into its fifth edition when Alexander Selkirk died, at the age of forty-seven, on 13 December 1721. Ironically, his death took place while his ship was on antipirate patrol off the coast of West Africa. The best-seller's frontispiece was still the drawing of a man in goatskins, an image that was to become the icon to represent a stranded castaway. And in *Serious Reflections* the printer had included a map of Crusoe's island to show the location of the episodes which would become the stock-memory of generations of children. Here is Robinson Crusoe with Man Friday standing beside him, both dressed in goatskins. They are on the seashore, muskets on their shoulders, sternly dealing with sailors from a ship anchored in the bay. The sailors may be the mutineers who have seized the vessel, or they may be the law-abiding crew who are appealing to Crusoe for help. In the woodlands behind the two men is a glimpse of a ladder, the entry to the camouflaged stockade which Crusoe laboriously constructs as his refuge. Farther inland there is the other stockade, his "country bower," in which reclines his talking parrot, Poll. A banner issues from its mouth with the immortal (and misspelled) line "Poor Robin Cruso." Dotted around the perimeter of the island with its pleasant hills and dales are various bands of cannibals engaged in ghoulish activities—disemboweling a captive before eating him, dancing around their cooking fire with human limbs and scraps dotted behind them, and, in the top right-hand corner, fighting their battle when Crusoe attacks them.

The topography is a helpful fantasy. It is a diagram to assist the reader to follow Robinson on his exploratory walks around his desert island, carrying his gun, with a basket of provisions strapped to his back and sheltered by his great umbrella. It is an island terrain of the imagination. Yet Defoe was at pains to give the impression that the island itself really did exist and was to be found off the coast of South America, where the Atlantic Ocean meets the Caribbean Sea. The title of the first volume of Crusoe's adventures brazenly states that it was the memoir of "Robinson Crusoe of York, Mariner: Who lived Eight and Twenty Years, all alone in an uninhabited Island in the Coast of America, near the Mouth of the Great River of Oroonoque; Having been cast on Shore by Shipwreck, wherein all the Men perished but himself. With an Account of how he was at last strangely delivered by Pyrates." The text describes how the island is near enough to the mainland for Crusoe to see its mountains on the horizon, and the gulf that separates him from the continent is narrow enough for cannibals to paddle across in canoes and regularly hold human feasts on the strand. More precisely, the text states that the island lies at 9 degrees 22 minutes north latitude, and the island of Trinidad is visible to the west and northwest. The fourth edition, which appeared in early August 1719, even had a world map appearing in the front of the volume, on which "R. Crusoe's I[sland]" was placed just off the delta of the Orinoco.

There is now no such solid island near the mouth of the Orinoco. Nor was there one in Defoe's time. There are only low shoals and shifting banks laid down by silt from the river delta or heaped up by current-driven sand. Robinson Crusoe's island off the Orinoco is an invention. It is in the same category as the specious claim that the book of his "surprizing adventures" was written "by Himself."

Yet the island is not entirely a mirage, either. Like the Great Roc lifting the castaway Sindbad the Sailor from his shipwreck shore, Defoe plucks Robinson Crusoe from the Pacific island where the *Duke* found Alexander Selkirk, carries him through the air at whirlwind speed, and sets him down on an island in another ocean, far away. More precisely, he puts him 2,700 miles distant, on the opposite side of South America. This was a deliberate landing. Defoe was a good geographer. He was knowledgeable enough to write the preface for a large and authoritative maritime atlas, and he deposits Crusoe in a picturesque region which he knew would fascinate his readers—the Caribbean shore with its hurricanes and heats, its blue seas and lush jungles. Here flourish exotic plants and animals that Defoe's contemporaries, genuine travelers, were meeting for the first time—manatees they confused with mermaids, palm trees that tasted of cabbages, howler monkeys who pelted fruit at passers-by, alligators ambushing pedestrians in the forest, bushes with sap so toxic that you broke out in a rash if you walked too close. And it was an area that Defoe knew in considerable detail, though he had never been there himself. He had already spent years lobbying for the foundation of new English colonies in Central and South America and gathering information about the best possible sites to do so.

With Robinson Crusoe's unnamed island safely located in the Caribbean, Daniel Defoe could rapidly enhance his narrative with half-remembered and tantalizing snippets of geography and local color. Defoe wrote astonishingly fast. For nine years he had produced a newspaper single-handed, writing every article in it, and publishing as often as three times a week even when he was locked up in prison. Such a literary prodigy had neither the time nor the inclination for detailed research on background material for a quick novel about a luckless castaway. It is estimated that Defoe dashed off the *Strange Surprizing*

Adventures in less than six months. He scattered his story with gritty details from his memory as briskly as shaking sand to dry the wet ink on a page of parchment. And placing Crusoe on the Spanish Main, the Caribbean shore of Latin America, gave Defoe a special bonus: he could write about his favorite theme—pirates. Defoe was an avid fan of pirate lore. He read everything he could about them, their deeds, their customs, their trials and escapades. He wrote books and plays about pirates, both fictional and real, and for a long time scholars believed—though this theory is now largely discarded—that the mysterious "Captain Johnson" who wrote the main source of all pirate stories, *A General History of the Robberies and Murders of the most notorious Pyrates,* actually was Defoe.

In the end it is pirates who give Crusoe his chance to escape his island.

So where did Defoe find the idea of an imaginary Crusoe's island? The Duke's ex-buccaneer pilot, William Dampier, provides a clue. He too wrote a best-selling book about his adventures. Dampier's book has a sober map of real places in and around the Caribbean. Here are genuine islands and coastlines, instantly recognizable when compared to a modern atlas, and accurately drawn by a leading London cartographer, Herman Moll. The map of the Caribbean and Spanish Main in Dampier's book summarizes what was publicly known about Caribbean geography when Defoe was writing *The Strange Surprizing Adventures,* and Dampier's book was one of Defoe's main sources for Caribbean geography. It locates the islands whose names turn up frequently in the pirate and adventure narratives that Defoe was also reading. Here are the locations for real maroons and castaways and the rendezvous of buccaneers—Aves, the "island of birds' off Venezuela; Golden Island in the San Blas archipelago off Panama; the Moskito Shore of what is now Nicaragua and Honduras; and several islands named Tortuga because turtles came ashore to lay their eggs on so many Caribbean beaches that island after island was given the Spanish word for turtle. One of these Tortugas lies less than three days' sail from the spot where Robinson Crusoe is alleged to have spent his lonely days.

And Crusoe is not just a clone of Alexander Selkirk. Crusoe, like his island, is a composite. The "surprizing adventures" of the man in goatskin garb quickly diverge from what happened to the cranky Scots sailor. Selkirk leaves the *Cinque Ports* of his own free will to go to live on the island, but Robinson Crusoe is a castaway, the sole survivor of a shipwreck. Selkirk had only his meager supplies from Captain Stradling and nothing more, but Robinson Crusoe spends his early days shuttling on a raft between the beach and the shipwreck so he can salvage all manner of useful goods from the wreck—muskets, kegs of powder, bags of nails and spikes, hatchets, crowbars, and even a grindstone. Crusoe encounters cannibals and enlists Friday, whereas Selkirk is never visited by native peoples. Selkirk spends fifty-two months on his island; Crusoe is stranded for a nearly impossible twenty-eight years. In the end Crusoe is much more interesting and diverse than Alexander Selkirk, and more complex. To inhabit his island of magpie geography, Defoe assembles his hero from a jumble of half-remembered tales of adventures, maroonings, and shipwrecks drawn from real life. When Defoe died twelve years after writing Crusoe's story, his private library was sold at public auction. The auctioneer's bill of sale cites volume after volume of travel books. Some of them could well have provided events and details that Defoe included in his novel.

No one has been able to find any hard evidence that Defoe met Alexander Selkirk in person. If he had, Defoe would have realized at once that his hard-working, God-fearing Robinson Crusoe was a continent apart in character, as well as location, from the Scots maroon. Trawling court records, Selkirk's biographers have discovered that Selkirk's true character was appalling. He was a troublemaker, cheat, and bully. At home in Scotland he beat up his close relatives during family rows, and after his return with Woodes Rogers's expedition was embroiled in a brawl with a shipwright in Bristol. A warrant was issued for his arrest on a charge of assault. He treated his "wife," Sophia Bruce, abominably. She came from Scotland to London, presumably to marry him, but he delayed their wedding, then neglected her. Two years later, after he joined the Navy, he probably committed bigamy by marrying another woman, his landlady in Plymouth. The result was that after Selkirk's death at sea, two women showed up to claim his back pay from the Navy and what seems to have been the remnants of his booty from the South Sea—four gold rings, a silver tobacco box, "one gold head of a cane," a pair of gold candlesticks, and a silver-hilted sword. Each woman produced a will made out in her favor, and Sophia claimed that her husband must have been drunk when he married his landlady. The ex-landlady countered with the claim that Selkirk had "solemnly declared . . . that he was then a Single and unmarried person, and was very importunate" in his courtship. She won her case. Selkirk, evidently, could create his own plausible fiction.

Crusoe uses a raft to salvage supplies from the
wreck of his vessel.

Chapter II
ISLA ROBINSON CRUSOE

In 1966 the president of Chile, Eduardo Frei Montalva, signed a decree to rename the island where the *Duke* found Selkirk. It was to be called Isla Robinson Crusoe in future. Similarly rebranded was one of its neighbors, a slightly larger island one hundred miles farther out in the Pacific. It was dubbed Isla Alejandro Selkirk. No one seems to have found it strange that the new names commemorate a fictitious foreigner and a heretical, cantankerous sailor who came to Chile to plunder its citizens and sack or its towns and churches or hold them for ransom. Previously, the islands had been referred to—when anyone bothered to refer to them individually at all—as Más Afuera and Más a Tierra. This offhand description means nothing more than "Farther Out to Sea" and "Closer to Land." Collectively the two islands and some small islets had long been labeled in a more conventional way—after their discoverer, the Spanish navigator Don Juan Fernandez. Sailing southward from Peru toward Chile in November 1574, Don Juan abandoned the usual coasting route, which is a hard slog against the prevailing winds and adverse north-flowing currents. He tried a wider-than-usual loop offshore into the Pacific, and succeeded in halving the usual voyage time, a feat so astonishing that he was accused of black magic. One result was that he acquired the nickname "the Witch"; the other was that he stumbled on these far outliers of land.

The islands' new names, it was hoped, would lure tourists. Remote as the islands are, there had been sporadic tourism between the two world wars. Excursion boats would bring tourists from Valparaiso on the mainland coast to spend a few days on Más a Tierra. Sometimes they were greeted by an enterprising islander paddling out on a home-made raft and wearing a goatskin costume and with a parrot or dog as his shipmate. He would peddle some local goods or, for a few coins, take the visitors ashore to guide them around "Crusoe's Cave" and "Crusoe's Lookout." But these charades had ceased by the time the Island of Robinson Crusoe got its new tag. The publicly available access from the outside world was aboard a veteran supply ship which set out from Valparaiso about every six weeks and took three days to chug slowly across a stretch of water notorious for its fickle currents, poor visibility, and sudden gales.

The newly christened Island of Robinson Crusoe received an airstrip as a baptismal present, and light aircraft began to ferry tourists back and forth, and airlift "lobsters" to the mainland on a one-way journey to the expensive restaurants of Santiago and Valparaiso, or even Paris. The crustacean *Jasus frontalis* is actually a crayfish. It lacks the heavy front claw that is the mark of a true lobster. But the Spanish word *langosta* does not distinguish between lobster and crayfish, and no one on the island pays any heed to the distinction. What matters is that the scrabbling pink crustacean, which was food and "jellies" for Alexander Selkirk, is more lucrative than tourists and is the economic mainstay of the islands. They are no longer caught as easily as when the *Duke*'s boatmen could pluck them from the shallows with their bare hands. Now they are trapped in double-chambered square pots of maqui wood lowered into forty to two hundred feet of water on lengths of rope. Nor are the *langosta* as large. At the end of the nineteenth century, monstrous crayfish four feet in length were recorded. Today they are exceptional when they reach half that size. The crayfish season runs from October 10 to May 15, and urgent consignments leave the island by air. The rest of the catch is packed alive into cardboard cartons, sealed with parcel tape, and sent aboard the humdrum supply ship *Navarino*, which trundles across to Valparaiso. Every couple of months she arrives with as many as sixteen thousand crayfish in her hold.

Transportes Aereos Isla Robinson Crusoe also has a trap on a rope, but to catch tourists. The airline uses the obsolete Los Cerrillos airport in the south of the country's capital, Santiago. The modest terminal building has a glass door leading to the concrete apron, where the aircraft load up. Crawling past the door in front of me comes a battered van, then a taut blue rope, and finally, like a toy on a string, a sturdy, well-worn aluminum-silver aircraft. The driver of the van steps out of his cab, unhitches the tow, and parks the van. Then he returns on foot, pushes a trolley in through the door for his passengers' luggage, and finally goes back outside and climbs into the cockpit. He is the pilot. Air Robinson Crusoe is a no-frills airline and I am grateful to see their only aircraft has a pair of engines.

The flight to Robinson Crusoe Island takes three hours from Santiago, and travels straight out to sea. This is a trip with a halfway point-of-no-return. There are no alternative landing places if there is a problem. You either continue directly ahead for the island, or the plane turns round and tries to reach the coast of Chile before it is obliged to ditch in the water. It is a bleak prospect. Beneath you is a wind-flecked sea where the strong winds that baffled Don Juan Fernandez the sailor blow steadily northward, whipping up crests on the cold waters of the ocean current flowing out of the Antarctic. The ride in the little plane feels very lonely and exposed. In early November, the tourist season is only just beginning. The other passengers that day are a returning islander with a selection of groceries crammed into a rucksack, and a gray-haired and enthusiastic Chilean gentleman wearing a tweed cap. He is a retired engineer. He has traveled all over Chile but has never been to Juan Fernandez. Hardly any Chileños ever go there, he says. I note that he still calls the island by its old name and uses Juan Fernandez to mean Más a Tierra on its own, and also the entire archipelago. I also observe that the brown paper bags containing our Aerolinas Robinson Crusoe sandwiches are printed with an antique map of the island originally drawn by an English buccaneer, Bartholomew Sharpe, eighteen years before Daniel Defoe launched Robinson Crusoe on the world.

The balmy image of Defoe's island does not survive the first glimpse of Isla Robinson Crusoe. The island thrusts aggressively out of the Pacific, stark and jagged. It looks exactly what it is—the craggy ridge of a submarine mountain chain. The Juan Fernandez Dorsal is a ridge 250 miles long and 30 miles wide that is an active volcanic zone. Robinson Crusoe Island has had four million years to erode into its present saw-tooth form. Along its length are sharp crests, slashes of deep ravines, and steeply angled slopes. Many end in tremendous black precipices that fall sheer into the sea. There is scarcely an acre of flat ground. The aptly named Anvil is a great solid black stump of mountain that dominates the western end of the island. Its flat top is soaked for most of the year in mists and cloud, and would make a fit setting for Professor Challenger's Lost World. The Anvil is such a dismal and discouraging sight that no one scaled this highest point on the island for two centuries after its discovery, and the first people to reach its summit were a pair of convicts who were promised their freedom and fifty dollars if they succeeded in making the soggy climb (they did, in 1796). Seen from the air Robinson Crusoe Island offers not the slightest hint of the low, gentle, fertile island where the hero of Defoe's novel wanders over pleasant hill and glen with his dog at his heels and gathers wild fruits. From the air I could see very few beaches, all but one composed of tumbled rock and shingle. Only on the western end of the island, at the farthest point from any chance of settlement, is there a single sandy beach where Crusoe could have found the imprint of Man Friday's foot. And of course Man Friday would have had to have paddled across 400 miles of rough sea to get there.

Our pilot has been steering his way around the coast and now overflies the little town of San Juan Bautista to let the citizens know that he has arrived, then scoots off to the west. He seems intent on suicide, aiming the aircraft at a cliff face only at the last moment lifting the little plane over the cliff edge to set it neatly down on the sloping runway of packed red volcanic soil. It is like landing on an aircraft carrier.

We walk from where the plane is parked near a pile of fuel drums, and take a rutted zigzag track down the nearest cliff face to a semicircular bay. It is obviously a drowned volcanic crater. Here the municipal motor launch is waiting at anchor, sensibly clear of the heaving swell which surges up against a rickety jetty. The orange-painted launch comes to collect passengers when alerted by radio by the approaching pilot, and it is a two-hour boat ride along the coast to get back to San Juan Bautista. On the way the launch passes curtain after curtain of grim cliffs, and every sea mile confirms the impression that Isla Robinson Crusoe is at best a forbidding location. The cliffs are built of layer upon layer of compacted volcanic ash, a vast *mille-feuille* crumbling and dripping at the edges. Sometimes the tiered layers of the cliff face are as white as wood ash, more often they are alternating bands of buff or beige with occasional terra-cotta. All are peppered with dark embedded lumps of hardened lava bombs. Every so often there gleams a vertical vein of basalt running jaggedly down through the ash layers. The basalt has hardened and splintered into chunks and shards, hexagons and crosses that look like rock candy. Every sense tells you that this island is a stark and alien intrusion in the ocean. For mile after mile there is no accessible landing place. The only shore is rock-bound ledge, sheer cliff, or screes of volcanic boulders against which the swell pushes sullenly. The sea under the launch's keel has the heavy cold feel and dense green of deep water. There are millions of potential nesting ledges along the ash cliffs, yet there are almost no sea birds. Only a few gannets glide past, or a scatter of rock doves bursts from the cliffs, dashes anxiously in a circle, and hurries back to land. Human activity is restricted to the occasional brief encounter with a crayfish boat. Its design is based on that of a motorized whale boat: about twenty-five feet long, double-ended and open-decked. It is manned by one or two fishermen who stand upright, bright yellow in their high-waisted oilskins. They wave briefly to the passing launch, then turn their attention back to the chore of locating the next orange buoy, leaning over to grab the tether line, and hauling the trap to the surface for inspection. When you look back a few minutes later, the fishermen have disappeared into the folds of the ocean swell.

Eventually the launch passes the mouth of a green, open valley, bare except for a grove of eucalyptus trees and the meandering gully of a dried-up stream, rounds a final cliff headland, and arrives at Cumberland Bay, so named by the commanding officer of a Royal Navy expedition who arrived there in 1741, twenty-two years after Alexander Selkirk departed aboard Woodes Rogers's ship.

To an arriving sailor Cumberland Bay is an uneasy place. The bay is open to the north-northeast and is poorly protected from gales and heavy swells from that direction. The holding ground for anchors is treacherous. Soft mud or sand would be better than the loose rocks and stones that litter the seabed. A vessel has to go worryingly close to the rocky beach before the water is shallow enough to anchor. A sudden change of wind, an anchor dragging, an anchor cable severed by the sharp stones, and the vessel will be cast up on the boulders within minutes. But the harbor's real menace is invisible. Woodes Rogers called them "flaws." They are freak wind gusts that suddenly sweep down the steep slopes of the valley and strike an anchored vessel with shocking force, tearing out the anchor, breaking spars, and shredding sails. One buccaneer map labeled the place "Windy Bay."

Two other anchorages on Robinson Crusoe's island—Puerto Ingles and Puerto Frances—are even less secure, so Cumberland Bay is where Woodes Rogers and Captain Courtney brought the *Duke* and *Duchess* to refresh their crews, and it is where the oarsmen in the *Duke*'s yawl saw the shaggy man in goatskins beckoning them urgently from the rocky beach.

San Juan Bautista's unpaved main street runs parallel to that same beach. It is a two-minute stroll from the concrete pier, past the harbor master's office with its blue and red Chilean flag on a pole and two Dobermans chained underneath the porch. Appropriately, on the day I arrived, a giant scarlet *langosta* on wheels lay stranded on the roadway. It was the most colorful item in the place, a carnival float made from cardboard and old oil drums and abandoned after the Discovery Day parade. A handful of the houses by the central plaza have two stories and are built of wooden boards, but most of the houses on main street are little more than boxes, their walls made of plywood. Every second cabin is both shop and dwelling and offers a near-identical small selection of tinned goods brought in on the *Navarino*. The newer, smarter houses occupy the steeply rising slope behind the main street. Built in chalet style, they give San Juan Bautista an alpine air. Nine out of ten houses, whether on the street or along the beach or on the upper slopes, look out over the anchorage. It is as if, like Alexander Selkirk, the inhabitants are watching for a ship to come to rescue them.

The present islanders are comparative newcomers. The longest established family is the Charpentiers—the first of whom arrived in 1889. Two years later, when the commercial *langosta* fishery began, the total population of the island was only fifteen persons. Today the population has barely reached six hundred—virtually all of them living in San Juan Bautista, as Alexander Selkirk Island, formerly Más a Fuera, has no permanent inhabitants at all—and the population has been hovering at that level for half a century.

The notice board outside the harbor master's house confirms the predictable claustrophobia of the place. I count fifty-two individuals on a civil list announcing boat registrations. Again and again the same family names appear—Recabarren, Celedon, Gonzalez, Rivadenaria, Green, Charpentier. Some are interrelated. There is an Aldo Recabarren Green and a Teodoro Rivadeneira Recabarren. The owners of the names whom I meet are uniformly short, stocky, and cheerful. Two *langosta* boats return to the anchorage and their crews come ashore and clump past me in their sea boots. One of them cheerfully holds up a spasmodically flipping crayfish in triumph. He has every reason for his smile. The legal retention size for a *langosta* is four-and-a-half inches along the tail, and even when sold on the island such a modest catch fetches sixteen dollars. Purchasers are found in the kitchens of a half dozen tourist chalets whose names repeat the familiar refrain—the Hosteria Villa Green, Hosteria Martinez Green, Cabaña Charpentier, and by way of variety the Aldea Daniel Defoe ("Now Closed". . .). In such company the Cabaña Dafne and Rita seem positively exotic.

The record of human settlement on Juan Fernandez Island, as Isla Robinson Crusoe is still habitually called, is like a faulty newsreel winding through a worn projector. Brief, jerky sequences of activity abruptly end in intervals of black. Each scene begins with men arriving in an empty space, busily rushing here and there, then stopping as if in freeze-frame. Suddenly the screen goes dark. After some moments the film briskly starts again, the same setting is immediately recognizable, but it is once again empty until the screen is abruptly filled with more activity of arrival, different people this time, more animation, and again brought to an end by yet another break, followed by nothing but darkness.

The first stuttering attempt to make something of Juan Fernandez was seventeen years after "the Witch" discovered the islands in 1584. Captain Sebastian Garcia applied for, and was given, a grant of five hundred *cuadras* (blocks or squares) of land for development on what was to become Isla Robinson Crusoe. Garcia had been running a shipping service for the kingdom of Chile, and probably imagined that a profitable way station could be developed on the route that Don Juan Fernandez had pioneered. Garcia put a few settlers and some goats on the island. Within five years all the settlers had given up in disgust and returned to the mainland, leaving the goats behind. Three years later a similar attempt to settle sixty indigenous South Americans as colonists also failed, watched by the goats, which were now feral. For the next three hundred years the goats were witnesses to an extraordinary succession of visitors, few of whom stayed for long.

Juan Fernandez always *seemed* so attractive to these new arrivals. Twenty-nine-year-old Jakob Le Maire was disappointed "for not being able to stay longer" at what he called "so pleasing an isle." He was the first non-Spaniard to record a visit here and had arrived with the same ambition as Columbus—to find a new route to the wealth of the China and Japan. His father, Isaac, a wealthy Dutch merchant, had given him command of an expedition to explore for a more southerly course than the usual entry into the Pacific through the Strait of Magellan. Guided by the veteran pilot Willem Cornelius Schouten, the two-hundred-ton *Eendracht* succeeded in doubling the southern tip of the continent, steering past a steep rocky headland. Here, according to the official account, the sailors threw their caps in the air and shouted "We name it Cape Hoorn after our beloved village of Hoorn." Arriving off the future Robinson Crusoe Island in March 1616, Schouten did not like the look of the anchorage and wisely preferred to send small boats to see what they could find by way of provisions. His landing party came across the inevitable goats, the usual crayfish, some half-wild cows, and traces of human visitors. The latter had been left by Spanish sailors on the by-now conventional Juan Fernandez sailing track who had been stopping off to replenish with fresh water, cut firewood, catch fish, and kill seals and sea lions for oil. Le Maire's men refilled their casks with good clean water from the island's springs and made a splendid catch of fish, sailing onward very enthusiastic about the island's potential.

Le Maire's endorsement meant that the next Dutch fleet to round the Horn headed straight for the island to rest and recuperate. Once again they were wary of the anchorage, and laboriously, cautiously, felt their way in, as "it was necessary to come within half musket shot of the shore." But it was worth the effort. They found pleasant woodlands, easy watering, and the fish so eager that they were jostling for the bait before the hooks had sunk six inches below the surface. In fact, six Dutchmen— three soldiers and three gunners—asked to be left on the island when that fleet sailed onward, because they felt too ill to continue with the voyage. They were the first deliberate maroons—nearly 80 years before Selkirk expressed the same wish. What happened to the six Dutchmen is not known. They may have been picked up by the Spanish. More likely, they died on their refuge, though their skeletons were never found.

It was no surprise that Juan Fernandez was a haven beckoning any seafarer who succeeded in entering the Pacific in those early days. Whether sailing through the Strait of Magellan or around the Horn, the entry to the Pacific was a hellish ordeal. It involved weeks of handling the ship in rain or sleet and snow, heavy seas, bad visibility, adverse gales and biting cold. Sailors claimed that the stress of one trip to the Pacific was the equivalent of two round trips to the East Indies by way of the Cape of Good Hope. Le Maire's men pioneering the Horn route met "such rain, hailstorms and changeable winds that course had to be altered repeatedly and at every opportunity. In spite of it being midsummer, the cold was appalling and frequent southwesterly gales forced us to sail under reduced canvas." Huge albatrosses landed in the rigging—the largest birds the sailors had ever seen—and when the starving men tried to kill them for food, the birds reacted viciously. It was claimed that sailors fell from the rigging, their skulls shattered by the great beaks. Captains bound for the South Sea via the Horn or the strait sometimes chose not to tell their crews where they were going for fear they would not sign on for the voyage. To hide the deceit the ship owners did not load warm clothing aboard. So when the vessel did reach southern latitudes the wretched sailors were even less prepared for the freezing conditions than they could have been. Vessels calling at the coast of West Africa to take on fresh provisions before the long slog across the South Atlantic often loaded up with disease as well. By the time they reached the tip of South America the crews were decimated by illness. Some captains waited at the entrance to the Straits, hoping to pick a weather window. Unfortunately their delay often stretched into weeks, sometimes months, and the crews were reduced to living off penguins and raw shellfish. During the passage itself iron discipline was needed to stiffen the resolve of ships' crews. In 1599, the vice admiral of a Dutch squadron became perhaps the most senior maroon in history when he was accused of faint-heartedness and was sentenced to be set ashore and abandoned in a region where the natives—the Patagonians, or "Big Feet"—were rumored to be eleven feet tall, red-haired, and fond of eating human flesh. The reports were exaggerated, but the inhabitants of Tierra del Fuego did ambush landing parties and, not content with picking off stragglers, would dig up the bodies of men buried by their shipmates and shoot them full of arrows. The Dutch vice admiral was not heard from again.

The harsh facts of maritime geography were still the same when Woodes Rogers and Captain Courtney rounded Cape Horn, aware that they had scurvy onboard. The prevention and treatment of scurvy was known to many captains—Le Maire's expedition had taken on 25,000 lemons in Sierra Leone, and just 10 milligrams of vitamin C per day is enough to fend off the sickness—but scurvy was still commonplace during voyages of longer than three to four months. William Hutchinson, a writer on marine architecture, himself contracted scurvy in 1738–39 on a voyage to the East Indies and described how it felt. The symptoms began to appear after four months at sea when his shipmates "took to their hammocks below and became black in their armpits and hams, their limbs being stiff and swelled, with red specks and soon died." Hutchinson determined to fight off the effects. "I therefore kept exercising in my duty and went aloft as long as possible, until forbidden by the officers who found it troublesome to get me down with safety as I frequently lost the use of my hands and feet. . . . I then endeavored to be useful below and steered the ship till I could not climb by the notches of the fore hatchway, upon deck, which I told the Captain, who then ordered the carpenter to make a ladder that answered for the purpose for the sick, who were able to get upon deck for the benefit of exercise and pure air, as that below being tainted by so many sick. I thus struggled with the disease so that my armpits and hams grew black but did not swell, and I pined away to a weak and helpless condition, with all my teeth loose, and my upper and lower gums swelled and clotted together like jelly, and they bled to that degree that I was obliged to lie with my mouth hanging over the side of my hammock to let the blood run out, and to keep it from clotting so as to choke me."

The scurvy victims aboard the *Duke* and *Duchess* knew that the island of Juan Fernandez held out a lifeline. It was common knowledge that several species of native plants on the island were edible, and that visiting mariners had left behind small gardens planted with greenstuffs specifically to serve as antiscorbutics. This random gardening was not necessarily altruistic. The men who planted the vegetables expected to return and eat them. By the time the *Duke* and *Duchess* appeared on the scene, the island had served for nearly half a century as a forward base for buccaneers.

The buccaneers first irrupted from the Caribbean into the Pacific by walking through the jungles across the Isthmus of Panama, the narrow waist of the Americas. When they reached the Pacific beach, they relied on hiring or stealing canoes from the Indians and using them to board and capture Spanish coastal vessels, which they then converted into sea raiders. Their prizes were small vessels, often in poor repair and in need of frequent maintenance, and they were inadequate to carry food and water for large groups of men. The buccaneers had to find places where they could mend these small vessels out of reach of the Spanish forces and, if possible, lay up caches of food and materiel. The Galápagos islands in the north and Juan Fernandez in the south were both suitable as they were so far away from the mainland; Juan Fernandez was the more popular of the two because it had the better water, and the strong currents around the Galápagos made the approach there uncertain. Buccaneers came there to scrape and patch worm-infested hulls, replace worn rigging, divide up their spoils, and argue over their past mistakes or future prospects.

A particularly notorious gang of these cutthroats, under Captain Edward Davis, came annually to the island between 1684 and 1687, and when their ship finally headed for home, they left behind another company of proto-Crusoes. Nine of the buccaneers—five white sailors and four negro boys—had lost their share of the plunder through gambling, and decided that rather than return home empty-handed they would remain on the island, hoping to be picked up by the next buccaneer ship and resume their plundering. They were allocated a small boat and some cooking equipment, axes, corn seed, and enough basic provisions to set up camp. For nearly three years they got along very well. They planted and harvested the corn, caught and tamed wild goats, and cultivated and enlarged the gardens of turnips and vegetables planted by earlier visitors. Their little colony was only disturbed by the arrival of a Spanish squadron checking the island for pirates. One of the buccaneers, named Cranston, gave himself up to the Spaniards, but the rest kept up a guerrilla warfare, hiding in the bushes, ducking down into underground hideouts and evading the Spaniards until they withdrew. Their stubbornness was rewarded when in late 1690 a privateer ship, the *Welfare,* called in to the island and the captain asked them to join the crew. Coyly the residents refused to join unless they were given shares in the privateering expedition. Otherwise they would prefer to remain on the island, or so they claimed. When the *Welfare*'s captain rejected their demands, the eight came aboard rather than continue in their exile. Smugly one of them boasted that he would reform the privateer crew in much the same way that his "hermetical life" on the island had improved the morals of him and his colleagues. But, wrote one of the *Welfare*'s officers, "He found himself much mistaken, for instead of the good he proposed to do, he again learned to drink and swear." It seems that, like Alexander Selkirk, who also lost his air of lonely introspection after months in London, maroons soon reverted to their former ways once they had left their solitude.

Selkirk's ship, the *Cinque Ports*, was an ocean-going galley, a hybrid vessel designed to be both rowed and sailed. In theory a galley was ideal for the purpose of privateering in the South Sea—she could make the passage from Europe under sail and then cruise the South American coast searching for her prey. When the wind dropped, her crew could rig the long oars called sweeps and row her into river mouths or pursue prizes whose sails were hanging slack. In practice, very little rowing seems to have been done. Perhaps the crews were unwilling or too weak to pull the heavy sweeps. During calms they found it easier to chase their prey using small boats which they had towed along behind the galley or kept stowed on deck. In her "letter of marque and reprisal," the *Cinque Ports* is described as being 130 tons, with twenty guns and a crew of ninety. But William Funnell, the sailing master aboard the accompanying *St. George* as was Selkirk on the galley, states that the galley was just ninety tons, with sixteen guns and sixty-three men. In either case, the *Cinque Ports* was small and overcrowded. However, she was a new ship and, according to Selkirk himself, was "in very good Condition as to Body Mast and Sayles." His only complaint was that she "wanted Sheathing," this being the layer of planks and sometimes lead plates nailed to the outside of the hull and intended to shield it from the gnawing attack of shipworm as well as to discourage the growth of barnacles and weed. This "want of sheathing" would be a contributory factor to the galley's eventually having to limp to Juan Fernandez to find and repair leaks, and to the loss of her sailing master.

The *Cinque Ports* and the *St. George* completed their fitting out in the southern Irish port of Kinsale in the summer of 1703, and on 11 September set sail for the South Sea. Two ships with no commercial cargo and carrying at least two hundred men and thirty-two guns was clearly not on a peaceful merchant venture. In fact the plan was to intercept and rob that perennial target, the Manila Galleon. The piratical nature of the expedition was underscored by the fact that its "Purser and Agent," the chief keeper of accounts, was an ex-buccaneer who was serving a jail sentence when the expedition was being organized. The expedition had to delay its departure until he was released. He shipped out aboard the *St. George* at the insistence of the expedition's overall commander, William Dampier, a former colleague in piracy who is a principal, if not pivotal, figure in the creation of Defoe's story of Robinson Crusoe. It is a map from his book of travels, *New Voyage Round the World*, that shows the nonexistent islands off the mouth of the Orinoco, one of which Defoe seems to have selected to be "Crusoe's island."

William Dampier's portrait, painted by the artist Thomas Murray in 1697 or 1698, is now in the National Portrait Gallery in London and shows how their commanding officer must have looked to the crews of the *St. George* and *Cinque Ports*: long-nosed, with a pallid complexion, high forehead, and dark eyes, he gazes sardonically at the artist. The puffiness below his eyes gives the impression of a man suffering from a hangover, and his lower lip slightly protrudes, leaving him with a vaguely petulant and dissatisfied expression. At the time of his new expedition Dampier was the best-known navigator in the English-speaking world, and he had promised "Vast Profits and Advantages" to sponsors if they invested in the new project to launch a raid into the Pacific drawing on his own considerable experience as a buccaneer. Now fifty-one years old, he had made several voyages to the Caribbean, twice circumnavigated the globe, and served in every sea-going capacity, from foremast hand on a merchant ship to captain of a Royal Navy exploring vessel. Yet only the previous year Dampier had come home from a Royal Navy voyage of discovery to face a court-martial. The court heard how the expedition had scarcely left home waters when Dampier had a blazing row with his lieutenant, George Fisher, beat him with a cane, put him in irons, and dumped him in Brazil to be sent home as a prisoner. After hearing the evidence the judges court found Dampier "guilty of very hard and cruel usage towards Lieutenant Fisher," fined him all his pay for the expedition, and pronounced that "Captain Dampier is not a fit person to be employed as commander of any of his majesty's ships."

The strictures of a Navy court-martial carried no weight with the sponsors of the new expedition, or perhaps they thought that a hot-tempered ex-buccaneer given to thrashing his shipmates was the perfect leader for an enterprise manned by former jailbirds and adventurers. Their commander's irascible behavior on the first stage of the voyage of the *St. George* and the *Cinque Ports* reflected his reputation. Again Dampier had a heated row with his senior lieutenant, and again the quarrel ended with the subordinate's being ordered off the flagship, this time in the Cape Verde Islands, where the unfortunate officer was abruptly set ashore at midnight with his sea chests and his servant, and the ship sailed next morning without him. His replacement lasted only as far as the coast of Brazil. A violent quarrel with Dampier ended when the new first lieutenant stormed ashore, accompanied by eight disgruntled sailors from the *St. George*. A change of officers aboard the accompanying *Cinque Ports* was to prove just as disruptive. Her original captain, Charles Pickering, died during the Brazilian stopover and was replaced by the twenty-one year old first officer, Thomas Stradling. He was a "gentleman mariner" who kept a monkey as a shipboard pet. This was the man whom Selkirk, with his working-class origins and fractious nature, would soon come to detest, and he was not alone. By the time the *Cinque Ports* dropped anchor at Juan Fernandez, the entire crew of forty-two men was at loggerheads with Stradling and walked off the galley, leaving only the captain aboard with his monkey.

Dampier arrived at the island two days later with the *St. George* and with his reputation as a skilled navigator badly dented. He had been to Juan Fernandez on two previous occasions in the company of buccaneers, yet according to Funnell, the famous navigator failed to recognize the island when it came in sight from the masthead. He mistook it for another island and wasted a couple of days sailing in the wrong direction, looking for the real Juan Fernandez. Realizing his error, Dampier eventually doubled back, only to compound his mistake by putting in at the treacherous anchorage at Puerto Ingles. No explanation is given for this erratic conduct, but Funnell, who had come to dislike his captain and was making notes for a very caustic description of the expedition, leaves no doubt that in his opinion William Dampier was overfond of strong drink. Eventually the *St. George* shifted to the safer anchorage at Cumberland Bay, and Dampier cajoled Stradling's men into ending their strike. Funnell does not say how this was achieved, but according to his biographer, Dampier's "highest idea of discipline was calling his subordinate officers 'rogues, rascals, or sons of bitches.'"

The element of farce continued. It was customary after the long and arduous passage around the Horn to unload the battered ships, put as much as possible of the gear and cargo ashore on the beach at Cumberland Bay, clean and disinfect the hulls, make good any damaged spars and rigging, and generally put the vessels in good order. The men of St. George and Cinque Ports were half way through this routine when their lookouts spotted a strange sail on the horizon. A hectic scramble followed as the men rushed to get back aboard. There was wild speculation whether the strange sail could be a Spanish warship that must be intercepted or a passing merchantman to be plundered. Either way, the distant vessel should be no match for the two well-armed English vessels. The embarkation became a burlesque. In their haste to make sail, Dampier and his people left behind five men "who were gone to the west part of the island and knew nothing of our going out against the Enemy." They also abandoned a miscellany of various anchors, ropes, water casks, and "a Tun of Sea-Lions Oyl" with other stores scattered on the beach. The St. George slipped her cable, leaving one of her small boats, the long boat, attached to the anchor rope as a marker. But her second boat, the launch, was taken along in tow. During the chase this craft was towed under and had to be cut loose and was lost. The Cinque Ports also hoisted sail in such a hurry that Stradling's men omitted to retrieve a small boat which was tied up behind the galley. By the time the ship was under way, it was either impossible to pull this tender against the flow of water, or it had been forgotten in the pandemonium. The ship hurried on until the strain on the tow rope increased and it broke. The tender drifted free with its occupants—a sailor and a dog. Neither Stradling nor Selkirk his sailing master gave the order to turn back to pick them up.

By 11 P.M. the privateers had caught up with their quarry, only to discover that they had set upon a prickly opponent. The strange vessel was a well-armed French merchantmen, the four-hundred-ton St. Joseph with thirty-six guns, and—though the privateers did not know it at the time— she was one of a three-ship squadron in the area. In daylight the following morning the two privateers closed in for the attack in characteristically bungling fashion. The *St. George* sailed into the way of the *Cinque Ports,* impeding her line of fire. The French captain noted that "the smallest of the two [privateers] fired but eight or ten guns at him and then fell astern, and did not come up again during the fight, as he believed, for want of wind." This was the *Cinque Ports,* the galley supposed to be ideal for these calm conditions, and Stradling's faint-hearted action cannot have endeared him to Selkirk and the rest of his crew.

Meanwhile the *St. George* managed to close with the enemy and began to exchange cannon fire. The two ships, reported the French captain, then "fought. . . broadside and broadside for more than six hours" and his own crew took heavy casualties, with many killed and at least thirty-two men badly wounded. Nine men aboard the *St. George* lost their lives. Then, just when it seemed that the Frenchman was about to surrender, Dampier abruptly ordered the attack to be broken off. Dampier later made the excuse that his crew was still weak from their ocean voyage and many of them had fled below decks in fright. Funnell, by contrast, said that it was Dampier who was the coward, and his crew had urged him to finish off the fight. John Welbe, another of Dampier's crew, agreed with Funnell's assessment. Dampier spent most of the action cowering "upon the Quarter-Deck behind a good Barricado which he had order'd to be made of Beds, Rugs, Pillows, Blankets etc." In this spirit of mutual acrimony the two ships turned back to Juan Fernandez.

Luckily for the drifting sailor and the dog, the remaining two ships of the French squadron had now arrived off Juan Fernandez, seen the loose ship's boat, and rescued the castaways. They then proceeded to Cumberland Bay, where they found the ships' stores abandoned by the English expedition and helped themselves. They also seized three of the five men who had been marooned, though the other two managed to run away and hide. So when Dampier and Stradling returned to the island, they found the French in occupation. The *Cinque Ports* crept in under oars to investigate and was met with gunfire and hastily retreated. Dampier decided that the Frenchmen would be difficult to dislodge, and regretting the loss of the ships' stores, sailed off to begin his campaign on the mainland. He had added two more men to the growing list of maroons abandoned willy-nilly on Juan Fernandez.

The French ships had long since left Cumberland Bay when the *Cinque Ports* eventually limped back to Juan Fernandez for repairs. Now the galley was cruising on her own. In the intervening six months Dampier had succeeded in alienating most of his officers; Stradling had parted company with the expedition commander; and Selkirk's dislike of his young captain had deepened. The main reason for his hostility was the one that bedeviled so many piratical enterprises: the division of booty. The *Cinque Ports* had captured a Spanish vessel, *Ascension,* and Selkirk felt he had not received his fair share of the plunder. He was already thinking of leaving the ship. Arriving back at the island, the *Cinque Ports* found the two men who had managed to escape the French. The refugees were fit and well, and their experiences on the island must have influenced Selkirk's decision to stay on. If the two men had managed to survive for half a year, then so could he. Of one thing Selkirk could be certain—when he told his captain that he intended to stay behind on the island while the *Cinque Ports* sailed away to continue her privateering cruise, Stradling would raise no objection. Selkirk would be just another in a succession of men left behind.

The items that Selkirk took ashore suggest that he left with his commander's tacit agreement, if not encouragement. "He had with him his clothes and bedding," wrote Woodes Rogers, "with a firelock, some powder, bullets, and tobacco, a hatchet, a knife, a kettle, a Bible, some practical pieces, and his mathematical instrument and books." The cooking pot and hatchet and gunpowder would have come from ship's stores with Stradling's permission, and possibly the firelock as well. In *The Englishman,* Richard Steele adds that Selkirk also took "a Sea Chest"—and thus lends some support to the idea that the sea chest now stored in the Royal Museum of Scotland is Selkirk's. Also, according to Steele, Selkirk had "a large quantity of Bullets" but only a pound of gunpowder, so Stradling was being parsimonious or Selkirk was not intending to do much hunting or, perhaps most likely, the galley was running low on this essential privateering materiel. Selkirk actually had more tobacco, "a few pounds," than gunpowder.

The remainder of his kit was his personal property—his clothes and bedding, a flint and steel, his knife, and his "mathematical instruments." These last would have included some sort of angle-measuring instrument, most likely the device known as a navigator's backstaff, which Selkirk normally used for measuring the altitude of the sun, moon, and stars. As sailing master he would then establish a ship's latitude position by collating the results against the columns of figures in what Steele called his "Pieces that concerned Navigation," i.e., his books of navigation tables. These Selkirk also took off the galley with him, possibly also a sand glass for measuring the pace at which a logline ran out from the stern of a vessel and thus calculating the vessel's speed, and a "perspective glass," or telescope. Together they were the tools of Selkirk's trade and, with the exception of the telescope, were useless to him while he was on the island. But they would make him a very welcome recruit to any vessel that happened to call at Juan Fernandez. Few captains would miss the chance to take on board a navigator who came so ready equipped. By every indication Selkirk was expecting to stay on the island for only a short time. He may even have anticipated that he would be able to leave before his gunpowder or his tobacco ran out. He cannot have anticipated that his sojourn would drag on for four years and four months.

In a final gesture of meanness, Stradling, according to Steele, gave Selkirk only enough food to last just two meals. After that he would have to forage.

The ease of catching fish at Juan Fernandez had been renowned since the time of Le Maire's visit. Shoals of mackerel, cod, rock salmon, tuna, and vidriola feed in the rich waters off the island, particularly the northeast corner, and the Dutch had taken two tons of fish in a single day. Yet there is no mention that Selkirk took with him a net or any hooks and lines. Perhaps he planned to spear fish in the shallows or expected to live off shellfish collected along the shore. This required no equipment. But Selkirk soon found that he was relying so much on catching and cooking the ever-present crayfish that he grew sick of the taste. Steele maintains that the Scotsman "found great quantities of Turtles, whose flesh is extremely delicious, and of which he ate very plentifully on his first Arrival, till it grew disagreeable to his Stomach, except in Jellies." Steele was wrong. Turtles are not found on Juan Fernandez, and Steele was confusing turtles with the *langostas*. It was a natural mistake, as we shall see, because turtles were the customary food of castaways and maroons.

Expecting a short stay, Selkirk made little attempt to order his daily life or plan for the future. He ate casually, only when he was hungry, and he stayed up late into the nights tending a fire to keep it burning brightly. He discovered that the wood of the "pimento trees," *Myrceugenia fernandeziana,* a shrub of the myrtle family, burns with a radiant steady flame. It served him "both for firing and candle, and refreshed him with its fragrant smell." Woodes Rogers also claimed that Selkirk ignited his fire by rubbing two pimento sticks together. This seems unlikely, as the firelock on his musket would have served the same purpose, even if he did not have the flint and steel that Steele lists as part of his equipment. A man who does not go hunting nor builds a permanent shelter, but walks the beach to gather "lobsters" and sits through the night tending a bright fire is a man who does not expect to stay long. For those first few weeks Selkirk was biding time, keeping a beacon alight, and expecting to be picked up soon by the next passing ship.

Gradually, as no ship appeared, he began to grow despondent. The weeks of solitude lengthened into months, and still no pickup came. It was at this stage that Selkirk became deeply depressed and morbid, oppressed by a growing sense of loneliness. "The Necessities of Hunger and Thirst were his greatest Diversions from the Reflection on his lonely Condition," wrote Steele. "When these Appetites were satisfied, the Desire of Society became as strong a Call upon him. . . . He grew dejected, languid, and melancholy, scarcely able to refrain from doing himself Violence." Woodes Rogers adds that Selkirk "had much ado to bear up against melancholy and the terror of being left alone in such a desolate place" and it took him eight months to come to terms with his predicament. According to Steele it was even longer, eighteen months, before Selkirk regained his mental equilibrium, and his gloom was enhanced by "Monsters of the Deep which frequently lay on the Shore [and] added to the Terrors of his Solitude; the dreadful Howlings and Voices seemed too terrible for human Ears."

These fanciful "Monsters of the Deep" were the enormous herds of fur seals and elephant seals that congregated at the island. There were so many of these animals—at least three million fur seals, according to a calculation for 1793—that it was difficult to find enough space between their recumbent bodies to walk along the shore. "They lay about in Flocks like Sheep, the Young-ones bleating like Lambs" was how Edward Cooke put it. "Some of the Sea Lions [more probably bull fur seals] are as big as our English Oxen and roar like Lions. . . . Both the Seels [*sic*] and Lions are so thick on the shore that we are forced to drive them away before we could land, being so numerous that it is scarcely credible to those who have not seen them." The never-ending roaring, moaning, and grumbling of these animals was Selkirk's torment, not any fear of physical harm. Buccaneers and privateersmen were long since used to the animals, and for amusement had developed a particularly cruel sport. Forming a circle around a cumbersome elephant seal, they would "prick" the beast with half-pikes and then jump back as the animal tried to retaliate or lumber away. The coup de grace was a pistol ball fired down the animal's throat at close range.

It was a sign of Selkirk's return to normalcy when he began to crop the herds of seals for food. As soon as he was "unruffled in himself," says Steele, "he killed them with the greatest ease imaginable. . . . For observing that though their Jaws and Tails were so terrible, yet the animals being mighty slow in working themselves round, he had nothing to do but place himself exactly opposite to their Middle and as close to them as possible, and he despatched them with his hatchet at will." A lusty fur seal, observed Cooke with a butcher's eye, "cut near a foot in the fat."

The wildlife of the island posed no threat to Selkirk. "He saw no venomous or savage creatures on the island," Woodes Rogers notes, "nor any other sort of beasts but goats." The most noxious creatures were hordes of rats, which had hitch-hiked there aboard visiting ships. They were genuine pests, fearless and hungry, and they bit Selkirk's feet as he slept and they chewed on his goatskin clothes. In defense he befriended a number of the wild cats which lived on the island. They were also refugees from visiting ships, and, wrote Funnell, "of the finest colour I ever saw." There were so many of these cats that Selkirk began by treating them as just as much of a nuisance as the rats. But when the rat infestation became unbearable, he began to attract the cats with tidbits of goat flesh until they took up residence in and around his huts and soon disposed of the rat problem. "He fed and tamed numbers of young Kitlings who lay about his bed, and preserved him from his Enemy," observed Steele. "Hundreds [of cats] would lie about him," according to Woodes Rogers, who also created the celebrated conceit that Selkirk taught the cats and tame young goats to dance with him as a diversion, though it was probably nothing more than the Scotsman singing and dancing to himself while his tame menagerie looked on.

Oddly, Selkirk found no dogs on the island to domesticate as his companions. Dogs as well as cats could have come ashore as escapees or survivors, but none had survived. Dogs were often carried aboard ships which called at the island. There was a dog in the small boat that broke adrift from the stern of the *Cinque Ports,* and the *Duke* arrived with a bulldog aboard, which Woodes Rogers sent ashore to help the men hunt goats. More surprising, no dogs remained of the fierce mastiffs that it had been Spanish policy to release on the island. The most recent release had been just fifteen years earlier, when Admiral Antonio de Vea of the Spanish navy's Southern Fleet, the Flota del Sur, had made a sweep of the area. The theory was that the marooned dogs would attack the goats as food and exterminate them. This in turn would deny the buccaneers and pirates an important source of rations. But the theory did not work. The mastiffs died, and the goats survived. Prior to Selkirk's visit, nearly every buccaneer who came to the island reported finding an abundance of goats, and there are no reports of wild dogs, though Funnell had heard rumors that the Spaniards had deliberately released dogs with rabies.

Technically, the climate of Juan Fernandez is Mediterranean. But Selkirk must often have been reminded of his native Scotland. The island weather is damp, windy, and fickle. The overpowering influence is the surrounding ocean. Its weather system brings over 40 inches of rain each year, and although the average temperature is a mild 15° Fahrenheit, the daily conditions veer abruptly from warm sunshine to gusts of cold wind and rain showers. Selkirk came ashore to the best of the weather, in October, when the summer dry season is beginning. But there are still showers and damp, muggy days, and he was in a place where the sun shines for less than 40 percent of the daylight hours and the relative humidity is high. In this environment it is difficult to keep anything properly dry without decent shelter. Yet Selkirk constructed only a rudimentary lodging: two huts made of pimento branches, covered with grass and lined with goatskins. Once again, he did the minimum, only enough to tide him over until he could leave.

His chief fear was illness. He was haunted by the anxiety that before he was picked up by a ship he would fall sick or be injured so badly in an accident that he could not forage for himself. The result would be slow starvation. He needed to keep food in reserve for such an emergency, but lacked salt to preserve his staple diet of goat's meat. He could have smoked the flesh or dried it in the sun, or turned to some form of gardening to build up a stock of food. Instead, "The Precaution he took against Want, in case of sickness, was to lame Kids when very young so as that they might recover their Health but never be capable of Speed. These he had in great Numbers about his Hutt."

This dread of a lonely death was justified. Selkirk came very close to being killed in a hunting accident. The event was clearly a traumatic experience for the Scot because he described it in detail to both Woodes Rogers and Steele. He had been chasing a wild goat through the hills and "pursued it with so much eagerness that he catched hold of it on the brink of a precipice of which he was not aware, the bushes hiding it from him, so that he fell with the goat down the said precipice, a great height, and was so stunned and bruised with the fall that he narrowly escaped with his life." When Selkirk recovered consciousness he found himself lying on top of the dead goat. The animal's body had cushioned his fall and saved his life. But he was so badly bruised and shaken that "he was scarce able to crawl to his hut which was about a mile distant, or to stir abroad again in ten days."

Yet the most astonishing fact of his entire stay is that Selkirk never made the effort to explore his island fully. The terrain is exceedingly difficult, with high ridges, steep inclines, and treacherously loose soil; and the Anvil and the other high peaks remain out of reach. Yet even a cautious explorer would take no more than a week to investigate its 40 square miles. But for four years Selkirk was content to stay where he was, overlooking Cumberland Bay and restricted to the eastern two thirds of the island. He told Woodes Rogers that it was too difficult to gain access to the long northwest spur, though this was where there were many goats. It seems a poor excuse for someone who was so fit and agile. The truth was that Selkirk elected to remain within self-imposed limits. Whether through caution, inertia, lack of curiosity, fear of an accident far from his huts, or disinterest, he made his small world even smaller than it was.

What would remind the Scotsman of four years and four months of his life if he went back to his island now? Would anything be familiar? Of course he would recognize the contours of the steep slopes rising toward the Cordon Central, the ridge that links the massive block of the Anvil with the sharper summit of Cerro la Piramide. This is the woodland and brush country where he lived and hunted. But the trees on the lower slopes would now seem very strange—eucalyptus, pines, cedars. They were not there in his time, nor was the exuberance of gold and orange and yellow nasturtiums growing along the rocky banks of the streams, nor the clusters of morning glories beside the beach. All these are more recent immigrants. Like the goats that fared better than humans, pioneer plants root more firmly than men on the Island of Robinson Crusoe. For millennia the island was a botanical wonder, a Galápagos of unique plant species that evolved in isolation, and it still has more endemic plant species for its size than any other oceanic island in the world. But the majority of these native species have retreated and are now found only in a few last strongholds of native vegetation high up in the mountains. They have given ground to more powerful invaders—chiefly the maqui bushes, which the fishermen cut to provide wood for their *langosta* pots, and to the humble blackberry.

In Selkirk's time the lower slopes were covered with native trees—sandalwood and myrtle, including the "pimento" tree whose branches gave the bright flames of his signal fire. A byword to the hungry sailors was the "cabbage tree," actually a native palm, *Juania australis*. It sprouted a budlike cluster of leaves "as good as any garden cabbage I have ever tasted," in Funnell's opinion. He compared its trunk to a bamboo growing "small and straight with several knots or joints about four inches from each other,. . . void of any leaves except at the top in the midst of which the Cabbage is contained." At the head of the tree fanned out an array of branches twelve or thirteen feet long. The "cabbage" itself was cut out from the bottom of the branches and was about six inches in circumference and "as white as milk." From the base of the cabbage dangled spectacular bunches of berries the color and size of cherries. They tasted "much like English haws" and had a stone in the middle. "We never climb up to get the fruit or cabbage," noted Funnell, "because the tree is so high, and there is not anything to hold by, so a man would find it a hard matter to get up." Instead, "which we always do to get the cabbage," the sailors cut down the entire tree.

As a result the cabbage trees were already a dwindling resource by Selkirk's time. Today he would have to ascend almost to the watershed of the Cordon Central, 1,640 feet above the sea, before he came across his first specimen of the palm. Though no longer felled for food, the "cabbage tree" was cut down to make souvenirs from its handsomely patterned wood. Only a thousand of these trees survive.

Most surprising of all, today Selkirk would find no goats. After four hundred years as the island's most successful residents, goats have disappeared from the Island of Robinson Crusoe, though about four thousand remain on Isla Alejandro Selkirk. Rangers of CONAF, the Chilean Parks Service, shot them as threats to a fragile ecosystem after the island was designated in 1977 as a World Reserve Biosphere; it is now listed among the dozen most threatened bioreserves on the planet. The rangers would like to dispose similarly of all the rabbits and rats, cats and mice, thrushes and sparrows that have joined more than two hundred introduced plant species, "weeds" in botanical parlance, in eroding the original ecosystem. Selkirk would also find it difficult to find enough feral cats to tame, but the feline role in the destruction of birdlife has been assumed by another escaped pet, the coati, a raccoon-like omnivore. Marauding coatis eat the eggs of, among others, the island's most endearing native bird, the tiny Juan Fernandez hummingbird. The male weighs less than half an ounce but sings a powerful song to attract the female, and the two hover together in an exquisite mating flight. The dark maroon plumage of the male bird, the color of drying blood, is so different from the green, white, and brilliant blue of the female that for a time it was thought they were different species. Funnell was much taken with the tiny flittering bird and judged it to be "about the bigness of a Bee. It hath a bill no bigger than an ordinary Pin." In the evenings as the privateersmen made camp on shore, the birds, which had been scarce by day, would appear in the gloaming and "come humming about us." Today there are less than twelve hundred of these unique hummingbirds left, a huge decline since Funnell's time, when "if it was dark and we had a fire, before morning we should have a hundred of them fly into the fire."

Against all odds, it is the seal population of the island that preserves a sense of the natural world in which Selkirk lived. The prodigious numbers of seals, sea lions, and elephant seals never failed to astound early visitors. In the breeding season their bulbous bodies carpeted every beach and rock ledge "in so much that we were forced to kill them to set our feet on shore." Many sailors complained of the taste of the dark, almost black seal meat and would not eat it, but few had any scruples about butchering the animals to satisfy their colleagues, who compared the flavor to roast mutton. The seals were so easily despatched—a "tap on the nose" would do the job—that sailors from a Dutch squadron in 1624 came to regret their own wantonness. They turned to killing the seals for fun when they completed their victualing and left so many dead seals rotting on the beach that the carcasses turned putrid, the air began to stink, and the sailors were reluctant to come ashore again.

This slaughter was nothing compared to what was to follow. At the end of the eighteenth century a market for sealskins developed in China in the wake of the declining trade in sea otter fur. The price of a sealskin was cheap, about fifty cents. But if a sealing captain could cram enough pelts in the hold of his ship and bring them directly to a Chinese port, he could make a handsome profit. The endemic Juan Fernandez seal was particularly desirable. The animal has a magnificent thick "two hair" pelt, with an outer and inner layer of hair, and commanded a premium price. Whalers and fur traders had hunted Juan Fernandez seals only sporadically until, in 1793, an American captain by the name of Steward began sealing operations in the archipelago in deadly earnest. Effectively a poacher, he ignored the Spanish colonial authorities and swooped down on the enormous herds of seals. Men were set ashore to walk up to the massed animals and club them on the head one by one. The killers' arms grew tired from swinging their bludgeons. Steward's ship, the *Elisa,* took the first cargo of Juan Fernandez seal skins direct to China. It was the start of a grotesque bonanza. In the next ten years the islands were effectively pillaged of their seal population. In 1798, Captain Edmund Fanning came into Canton with his ship, *Betsey,* stuffed with nearly a hundred thousand fur skins, nearly all from Más Afuera, the future Isla Alejandro Selkirk. As many as fourteen sealing ships would anchor off the island at one time while their crews went about the carnage. Some captains put slaughter gangs ashore and sailed off for a few weeks to another hunting ground. When they returned, they expected to find piles of flayed skins stacked on the beach, ready to be loaded aboard. The treatment of the shore crews was on a par with the brutality of the operation. In 1808 the American sealing ship *Nancy* visited Easter Island and forcibly kidnapped twelve men and ten women islanders. The plan was to take them to Más Afuera and put them ashore as slaves, to kill and skin seals. It would have been yet another case of forcible marooning had not the captain of the *Nancy*, three days after leaving Easter Island, allowed his captives out of the hold and up on deck. All the Easter Islanders promptly flung themselves overboard and tried to swim away. Efforts to drag them back into the ship failed. So the *Nancy* kept her course, and the islanders were left to drown at sea.

The seal population of the islands collapsed before this onslaught. Another American captain, Amasa Delano, reckoned that three million skins were shipped out during the period 1797 to 1804. He himself took a hundred thousand skins. There were fewer and fewer sightings of Juan Fernandez seals. By the mid-twentieth century the animal was believed to be extinct.

Fortunately, the impression was wrong. Small groups of seals survived. They must have continued to live and breed on islets and in hidden coves, and in 1965 the Juan Fernandez seal was rediscovered, to the surprise and satisfaction of zoologists. Today the population is estimated at twelve thousand individuals and is increasing steadily. The *langosta* fishermen of San Juan Bautista regarded the seal resurgence with sour suspicion at first. They assumed the animals were eating the precious *langostas*, and surreptitiously shot the seals when they had the chance. Now they have been persuaded that the seals are more likely to be eating octopus, the *langostas'* predator, and they leave the seals alone.

The main seal rookery lies below the high razorback spur that forms the western arm of Isla Robinson Crusoe. Here the terrain is utterly different from the evergreen area where Selkirk lived. The high ridge is bare and massively eroded into a moonscape of crumbly white soil. The wind from the ocean lifts across the crest, raising plumes of fine dust. In this desert landscape the only surface water is occasional seepage oozing from seams in the layers of the pale earth that gives the zone its name—Tierras Blancas. Rain seldom falls, and the runoff carves deep gashes in the badlands that grow steeper and steeper until they fall away as the cliffs encircling the rookery. First seen from high on the ridge, the seals are no bigger than small dark slugs scattered across the rock ledges far below. Then, in the swirl and foam of the waves that lap the rocks, the swimmers are visible, dozens and dozens of animals bobbing and floating in the backwash, rising and falling with the swell, a corona of sea mammals. Descending out of the sound of the wind on the ridge, you begin to hear the clamor. The sounds of the rookery come rising on the updrafts. Thinly at first, but then louder and louder as you follow the path downward, the sound is reflected and echoed by the cliffs, until it becomes an uproar. This is the constant clamor Steele described as "dreadful Howlings and Voices . . . too terrible to be made for human Ears." It is a cacophony of moaning and braying, barking and hissing, bubbling and trumpeting. Closer, it is possible to distinguish the mewling squeaks of the seal pups, which Cooke compared so well to the bleating of lambs. Their mothers have higher-pitched cries, and overlaying everything is the astonishing roar and belch and chuffing sounds of the huge bull seals. These are hulking creatures, with massive shoulders and upper bodies bulked out by a great mane of magnificent silver or pale brown fur. In the breeding season they are to be treated with respect. They rear up in a tremendous show of defiance, weave their heads from side to side, puff out their manes like bloated cobras, open their mouths to reveal great yellow fangs, and bellow aggressively. "They roared as if they had been Lyons," wrote Basil Ringrose, a buccaneer, in *The Adventures of Captain Bartholomew Sharpe and Others in the South Sea*, published in 1685. "Two of our men could not kill one of these animals with great stones."

Late October is the seals' birthing season, and newborn seal pups lie larvalike, three or four at a time, in rock crevices. Only a few hours old, the babies are already capable of crawling. They labor their way over the rough stones to reach their mothers and suckle. Encountering another infant, they hiss and bicker, miniature versions of their fathers, who keep up a constant bullying watch over their harems. Straying females are chased back into the group. If a strange bull intrudes there is out-rage. The defending male lumbers to the attack, moving across the rocks with surprising speed while he utters a threatening chuffing sound like a giant blacksmith's bellows working frenziedly. At touching distance he rears up in display and roars. If his authority is still challenged, the two males press up against one another like sumo wrestlers. They push and shove and twist their heads from side to side, mouths wide open, fangs and red gullet displayed, seeking to shove the opponent back from the ring. But there is a more dangerous side. If an opening presents itself, there is be a lightning-fast lunge and a cruel bite with teeth designed to grip and kill large fish. A gobbet of flesh flies from the gouged wound, and the victim suddenly turns and flounders away, leaking blood and pursued by his trumpeting victor. The contest usually ends with the de-feated male solitary and forlorn on a rocky outcrop or, very occasionally, as a battered and bloated corpse floating on the tide, the buoyant carcass gradually flayed by the rocks.

"I suppose they feed on grass and fish," wrote Ringrose, "for they come ashore by the help of their two fore feet and draw their hinder part after them." Hauling out is the zoologists' term for the apparently cum-bersome process, but its awkwardness is deceptive. I pitched a tent on the edge of the rookery, hoping to hear the sounds that disheartened Selkirk on his first few nights ashore. I picked a spot uphill and a hun-dred yards inland. As the sun went down, more and more seals began to haul out. They were coming ashore to rest for the night. The younger, more athletic males carefully avoided the territory of the big savage males on the more favored ledges close to the water. They waited for the surge of a swell to lift them onto an adjacent shelf, and then set off in-land to find their couches. A six-foot scree of broken rock was no obsta-cle. They clambered up as if their flippers were gripping claws, and to my consternation the younger males appeared on the slope I had se-lected and began to range toward me. One by one they found suitable spots and lay down to rest. I realized that I was camped within the fringe of the rookery. I waited for darkness. Sure enough, the sneezes, roars, and burps of the colony diminished but never grew quiet throughout the night. And, lying there, I discovered something that no buccaneer had reported: the groaning, bubbling, grumbling talk of the seal is per-vaded by an oily miasma of mustiness. Their breath and body odor is the smell of rotten fish.

It is a peculiarity of the buccaneers and pirates and privateers who raided the South Sea that they chose to write books about their ex-ploits. They might have been expected to keep quiet about their pillage, torture, theft, arson, mutinies, and the rest. Instead they came home and paraded their feats before the public. This was chiefly an English trait. There were French and Dutch buccaneers who described their es-capades, but the majority of the buccaneer-authors were English. Seven English buccaneers or privateersmen published books boasting of their exploits off the coasts of South America before Defoe penned his story of Robinson Crusoe. Besides Woodes Rogers and Edward Cooke, who both described Selkirk's rescue, there had been Funnell and Dampier and Welbe, who accompanied the expedition that took Selkirk to the Pacific. Before them, Basil Ringrose's *Adventures of Captain Bartholomew Sharpe and Others in the South Sea* was so popular that it was reprinted in two travel collections, and a seventh book was written by a buccaneer-surgeon, Lionel Wafer, whom we shall meet later. Every one of these publications mentioned the island of Juan Fernandez before Defoe took up his pen.

Daniel Defoe was at yet another crossroads in his life when he sat down to write *The Life and Strange Surprizing Adventures*. . . . Highly intelligent and ferociously hard-working, he was willing to turn his hand to almost any occupation. Yet his schemes rarely worked out quite as he hoped. His first enthusiasm had been commerce. He tried in turn to make money by wholesaling hosiery, then by underwriting insurance, and finally by running a brick and tile factory. When all these businesses miscarried, he turned to journalism, financial speculation, and a murky career as a spy, agent provocateur, and political propagandist for both main political parties of the day. In the course of these activities he wrote numerous political pamphlets, and also a book on moral instruction, which had sold very well. His robust literary style, vigorous wit, and a delight in exchanging strokes in the political fray meant that he spent much of his life gyrating from one crisis to the next. Twice bankrupt, he had been pursued through the courts for debt and sedition or on false charges made by his enemies. A warrant issued for his arrest on a charge of seditious libel in 1703 describes him as "a middle sized spare man, about 40 years old, of a brown complexion, and dark-brown coloured hair, but wears a wig, a hooked nose, a sharp chin, grey eyes, and a mole near his mouth." While Selkirk was preparing to set sail aboard the *Cinque Ports,* Defoe was exposed for three days in the public pillory. Famously, the London mob who approved of his satirical view of the failings of the government and the judicial system escorted him to the pillory, decorated it with flowers, drank his health, and bought copies of a satirical poem that Defoe had penned with typical feistiness while waiting for the sentence to be carried out. Now, eight years after Selkirk had come home with Woodes Rogers and six years after Steele the essayist had published his description of the maroon, Defoe launched yet another career: at the age of fifty-nine, with a wife and six grown-up children, he became a novelist.

The dictionary defines a novel as "a fictitious prose narrative of considerable length, in which characters and actions of real life are portrayed in a plot of more or less complexity." *The Life and Strange Surprizing Adventures of Robinson Crusoe* was the first widely read book in the English language to meet that specification precisely and still be remembered by the public at large. At the work's inception, Defoe knew what would sell well—another travelogue spiced up with a hint of piracy.

He built on Selkirk's experiences. Crusoe, like Selkirk, comes ashore with a knife, a tobacco pipe and a little tobacco. On his first night he is so scared of wild animals that he climbs a tree for refuge, in the manner of Selkirk hiding from the Spanish landing party. Hoping for rescue, he too makes trips to the top of a hill to look for passing ships and, later, lights a bonfire to attract their attention. Both Selkirk and Crusoe then pick a site for their habitation that overlooks the sea. In that dwelling both men keep navigational books and instruments. When their rescues are delayed, both Crusoe and Selkirk grow "dejected, languid and melancholy." To console themselves, both men spend a great deal of time reading the Bible and communing with God. For physical survival the two solitary islanders hunt goats—one with a musket, the other by hand—and tame a private flock. Both men finish up wearing goatskins and domesticating cats.

But Defoe gives each detail a new gloss. The cats are a good example. Recalling Funnell's comment that "there are in this island a great many wild cats of the finest colour I ever saw," the first land animal that Crusoe encounters is a wild cat. Crusoe has been salvaging items from the wreck of his ship and returns to the beach worrying that wild animals may have begun to eat the provisions that he has already placed on land. "But when I came back, I found no sign of any visitor, only there sat a Creature like a wild Cat upon one of the chests, which when I came towards it, ran away a little Distance, and then stood still; she sat very compos'd, and unconcerned and look'd full in my face as if she had a mind to be acquainted with me." Crusoe aims his gun at the animal, "but as she did not understand it, she was perfectly unconcern'd at it, nor did she offer to stir away, upon which I tossed her a bit of Biskit. . . . She went to it, smell'd of it, and ate it, and look'd (as if pleas'd) for more, but I thanked her, and could spare no more, so she march'd off."

Selkirk's and Funnell's wild cats have become Crusoe's cat, much more recognizable and behaving like domestic cats the world over. But then, several chapters later, the scene darkens as Selkirk's tame and helpful cats meet quite a different fate at Defoe's hands. Selkirk's living quarters, according to Captain Edward Cooke of the *Duchess*, were cozily draped with dozens of cats and "kitlings" lounging about and contentedly fending off the rats and mice. In Crusoe's domain the cats perform the identical service but then become too numerous for their own good. Crusoe worries that when he dies, his corpse will be eaten by his former pets. To reduce their number, he drowns kittens and shoots excess cats as vermin.

Defoe also tinkers with the landscape. He adopts the feature of Juan Fernandez that puzzled visiting sailors: one half of the island is green and fertile, while the other is dry and barren, and yet for some strange reason it is the barren half of the island that has the most goats. This is also true of Crusoe's island. It is as if Defoe had seen the map in Cooke's story of rescuing Selkirk. Cooke's *Voyage to the South Sea* has a chart of Juan Fernandez, accurately showing its bays and anchorages. The eastern half is decorated with a bosky forest of neat little trees and there is even a neat little sketch of a "cabbage tree." The other half has a note that reads, "On this end there is but little Wood but abundance of goats." To emphasize the point, the otherwise empty and treeless half of the island is embellished with two drawings of billy goats.

Defoe then adds a cave for Crusoe to live in. When Crusoe arrives, he finds only an overhang of rock under a cliff against which he erects a lean-to, almost as temporary as Selkirk's huts of grass and branches. But with time and energy, Crusoe gradually burrows back into the overhang and digs out a home for himself. Laboriously he excavates a sizable cavern, furnishes it with homemade table and chairs, builds a stout camouflaged stockade in front of it in case he is attacked, opens up a side entrance as a sally port, and makes himself an impregnable and comfortable refuge.

The cave is the centerpiece of Crusoe's world, the focus of his strenuous efforts to make the best of his circumstances, to learn how to fend for himself. His *Strange Surprizing Adventures* becomes a manual of self-help as Crusoe deploys the survival skills that will fascinate future generations of readers—how to bake pots, how to make clothes, how to till the soil, how to catch and train goats. Everything centers on the cave, Crusoe's snug home.

Selkirk never dug a cave nor lived in one. There is no cave in his story when told by Woodes Rogers, or by Cooke, or by Steele the essayist. The sailors who rescued Selkirk never mention a cave. Nor did any of the maroons and castaways refer to using a cave as their home. The home-in-a-cave belongs strictly to the "fictitious narrative" of Defoe's novel. Yet so convincing is Defoe's creation that Crusoe fiction has subsumed Selkirk fact. Today travelers take a twenty-minute boat trip from San Juan Bautista to visit "Crusoe's Cave." The assumption is that if Alexander Selkirk was the real Robinson Crusoe, then surely Crusoe's world exists on Juan Fernandez.

"Crusoe's Cave" as created on the island today is a perfect match for the theatrical imagination. The rusty barrel of an old cannon lies in the shingle in front of it and the cave looks as much the part as the islander who dressed in goatskins, took parrot and dog, and paddled a raft out to visit tourist ships. The cave is about 250 feet from the edge of the sea and its mouth faces northeast across the anchorage that is now called Puerto Ingles and was named Sharps Bay on Basil Ringrose's map. This is an old pirate anchorage. The cave is the very first feature to catch the attention—a deep cavity at the foot of the hillside where it slopes down to the beach. Inside, the cave is high enough to stand in comfortably, and is five paces deep and eight paces across. Its walls are scratched and pitted with tool marks. But a moment's familiarity with Defoe's description should raise suspicions that this cannot possibly be Crusoe's cave—even the cave of fiction. Robinson Crusoe's home was set high up, well back from the sea, and had an apron of open ground in front of it where Crusoe planted his crops. He did not want to be on the very threshold where any visitor first stepped ashore. But for 150 years visitors have wanted the cave at Puerto Ingles to be Crusoe's cave. In 1849 an American writer, John Ross Browne, came across a group of Californians there. They were hopeful forty-niners on their way round the Horn to reach the gold fields, and their ship called at Juan Fernandez. Browne found them hacking away the walls with pick axes to take away souvenirs, convinced that Robinson Crusoe and his cave were genuine. Half a century later the first man to circumnavigate the globe alone, Joshua Slocum, brought his yawl, *Spray*, for a similar visit. He sailed away delighted that he had "paid a visit to the home and the very cave of Robinson Crusoe."

Selkirk's story—truth, not fiction—has a similar myth-making power. Every tourist fit enough to make the exhausting climb sooner or later takes the footpath to "Selkirk's Lookout," high on the crest of the Cordon Central. Almost two thousand feet above the sea, it commands an incomparable view: on one side down to Cumberland Bay, on the other across to the southwest face of the island. According to firmly held belief, Selkirk climbed up here every day to scan the horizon for a passing ship. A plaque marks the spot, a bronze tablet left in 1869 by the captain and crew of a visiting British warship, HMS *Topaze*. The Victorian sailors failed to consider that "Selkirk's Lookout" must be in the wrong place. It does not command a view to the east, the direction from which the *Duke* and *Duchess* saw his bonfire as they were approaching. If Selkirk had a lookout—as he probably did—it would have been a place where he could watch for any ship standing in to Cumberland Bay, Puerto Ingles, or Puerto Frances. He needed a vantage point where he could ascertain whether the newcomer was friend or foe, a place from which he could flee and hide, or hurry down to the beach and greet—as he eventually did—Second Captain Dover and the oarsmen in the *Duke*'s yawl. His stay on Juan Fernandez dragged on far longer than he anticipated, but it was relatively uneventful. The key to his survival was patience and resignation. What happened next on his island was far more colorful.

The day *The Life and Strange Surprizing Adventures* . . . first went on sale to the London public, two more English privateer ships were already six weeks into an Atlantic voyage, bound for Cape Horn. Each captain had in his great cabin a copy of Woodes Rogers's *Cruising Voyage Round the World,* gifts from the "Owners," the merchants who had invested their money in this new enterprise, and a reminder that they expected their captains to repeat Woodes Rogers's lucrative foray into the South Sea. The investors had also recommended that the island where Woodes Rogers found Alexander Selkirk would be a suitable place to rest and recuperate before the two ships came home with their anticipated booty. Captain John Clipperton of the thirty-gun *Success* already knew the place well. An ex-buccaneer, he had been twice to the Pacific and had served there as mate to William Dampier in 1704.

Captain George Shelvocke of the *Speedwell* was, by contrast, starting out on his first voyage to the Pacific. A self-seeking rogue, he had served for thirty undistinguished years in the Royal Navy, reaching the rank of second lieutenant aboard a flagship. Now that he was retired from the Navy, his interest was money—how to make it for himself, and as quickly as possible. His path to the command of a privateer ship had been typically suspect. His former clerk in the Navy, Edward Hughes, had given him the job. Some years earlier Shelvocke had engineered the appointment of Hughes as purser aboard a naval vessel. It was a plum posting much sought after by unscrupulous individuals who made substantial sums by false accounting and peculation. By 1718, when Shelvocke had long since left the Navy and was out of work, Hughes had become a rich and successful merchant. With a group of like-minded investors he was putting together the finances for a two-ship raid on the South Seas. When Shelvocke approached him, Hughes repaid the earlier favor by promising him command of the expedition, though at the last moment the overall command was given to Clipperton, along with the larger ship, the *Success*. Shelvocke had to make do with the smaller, twenty-two-gun *Speedwell*.

Shelvocke proceeded to staff his ship with a motley collection of officers that included his nephew as ship's surgeon, a couple of ex-privateers, a Frenchman as second mate, and several landsmen who made no pretense at being mariners. There was also his son George whose official "quality," or rank, was listed as "Nothing." An observer commented acidly that George "knew nothing of sea affairs or indeed of any thing else that was commendable or manly. His employment in London was to dangle after the women, and gossip at the tea table; and aboard us his whole business was to thrust himself into all society, over hear every thing that was said, then go and tell his father. So that he was more fit for boarding school than a ship of war."

Before the ship sailed from Plymouth Shelvocke posted upon the cabin door the Articles of Agreement, the crew contract for voyage, for all to see. Hughes and his fellow investors, the "Gentlemen Owners," would receive half the profits of the venture. James Hendry, "Purser and Agent," would look after their interest. The remainder of the profit was to be divided into 650 shares, or "dividends," to be distributed in ever smaller amounts according to rank. Shelvocke would receive sixty shares, his first officer thirty shares, and the captain of marines twenty shares. By the time the lesser office holders such as the ensign of marines, the two surgeon's mates, and the cooper had received their allocations, there would be little left for the men who actually worked the ship—the able and ordinary seamen. It was a division of the booty which was to skew the outcome of the voyage.

Shelvocke was brisk in opening his account as a privateer. While the *Speedwell* was still in the Atlantic, he accosted a Portuguese merchant ship off the coast of Brazil. The vessel was not a lawful target for an English privateer as Portugal was at peace with England. So Shelvocke ordered the flag of imperial Austria to be hoisted. The flag, with its double-headed black eagle on a yellow background, was easily mistaken for a black skeleton on a yellow background—a pirate flag. After a musket shot across the bows, the Portuguese ship was suitably bamboozled and allowed Shelvocke's men to come aboard. They extorted several valuable "gifts," including a cash sum of three hundred *moidores* from the Portuguese captain and lengths of silk embroidered with gold and silver flowers. When their victim had gone on its way, Shelvocke directed that trimmings of this silk should be sewed to the pockets and cuffs of his officers' uniforms—the gold flowers to set off the red silk suits which the Owners had given the sea officers; the silver flowers to go with the green costumes of the marines. Shelvocke's son George obtained a cinnamon colored silk outfit, and Shelvocke himself sported a black silk suit with large silver loops across his chest. He must have cut a comical figure as he was, by his own admission, "very corpulent and crippled with gout." The deckhands used the off-cuts to fashion themselves "waistcoats, caps and breeches" in silk.

This early taste of booty led the *Speedwell*'s popinjay crew to calculate how much each man's share should be. When they looked again at their contract, they became suspicious. They had a feeling that the document was not the same as the one that had been nailed to the cabin door in Plymouth. It seemed to have been tampered with. It was much longer and "written by several hands and intertwined in a great many places." Led by one of the mates, Matthew Stewart, they demanded a new contract giving them a greater share of any plunder. They also insisted on an immediate share-out of booty as soon as a prize was taken. They had heard about the endless lawsuits that had delayed the payment of dividends to the men who came back to England with the Woodes Rogers expedition, and "it is known how the people aboard the *Duke* and *Duchess* were treated." If the crew thought they were controlling the matter, they were mistaken. Matthew Stewart was almost certainly Shelvocke's agent. He had started the voyage as Shelvocke's steward, been promoted to officer rank, and was now encouraging the crew to change the Articles of Agreement. One significant new clause gave Shelvocke a 5 percent increase in his share of the booty.

Simon Hatley, the first mate, knew all about the legal squabbles that had denied Woodes Rogers's crew a quick payout of their plunder. Hatley had been aboard the *Duchess* when Woodes Rogers picked up Alexander Selkirk from Juan Fernandez, and must have seen the Scotsman dressed in his goatskins. Now, as the *Speedwell* struggled her way around the Horn and was driven as far south as 61 degrees 30 minutes south latitude by constant bad weather, Hatley was to have another brush with literary history. For several days the ocean had been empty. The sailors had seen only the gray Southern Ocean waves and the low scudding clouds. There had been none of the usual fish life and birds normally encountered in those waters except for one "disconsolate black albatross," which, Shelvocke wrote, "accompanied us for several days, hovering about us as if he had lost himself." In his frustration at the slow progress of the ship, Hatley eventually interpreted the presence of the great black bird as an ill omen. He decided that if he could get rid of it, better weather would follow. After several attempts, Hatley succeeded in downing the bird with a well-aimed shot—but to little effect. There were another six weeks of heavy weather and headwinds before the *Speedwell* sighted the coast of Chile.

Hatley's deed lived on. Like other privateers before him Shelvocke published an account of his voyage when he came home. Fifty years later the book was read by William Wordsworth. He mentioned Hatley's killing of the albatross to his friend Samuel Taylor Coleridge, who was working on a poem. Wordsworth suggested the theme that slaying an albatross brought bad luck, and Coleridge immortalized the idea in "The Rime of the Ancient Mariner" with his verse:

> *God save thee, Ancient Mariner!*
> *From the fiends, that plague thee thus*
> *Why look'st thou so?—"With my cross-bow*
> *I shot the ALBATROSS."*

Wordsworth and Coleridge had little knowledge of sea custom. First Mate Hatley used a musket or a shotgun, not a crossbow, to bring down the bird, and albatross were sometimes killed for food by hungry sailors. They set special fishing lines, the hooks loaded with floating bait and trailed in the wake of the ship to catch the giant seabirds. But the ill luck which soon enveloped Hatley's ship at Juan Fernandez seemed to justify what became a lingering and gloomy superstition.

Shelvocke's enemies were to claim that their captain deliberately dawdled so that the *Speedwell* did not get to the rendezvous with the *Success* at Juan Fernandez on time. The *Success* arrived at Cumberland

Bay on 7 September 1719, long before her escort. It was ten years and seven months since the now-celebrated moment when the *Duke*'s yawl had found Selkirk standing on the beach. This time the boulder-strewn waterfront was deserted.

Captain Clipperton followed the usual routine: the ship was unloaded and cleaned, the crew set up tents ashore for scurvy victims—there were sixteen, of whom three failed to respond to the fresh diet and died—and shore parties went off to hunt goats and seals to replenish the ship's stores. Selkirk had complained about the lack of salt to preserve or flavor his food when he was on the island. Now the men from the *Success* found a cache of salt. It had been left subsequent to Selkirk's visit by visiting French ships. Clipperton's men used their convenient discovery to salt down goat's flesh for the forthcoming cruise along the Peruvian coast.

After a month, Clipperton could see no point in delaying further and decided to get on with the attack on the Spaniards. Before he left the island, he sent his first officer with a shore party to bury a message in a bottle. The note was for Shelvocke, to tell him the new plan, and to arrange a further rendezvous. The shore party erected a wooden cross to mark the place where they had buried the bottle. As insurance, they also cut a mark into a prominent tree near the landing place to let Shelvocke know that the *Success* had been at the island and left. Clipperton was too canny to leave his full name or the name of his ship in case the Spaniards found the mark and learned that a known privateer had returned to the area. So his men carved only his first name, and then the name of the ship's doctor, a man known to Shelvocke. The mark read

Captain John ——

W. Magee

1719

Clipperton was worried that the bottle might be dug up mischievously by two would-be Selkirks. They were part of a group of four sailors from his crew who had earlier taken it into their heads to stay behind on the island and had run off into the interior and hidden. Their plan was to find the huts Selkirk had left behind and live in them once their ship had left. Their flight was a spur-of-the-moment decision because they took no food or equipment with them, not even a flint and steel for making fire. Selkirk's captain had been glad to be rid of the Scotsman, but Clipperton was not so charitable toward deserters. He gave orders that the absentees were to be brought back to the ship and he sent out a search party to find them. Two were quickly caught. A party of goat hunters from the *Success* stumbled across the four runaways, and gave chase. The pursuit up and down the steep hills was so exhausting—the hunters said it was twice as difficult to chase men as goats in such terrain—that the hunters had to resort to firing shots at the fugitives to try to make them stop and give themselves up. Two of the runaways halted their flight, but their colleagues got away. The pair who were brought back to the ship confessed that their escapade had its drawbacks. For the first five days they had been extremely hungry and had to live off raw leaves from the cabbage trees. Life became marginally more comfortable when they managed to obtain fire from the embers of a campfire carelessly left behind by one of the hunting parties from the *Success*. Clipperton decided to waste no more time and effort looking for the other two stragglers, and at eight o'clock on the morning of 7 October gave orders to weigh anchor.

Thus, two more maroons joined the list of refugees on Juan Fernandez, though their tenure was brief. Clipperton captured a Spanish coastal vessel six weeks into his cruise, and his victims neatly turned the tables on their captors, who had been left behind on the prize. Waiting until the *Success* had sailed over the horizon in search of other prey, the Spaniards rose up and overpowered the English prize crew and retook their ship. Then they deliberately ran her ashore on the mainland coast so that their former jailers fell into the hands of the Spanish authorities. Under interrogation, the Englishmen revealed the existence of the buried bottle and the fact that there were two deserters living on the island. A Spanish patrol visited Juan Fernandez early in December, dug up the bottle, and its message, and captured the two runaways. Their stay as would-be Selkirks had lasted just two months.

The two men probably gambled on the fact that the *Speedwell* would soon arrive to pick them up. As it turned out it was a full three months after the *Success* had left the island that Shelvocke finally appeared in the offing and on 11 January 1720 brought his ship in leisurely fashion toward the island. As a ship commander, Shelvocke had proved to be as rude and abusive to his men as Dampier had been, and with the same result: members of the crew had deserted or were sacked at each Atlantic port of call so that the original crew of one hundred was down to about seventy men by that time they reached the Pacific. Furthermore, Shelvocke had stoked a seething row on board with one of his chief officers, a quarrel whose hostility equaled any dispute between Selkirk and his captain, Stradling. The chief malcontent this time was William Betagh, another former Navy purser who now held the rank of captain of the green-and-silver-clad marines. Betagh, along with Hatley, had been ringleader of the squabble over the revised crew contract, and Betagh and Shelvocke had been feuding ever since. Matters were made worse by the special instruction from the owners that Betagh was to be allowed to take meals in the captain's great cabin, and this threw the two antagonists together even more closely. Shelvocke found Betagh "insolent" and at dinner one day hurled his drinking mug at Betagh's head. Later he had Betagh placed under arrest and confined to the steerage. There, according to Betagh's version of the story, he had to lie for twelve to fourteen days, stretched out on the arms chest, with not enough head room to sit up, and watched over by a sentry with a drawn sword. Planning his revenge, Betagh started gathering material ready to denounce Shelvocke to the sponsors at the end of the expedition, much as Funnell had collected evidence to censure Dampier.

The *Speedwell*'s larder was so bare as she approached Juan Fernandez that for four days Shelvocke kept his vessel "standing off and on" so that his small boats could go fishing. As usual, Juan Fernandez's rich fishing grounds provided a generous catch and the *Speedwell* had salted five casks of fish before Shelvocke finally got round to sending a search party into Cumberland Bay to go ashore and look more closely for any traces of the *Success.* Very soon they came across the mark on the tree and realized that Clipperton had already left. Shelvocke was secretly pleased. He had a long-standing grudge against his fellow captain for accepting command of the larger, more prestigious *Success,* which Edward Hughes had originally promised to Shelvocke. Now he could blame his colleague for disobeying his instructions to wait for the *Speedwell.* Also, not knowing about the buried message in a bottle, he accused Clipperton of sailing off on his own account without leaving any information. More to the point, Shelvocke was now free to go raiding the mainland and Clipperton and his crew would have no share in the proceeds.

Shelvocke set off to attack the Spanish as soon as his ship had taken on fresh water. The cruise had only modest success. Its high point was the sack of the town of Payta, close to the modern boundary between Peru and Ecuador. The nadir was the capture of a coaster whose cargo turned out only to be guano, or "cormorant dung." With the capture of this guano carrier Shelvocke showed his true colors, according to Betagh, who was still gathering evidence against his captain. Aboard the *Speedwell* was a young marine officer, Ensign Gilbert Hamilton. He was a Scot and he spoke with a broad regional accent, and he was keeping a daily journal. His pithy summary of the incident, which he read aloud to his messmates, was "This geud day we a taen a sma vashel lodded wi turds." Naturally this raised hoots of laughter in the crew's quarters, and Shelvocke sent his son George from the captain's cabin to investigate the reason for the mirth. When son George reported the reason, Shelvocke himself stormed into the crew's accommodation and ordered Hamilton to stop keeping a journal, vowing there would be "no pen and ink work aboard his ship."

Soon afterward Shelvocke parted company with his foe, Betagh, who set off with Hatley in one of the prizes and never returned. Never one to lose the chance of blackening another's reputation, Shelvocke claimed that Betagh had in fact deserted because he was an Irish Catholic and secretly in league with the Spanish. Betagh counterclaimed that Shelvocke deliberately sent him and his crew away so that he would not have to share any of the booty with them. What Shelvocke did not realize was that although he was rid of Betagh, his gadfly was not about to let the feud drop.

So it was an already disgruntled crew that reappeared off Juan Fernandez under Shelvocke's command on 6 May 1720. There were still about seventy men aboard the *Speedwell*. Their numbers had been depleted by the departure of Hatley and Betagh and the various prize crews, but then increased by the acquisition of several blacks and Indians. These unfortunates were regarded as human loot, "liberated" from the Spanish colonists. A few might become free members of the shipboard community, but usually they were treated as little better than slaves and regarded with suspicion in case they betrayed the privateers to their former masters.

When the familiar outline of the Anvil came in sight, every man aboard the *Speedwell* knew that they had little to show for their efforts: their loot was meager, they were low on fresh water, the mainland coast was in uproar against them, and there had been a couple of narrow escapes from patrolling Spanish warships. The risk of being trapped in Cumberland Bay by a Spanish warship led Shelvocke to decide that he would not even anchor there. For ten days he again "stood off and on," sending boats to fill water barrels and bring them out to the ship. But it was such slow work that it was calculated that the men aboard were consuming more water than was being brought aboard. This, wrote Shelvocke, "made me think of anchoring in the road [the anchorage] for a few hours." He intended only to stay long enough to fill twenty casks. As it turned out the stay was over four and a half months.

The ship's cooper prepared the twenty casks while the *Speedwell* cautiously worked her way into the treacherous-looking harbor at Cumberland Bay. The poor holding ground and the rapid dropoff of the sea floor meant that the ship was only six hundred yards from the shore before she could anchor effectively. Even so close to land the depth was forty fathoms, or 240 feet. Everything now proceeded according to routine. The twenty empty casks were lashed together to form a raft. A long rope was rigged between the ship and the shore along which the raft was hauled to the beach. There the casks were unlashed, rolled to the stream, filled and bunged, and rolled back to the water's edge, where they were floated off to the ship. The sailors had done similar chores many times before, and by the morning of May 21 the *Speedwell* was getting ready to depart. The only men ashore were a party of woodcutters gathering firewood for the ship's cook.

Once again, Shelvocke dawdled. He does not say why. Only that "we were ready to go to sea, but had not the least opportunity in 4 days." The most likely explanation is that he was waiting for a break in the weather. It was now the southern winter and sailing conditions were at their worst. As for other sailing ships of her time, it was prudent for the *Speedwell* to wait for suitable conditions—an offshore breeze and little swell—to work her way out of an anchorage, particularly when she was moored so close inshore that a false move could send her onto the rocks. She needed expert handling in the crucial moments after the anchor lost its grip on the seabed, and before the vessel had adequate way to be able to be steered effectively. If she had been a galley like the *Cinque Ports* she might have rowed out of the bay, then set sail. If the waves and swell had been less, her small boats could have towed her out. As it was, Shelvocke and his crew simply waited.

On 25 May 25 the weather did change, but for the worse. A gale blew straight into the bay from the northeast, its most exposed direction. The *Speedwell* hung on her anchor, and continued to wait. As the waves and swell grew larger, driving into the bay, the ship rolled and pitched uncomfortably. It was overcast and rainy. But the anchor cable was new, and there was no need for alarm.

What happened in the next few hours depends on whose account is to be believed. According to Shelvocke, "A hard gale of wind came out of the sea upon us (a thing very uncommon as has been reported) and brought a great tumbling swell, so that in a few hours our cable (which was never wet before) parted." With her anchor cable snapped, the *Speedwell,* lying so close to the shore, immediately drifted toward the stony beach. Pushed by the onshore gale, the hull hit the beach within moments. It was providential, according to Shelvocke, that the ship struck where she did, on an open stretch of foreshore. If she had hit "a cable's length farther to the Eastward or Westward of the place where we did, we must inevitably have perished." As it was, the impact of her grounding was so severe "that as soon as she touched the rocks we were obliged to hold fast by some part or other of the ship, otherwise the violence of the shocks she had in striking, might have been sufficient to have thrown us all out of her into the sea." With the swell pounding the hull against the shore, the vessel began to break up rapidly. "Our main mast, fore-mast, and mizzen top mast went all away together," reported Shelvocke, and the planks began to splinter and to spring from their fastenings. The hull "bulged," opening up and filling with seawater.

The death of the *Speedwell* was remarkably quick. The water flooded her lower compartments so rapidly that very little gear could be saved from below decks. The surgeon's chest had been stowed below and disappeared underwater and "little or nothing preserved out of that," though—an echo of Alexander Selkirk—"we saved 2 or 3 compasses and some of our mathematical instruments and books." The loss of all three masts over the side left enough clear space on deck for the crew hastily to assemble a life raft from spare timbers. Launching the raft over the side of their doomed and disintegrating ship, the crew rode it into the shallows and scrambled through the surf and onto the beach. "Before it was quite dark we were all ashore in a very wet uncomfortable condition . . . [with] no place . . . to recourse to for shelter from the boisterous wind and rain except the trees; nothing to cheer up our spirits after the fatigue and hazard in getting from the wreck to the rocks, and no other prospect but that, after having suffered much in this uninhabited place, we might in process of time be taken away by some ship or other." During the evacuation just one man lost his life. Shelvocke entered his name in the list of those who never returned from the South Sea: "John

Hannah—drowned when the ship was cast away on the Island of Juan Fernandez."

Captain of Marines Betagh was to dismiss Shelvocke's account of this so-called "dismal accident" as a farrago of lies. What really happened, according to Betagh, who relied on hearsay from the sailors involved, was that Shelvocke *deliberately* wrecked his ship. Betagh's far-fetched theory was that Shelvocke planned the whole crisis in order to annul his contract with the backers of the expedition. He piled up his ship on the rocks so that he no longer used a ship provided by the merchant-sponsors, and so would be free to go plundering on his own account, without having to put aside a share of the spoils for his backers. As Betagh interpreted the situation, Shelvocke was expecting to be picked up by another vessel or to construct a vessel of his own. He knew that being cast away on Juan Fernandez was no great ordeal. Members of Shelvocke's crew had often heard their captain state that "it was not difficult living at Fernandez, if a man should accidentally be thrown there, since Mr. Selkirk had continued upon it four years by himself."

Betagh went to great trouble to support his version of events with statements from survivors of the wreck. The true scenario of the wreck, as sketched by Betagh, was that there was no gale that day, only a heavy swell. The "hard gale" was "a wind raised only in his [Shelvocke's] brain and of his own invention." In preparation for his disgraceful scheme, Shelvocke had secretly sent some of the ship's stores onto the beach during the watering operation. He also made sure that nineteen members of his crew were already on land, ostensibly cutting firewood but in reality prepared to rush down to the beach and help when the "accident" happened. Before the anchor cable broke, claimed Betagh, Mr. Brooks, the first lieutenant, had noted the danger of riding to only a single anchor when so close inshore. He warned Shelvocke and "advised slinging two of their heaviest guns" overboard and using them as drags in case the anchor rope snapped. But Shelvocke "rejected all these things with a steadfast tranquillity." Instead, as the *Speedwell* pitched and rolled on the swell, he ordered that a spring hawse—an additional rope—be attached to the anchor cable and be hauled in so that the ship came broadside to the waves. This maneuver, according to Betagh, was deliberately designed to exert extra strain on the anchor cable so that it snapped. Mr. Dodd, lieutenant of marines and presumably a confidant of Betagh, who was his ex-commander, noticed "about three hours before the ship went ashore some hands at work on the quarter deck hawling in a hawser (the spring) which was made fast to the cable." Dodd had no knowledge of ship handling and, puzzled, asked the gunner, Gilbert Henderson "what that was for." Henderson answered him "that if he would be rightly informed, he must go and ask the captain." Gunner Henderson's testy reply was probably a way of telling the landsman to mind his own business, but in Betagh's interpretation it had a more sinister tone: Shelvocke was putting into action his criminal scheme.

"Soon as the cable parted," Betagh continues, "Mr. Laporte his third lieutenant seeing immediate ruin, cried out 'Set the Foresail!' hoping thereby to do some good. And while Edmund Philips and other were actually upon the yard, Shelvocke hastily ordered them down, and taking the helm in his hand said 'Ne'er mind it boys; stand all fast, I'll lay her on a feather bed.'" It proved "a plaguey hard one," adds Betagh sourly. *Speedwell* had set out from England with four anchors and four cables, and it was inconceivable, Betagh wrote, that such an experienced mariner as Shelvocke did not have a spare cable and anchor ready to hand for such an emergency. "He brags of his being thirty years an officer in the navy; what then must we say to a man of such experience who will. . . save not an anchor and cable for a time of need? There is nothing can excuse it. . . either way it's very bad. His judgement and his honesty being both in great danger."

In his vengeful mood Betagh was overstating his case. It is difficult to imagine how any captain could destroy his ship with such a Machiavellian scheme. The outlook for Shelvocke's crew on the beach—wet, cold, hungry, and exhausted—was so bleak that no sane commander would have attempted such a ploy, certainly no one as careful to watch out for his own interests as Shelvocke.

For the first time in the English experience, the new residents of Juan Fernandez were genuine castaways, the involuntary victims of a wreck. They had not been left behind by accident or run away from their vessels or, like Selkirk, chosen to be left ashore. In this regard Shelvocke and his men were beginning their adventure on Juan Fernandez in circumstances that precisely mirrored Robinson Crusoe's crash landing on his desert island. Even as readers in England were enjoying Defoe's newly published novel, a group of survivors was facing the identical challenges that Crusoe had to deal with, and on the very same island known to Defoe from the story of Alexander Selkirk. There was, of course, one major difference: Robinson Crusoe was a solitary maroon, whereas Shelvocke, the leader of the castaways, found himself in command of nearly seventy men thrown ashore. But this, as we shall see, did not make his task any easier. The events now to unfold on Juan Fernandez illustrate the turbulent realities of shipwreck and survival at the time when Defoe created his masterpiece. They also offer a more lifelike alternative to Defoe's optimistic version of Crusoe's final days, when his hero organizes the smooth evacuation of a motley collection of sailors whom he has rescued from the cannibals and a visiting ship. Shelvocke's nature was far removed from that of the upright and competent Robinson Crusoe, yet the sea captain's escapade was to provide just as many colorful episodes as the fictional castaway's, and—unexpectedly—reach the same happy outcome.

Like Robinson Crusoe, Shelvocke's first priority was to recover as much material as possible from the hulk before *Speedwell* was broken up entirely by the waves. That evening, "All the Officers came to bear me company and to consult how we should contrive to get some necessaries out of the wreck if she was not quite in pieces by the next morning." After some discussion he "came to the resolution of losing no time in endeavouring to recover what we could out of the wreck." Then he and his officers lay down to sleep beside the campfire "wrapped . . . in what they could get . . . and notwithstanding the badness of the weather, slept very soundly."

But at first light next morning their decision to salvage the ship as a matter of urgency ran into a snag: Shelvocke found he could not persuade the ordinary seamen to swim out to the wreck and do the work. While the officers had been making themselves comfortable around a campfire, the rest of the men had wandered up and down the beach and into the woodland, searching for places to shelter from the rain where they could lie down and get some rest. Shelvocke went among them, giving orders to assemble on the beach for the salvage party. But they ignored him. Instead they devoted their energy to improving their temporary shelters. To Shelvocke's intense annoyance, in this way, "all opportunities were lost of regaining anything [from the wreck], but some of our small arms which were fished up . . . and in the meantime the wreck was entirely destroyed and everything that was in her lost, except one cask of beef and one of Farina de Pao [a type of flour] which were washed whole on the strand."

Shelvocke was being less than honest. Already he was developing his own agenda. In his description of the shipwreck on Juan Fernandez and the extraordinary events to follow, he is intent on emerging from the tale as its conspicuous hero. To do this he begins by painting the situation in the gloomiest colors: "I need not say how disconsolate my reflections were on this sad accident which had . . . thrown us out from the rest of the world, without anything to support us but the uncertain product of a desolate uncultivated Island, situated (I may justly say) in the remotest part of the earth." No help can be expected from the outside because the distant mainland is "90 leagues distant" and "in the possession of the Creolian Spaniards who have always been remarkable for their ungenerous treatment of their enemies." And he knows that "it was inevitably certain that our stay here will be very long" so "we must now be obliged to suffer all such hardships as would be consequent to our shipwreck."

As Shelvocke presents the situation the salvation of all rests on his leadership. Like Robinson Crusoe organizing Man Friday and the sailors he has rescued from the mutineers, he must work night and day to keep the men healthy. He must "think of some economy to be observed amongst the people in relation to the distribution of such provisions as should, from time to time, be got etc." Yet his account of the shipwreck and the days of survival is riddled with inconsistencies. On the one hand he claims that the wreck was an utter catastrophe and that he and his men barely survived with their lives and were thrown destitute on the beach. But it later turns out that he and his men have barrels of gunpowder, canvas to make sails, extra muskets, even four live hogs, and all manner of paraphernalia and useful materiel which must have come from the *Speedwell* at some stage. Some of it had been landed during the grounding of the ship. Shelvocke boasts that during the initial emergency he took care to bring with him his written commission, his "letter of marque," as well as "1100 dollars belonging to the Gentlemen Owners which were kept in my chest in the great cabin." This was some of the loot due to the sponsors, though "the rest being in the bottom of the bread room for security, could not possibly be come at."

There was also a serious flaw in Shelvocke's idea of leadership: it was entirely based on the social assumption of the day that a well-ordered community functioned smoothly if it was arranged by rank and class. "The people," as Shelvocke called the ordinary sailors, formed the base of the structure. They were expected to obey the orders given to them by the officers, who were usually, but not always, gentlefolk. The specialists and craftsmen such as the gunner, the cooper, the sailmaker, the armorer, and the ship's carpenter carried out their duties semi-independently but also under the overall direction of the gentleman officers. Barriers between the ranks were surprisingly porous, and changes of status could be sudden. The *Speedwell*'s first lieutenant, Edward Brooks, had been a deck hand on his previous voyage; and on the voyage out to Juan Fernandez Shelvocke abruptly promoted the cabin steward, Matthew Stewart, to the rank of mate. But if this ramshackle hierarchy was to work, it depended on everyone's knowing his place according to his present status. A foremast hand might become a captain, but until he did so, he was just one of "the people" in Shelvocke's opinion, and would be treated as such.

So Shelvocke began by attending to his own comfort. "I took some pains in finding out a convenient place to set up my tent; . . . and at length found a commodious spot of ground not a half mile from the sea, and a fine run of water within a stone's cast on either side of it, with firing [firewood] near at hand and trees proper for building our dwellings." In this pleasant glade he had his tent erected, and "thus secured ourselves as well as possible against the inclemency of the approaching winter." He notes condescendingly that "the people settled within call about me in as good a manner as they could." But they had to make do with improvised shelters of the sort that Selkirk would have recognized—shacks of junk timber and branches thatched with grass and leaves, while "others covered them with the skins of seals and sealions." A wretched few preferred to salvage empty water butts from the ship, rolled them under the shelter of trees, and slept in the barrels. Their woes contrasted with the well-being of the officers, who "used to pass our time in the evening in making a great fire before my tent, round which my officers in general, assembled employing themselves quietly in roasting crawfish in the embers; sometimes bewailing our unhappy state and sinking into despair; at other times feeding themselves up with hopes that something might yet be done to set us afloat again."

After these fireside discussions, Shelvocke decided—echoing Crusoe's thoughts as he resolves to build an escape craft—that "words alone were not sufficient, and I began to think it full time to look about me to see if it was really practicable for us to build such a vessel as would carry us all off this Island."

If Shelvocke had been less self-absorbed, it would have come as a no surprise that his crew now started to make trouble. He began by approaching the ship's carpenter, Robert Davenport, whose skill was essential to the project of building a new boat in which to escape from the island. He asked Davenport if he could build such a boat and was stunned when the carpenter rebuffed him rudely. "I was astonished at his cold indifference when he answer'd me that he 'could not make brick without straw,' and walked away from me in a surly humor."

He had better luck with the ship's armorer. Not as crucial to the boat building project as the carpenter, the armorer was nevertheless a pivotal member of a shipwright's support team. It was his task to do the blacksmith's work, to produce the fastenings, the bolts and nails and rivets that held the planks to the frames, and the dozens of special metal fittings required—rudder pins, shackles, drifts, and so forth. Above all, the armorer was the toolmaker. He could fabricate the metal chisels, awls, gimlets, and other tools for the boat builders. If both the carpenter and the armorer refused to help, then the boat building project would never get started. Shelvocke was not like Crusoe, who was an expert on self-help and successfully turned his hand to making furniture, basketwork, and other utensils. Shelvocke's role was to organize the craftsmen who already possessed the essential skills.

Shelvocke found that the armorer, John Popplestone, was ahead of him. When Shelvocke went to look for him, he came across the armorer on the beach picking over the wreck site. He had already salvaged a set of bellows to make a forge, and brought out four or five spadoes, heavy cutlasses, to melt down for steel. He told Shelvocke that it should be possible to scavenge plenty more scrap metal along the shoreline, and suggested that men should be set to work cutting trees as soon as possible and preparing charcoal to feed his smithy.

Encouraged, Shelvocke called together the men and explained the situation. The work would be long and arduous, he told them, but it offered them a chance of salvation. If they could build a rescue boat, they could get away from the island—"to which," he adds smugly, "they with one voice, consented, and promised to be extremely diligent in this important work and begg'd of me to give them instructions how to proceed."

Acting on the advice of the armorer, Shelvocke sent the members of the crew who had been ashore cutting wood when the *Speedwell* was wrecked to fetch their axes and then go to cut trees and make charcoal. The remainder "went down to the wreck to get the bowsprit ashore of which I intended to make the keel," and Shelvocke persuaded the surly carpenter "to go with me to fix on the properest place to build upon."

At once the crew made a happy discovery. Salvaging the bowsprit from the wreck, they found the top maul from the *Speedwell*. This was the heavy club hammer normally kept lashed to the upper section of the mainmast, where it was used for driving wedges and pounding on jammed fittings. When the mainmast toppled overboard, the upper section floated up on the beach with the top maul still attached. The heavy hammer was invaluable during the boat building, and "though of no small weight, would not at this time have been exchanged for its weight in gold." Any part of the mast itself must also have been useful salvage, but, characteristically, Shelvocke makes no mention of this bonus.

On 8 June, eighteen days after the wreck, the keel blocks were set in position. These were the blocks of wood on the beach on which the keel would rest while the boat was under construction. It was the first visible step in the construction, and Robert Davenport, the carpenter, went to work squaring and shaping the former bowsprit "with seeming good temper," while Shelvocke looked on. Suddenly the carpenter had a tantrum. He rounded on Shelvocke, swore at him, and shouted that he "would not strike another stroke" on the keel. He announced that "truly he would be no body's slave, and thought himself now on a footing with myself." Davenport's effrontery produced an immediate reaction from his captain—"This unreasonable exclamation," said Shelvocke, "provoked me to use him somewhat roughly with my cane."

It took only a few moments for Shelvocke to realize that hitting his recalcitrant carpenter with a stick was not the best way of encouraging

Davenport back to work. It also dawned on Shelvocke that the carpenter was not acting on his own. There were "sad ones" who were prompting him. So he quickly changed tactics, and offered the carpenter a "reward" or bribe. After some negotiation Shelvocke agreed to give the carpenter "a four pistole piece as soon as the stem and stern post were up, and 100 pieces of eight when the bark was finished." Knowing that his own reputation for honesty was already suspect, Shelvocke offered to place the cash with a stake holder, promising "the money to be committed to the keeping of anyone he [the carpenter] should name, till that time."

"This done," Shelvocke concludes with an air of satisfaction, "he went to work on the keel, which was to be 30 foot in length."

The length of the salvaged bowsprit determined the size of the keel, and this in turn governed the general proportions of the boat. "Her breadth by the beam was 16 foot, and seven foot depth of hold," Shelvocke noted. For a vessel intended to carry almost seventy men to safety, this was very small indeed. Even if the vessel was ever built, she would be dangerously overloaded.

The boat building proceeded very slowly. First there was the "chalking out," the drawing of her dimensions using charcoal or chalk and making patterns of the curves. Then the search for suitable timber took a huge effort. Earlier visitors to the island had commented that the eastern half of Juan Fernandez was covered with woodland, but few trees were suitable for boat building or masts. The best of the timber had already been felled. Now the *Speedwell's* crew was obliged to scour the high ground for the tallest and heaviest trees, searching for those whose bends and curves naturally matched those required for the frames of their makeshift vessel. When they found a suitable tree, it was very awkward to drag the timber down to the beach. To his credit Shelvocke sympathized with those who "were obliged sometimes to go a great way from the waterside, and after having cut it down it must be dragged up steep hills and other fatigues which tired the people to a great degree."

His chief ally was Popplestone, the armorer. He proved to be a workhorse. He "did not lose a minute's time from the work of his hands and contrivance of his head." Over the next few weeks Popplestone made the boat building team a "little double headed maul, hammers, chisel, files and a sort of gimblets which performed very well." He also produced a mold for making musket bullets and a large auger for boring "cartouche boxes," or cartridge cases. The wood for these cases came from the *Speedwell*'s gun carriages, which had washed ashore. To make them watertight they were covered in sealskin. The blacksmith then turned carpenter and while the larger vessel was under construction, began to build a small boat to serve as tender. If any one member of Shelvocke's crew could be rated as a true Robinson Crusoe, it was Popplestone, with his energy, self-discipline, and practical competence with every material, whether metal, timber, cloth, or skin.

Not everyone could be employed on the boat at the same time. There was not enough space around the keel and frames to work freely, nor enough tools to go round. Besides, only some of the men were handy with the improvised tools. So Shelvocke organized his labor force into two shifts. They worked on the vessel on alternate days, and those who were not working went off to find food.

The weather was too bad during the first few days to go fishing, so the food gatherers killed seals. At first it was an easy assignment because the seals and sea lions lay about on the rocks in their usual great herds, and the hunters had only to walk up and dispatch them. But their butchery was wasteful. Many of the castaways were reluctant to eat seal meat, although, for some reason, they were willing to eat the entrails. So the hunters killed the animals, cut out the edible organs, and left the carcasses. Soon the beach at Cumberland Bay was littered with the rotting corpses of seals, and there was a strong putrid stench in the air. The constant hunting reduced the numbers of animals drastically, and within weeks the surviving seals and sea lions had taken fright and left. They moved to other hauling out sites where they would not be disturbed by the human predators. It became rare to see seals on the beach at Cumberland Bay, and the hunters came back empty-handed or with only one or two dead seals for the pot. No longer were the sailors so fastidious about their food. They never acquired a taste for the rank-flavored blubber, but steaks of lean meat were quite palatable if roasted "till they were as dry as a chip."

Surprisingly, the sailors managed to catch only a few goats. Their hunters were hampered by a shortage of powder and shot for their muskets, and they were not as agile as Selkirk so they could not catch them by hand. The *Speedwell's* men had come ashore barefoot or wearing shoes that soon wore out. They laced pieces of goatskin and sealskin to their feet with thongs, but these were inadequate for the rough terrain, and they hobbled during the chase. The main reason for the lack of success in goat hunting, however, was that the Spanish policy of releasing dogs on the island at last seemed to be having an effect. The wild dogs had reduced the goat numbers, and the surviving goats had withdrawn to the high ground, where they were even more difficult to catch.

Their plan to eat goat meat foiled, the hunters turned to other game. The island was still overrun with feral cats, in spite of the wild dogs. These cats were "in size and colour exactly the same with our house cats," wrote Shelvocke, and they lurked in almost every thicket. There were so many that "there is hardly taking a step without starting one." The cats preyed on the colonies of small seabirds the Spanish called *pardelas,* a species of shearwater, which nest in underground burrows like rabbit holes. Now the cats in turn became prey for a small bitch, which seems to have come ashore as another of Speedwell's survivors. The castaways trained her up as a hunting dog, and the bitch was set on a cat hunt and "would catch almost any number they wanted in an hour or two." Some of the sailors acquired a liking for cat meat, and they assured Shelvocke that to dine on a single cat assuaged their hunger more than eating "4 or 5 seal or fish." They were exaggerating, and Shelvocke himself "could never be persuaded to taste them."

Whenever the weather permitted, the men went out in a small ship's boat, which had also been salvaged from the wreck, and caught fish. The ever-industrious Popplestone forged metal hooks, which the fishermen attached to lines fashioned by twisting together lengths of ribbon, large quantities of which washed ashore from the wreck. For a time the fishing was very successful, but then we "were deprived of the benefit of that [fishery] by the roguery of some of the people who did one night (for what ends I know not) set the boat adrift and she was lost." The loss of the little boat was a severe blow. As a replacement, some of the more ingenious sailors made themselves small coracles. They tied together slender branches into bowl-shaped wickerwork frames. Over these they stretched a membrane of sea lion skin. In these unstable basket boats they paddled out and managed to "catch the small fish near the shore, but dared not go out of the bay with them." Only when the armorer finally finished making his small boat did the fishing improve. By then it was 9 September and Shelvocke and his castaways had been on the island for nearly four months.

In all that time their accommodation had been miserable. Shelvocke described their huts as being "as mean and inconvenient as possible, some being made with the boughs of trees, some cover'd with seal and sea-lyons skins, and some with remains of the ship's sails." These flimsy shelters did not withstand the "flaws." Sudden gusts of wind came rushing down the valley and stripped away the coverings to "leave us. . . in bed, exposed to the weather." Equally inconvenient was the lack of any furnishings or utensils. The only cooking equipment was a few frying pans made from the lids of the *Speedwell*'s cooking pots. The ship's pitch ladle which had once done duty for melting and pouring pitch into the deck seams, was now a saucepan. The food, fish cooked in seal oil and flavored with wild sorrel, was barely adequate. Even the famed "cabbage trees" were a disappointment. They were awkward to find now that they had been cropped so often, and when found were difficult to cut down, so that they scarcely rewarded the effort. "The whole tree seldom affords above two pounds that is eatable," Shelvocke lamented. The last of the turnip gardens were stripped of their produce, and the sailors found a handful of pumpkins that had been planted by earlier visitors. They were so hungry that they did not wait for these vegetables to grow to size and ripen, but ate them while they were still hard and immature.

The mysterious loss of the ship's boat should have been a further warning to Shelvocke that more trouble was brewing. The carpenter's angry outburst had been the first symptom of a gathering malaise caused by poor diet, bad accommodation, boredom, and a growing sense of hopelessness. The crew of the *Speedwell* had never been a cohesive unit. Each man had joined the venture out of self-interest, to acquire booty. Now, in the tedium and discomfort of island life, any vestige of solidarity faded. They became disaffected and grumbled, and Shelvocke was the scapegoat.

Shelvocke realized that something was amiss when his senior officers began to avoid him. They were spending more and more time with the ordinary deck hands. Shelvocke was hurt. He was scornful that they "deserted from my conversation to herd with the meanest of the ship's company." Then he observed that work on the boat, which had made steady progress at the outset, was now trickling toward a complete halt. His officers were failing to exert their authority, and showed little enthusiasm for the project. When he met any of his officers and asked why they were negligent, their replies were evasive or downright pessimistic. One said that he did not think they would ever escape from the island; another referred to the half-built boat as "a bundle of boards." The ordinary sailors were even less cooperative. If Shelvocke asked them what was going on, they refused to answer his question and maintained a surly silence or muttered that they would do what the majority decided. All these signs confirmed Shelvocke "in the suspicion that I had had for some time before that there was a black design a kindling which was now ready to break out into a destructive flame."

Suspecting the worst, he told his son George to hide his letter of marque. The young man was to go secretly and find "some dry place of the woods or rocks" and conceal the document. It was Shelvocke's only form of insurance. Whatever his men decided to do, if they were caught by the Spanish and could not produce a letter of marque, they would be sure to be executed as pirates. The written "commission" was the expedition's only fig leaf of legality. Keeping control of the letter was the sole bargaining counter that Shelvocke could prepare.

The crisis came on an afternoon when Shelvocke realized that the only people in camp were him, his son, his nephew John Adams, the ship's surgeon, and Mr. Henry, the owners' agent. Thomas Dodd, the lieutenant of marines and Betagh's former subordinate, was also there. But he was an elderly man and was of no consequence because "for some reason best known to himself [he] had feigned lunacy and had a mind to act the mad man."

That evening Shelvocke learned why the camp had been deserted. Everyone else had gone to a meeting at the spot they called "the great tree." There they held a conference to decide a new structure for the expedition. The spokesman and prime mover was a midshipman whom Shelvocke disdainfully describes as someone "who both made and mended their shoes before the Speedwell was lost." He calls him "Morphew"—though his real name seems to have been William Murphy, a name that appears on the crew list—and he insinuated that Morphew was not only a cobbler by trade but a thief who had stolen a ship's boat on a previous voyage.

Morphew addressed the meeting to tell them "that they were their own masters and servants to none." He went on to say that although Shelvocke had been appointed as captain by the sponsors of the expedition, any future captain should hold the post only by the general consent of the crew. Shelvocke's command "was too lofty and arbitrary for a private ship" and he would have been better off staying in the Royal Navy where the sailors were "obliged quietly to bear all hardships imposed upon them." The decision of the meeting was that Shelvocke was formally deposed from his position as captain, and the entire crew placed themselves under "Jamaica discipline." Jamaica discipline was the code of conduct of the Caribbean buccaneers. Its main components were that all men had an equal vote in the running of the expedition; they could pick and choose their own leader; and—above all—any booty would be shared out according to the wish of the majority. *Speedwell*'s men had taken a step that changed them from privateers operating under a letter of marque to the status of pirates.

In the night the crew brought the new contract to Shelvocke's tent for him to sign. The opening paragraph informed him that "whereas the Speedwell was cast away . . . they were now of consequence at their own disposal, so that their obligations to the Owners and to me were of no validity; the ship being no more." Under these conditions "they had now thought fit to frame such articles as would be most conducive to their own interest." Their first key demand was that in future all booty should be divided equally among the crew. Nothing was to be set aside for the owners. The second clause laid down that "in all attacks by sea or land, and everything else, the people's consent was to be ask'd in general, every one to have a single vote, and their Captain to have two."

Examining the document more closely, Shelvocke noted that the mutineers had also decreased his allotment of shares in any booty. Under the previous agreement with the owners his entitlement had been sixty shares; now "I found myself reduced from sixty shares to six." When he remonstrated, he was told that "I might think myself well off since the Jamaica captains were allowed but four shares and they had given me two more out of regard they had for me." The mutineers also informed him that he was lucky to be asked to continue on as captain, and that they would only accept him if first he signed the Articles. "Otherwise they would not trust themselves under my conduct, because they should always be apprehensive that I had sinister intentions upon them." The mutineers had in mind the recent case of a privateer captain who had agreed to his men's demands verbally, but without signing a written agreement. Later, when the opportunity arose, "he denied them, and suffered eight of them to be hanged as pyrates, before his face."

"I was at a loss, not knowing what to do in this dilemma," Shelvocke pleads to his reader "and was distracted at the thought of subjecting myself to the caprices of a giddy mutinous gang of obstinate fellows who were dead to reason and in a fair way of being hardened in all kinds of wickedness." He claims that he had no alternative. If he did not sign, there was little chance that the rescue vessel would be built; or, if it was built, then he would probably be forcibly marooned on the island, or be murdered for the sake of the letter of marque and no one would ever know who committed the crime. As his final excuse, he stresses that he had already been betrayed by the other officers.

True to character, he signed the Articles.

Shelvocke hoped that once he signed, the mutineers would return to work on the half-built boat. But when he walked down to the building site early next morning, his hopes were disappointed. There was no one on the beach except the carpenter, Robert Davenport, and two or three assistants. They were at work on the hull, but Shelvocke was too petulant to give them much credit. They were still mutineers, as far as he was concerned, and their efforts were motivated "by the hopes of some money from me." He wondered what the rest of the crew were doing, and "what mischief they possibly might have in their heads, after what they had already done."

He soon found out. The next morning Morphew reappeared at his tent accompanied by Matthew Stewart, whom the crew had appointed as their spokesman and who was probably still in collusion with Shelvocke. The deputation came to demand "in the name of all the people" that Shelvocke hand over all the booty previously set aside as the owners' share. It included a stock of raw silver ingots valued at 750 pieces of eight, a large silver dish weighing 75 ounces, and 250 dollars in cash. Shelvocke had to agree to their demand, and the hoard was immediately shared out under the rules of the new Jamaica discipline.

At this stage Shelvocke's original ship's company had effectively split into a competing number of factions. There was the main body of rebels, led by Morphew and Brooks; a dwindling faction loyal to Shelvocke; the older and steadier men who shared the tent of George Henshal, the bosun; a few cantankerous individuals like Mr. Coldsea, the master—"the most quarrelsome turbulent fellow in the ship," who wanted nothing to do with any group; and six or seven craftsmen, notably the carpenter, who were still working on the boat. There was yet another, more dangerous, group on the periphery. About a dozen men had withdrawn from the camp altogether. They formed a band living in the hills. They contributed neither to the boat building nor the food gathering, but would come down in the evenings like brigands and extort rations. When they were caught trying to steal muskets and gunpowder, Shelvocke told them that next time they came within musket shot of the camp they would be treated as enemies.

There was one more indignity Shelvocke had to endure: the entire body of mutineers came again to his tent and demanded that he hand over all the muskets in his care. The mutineers, Shelvocke claimed, feared that he might lead a counter-uprising, possibly with the assistance of the bosun's faction. The confrontation over the muskets led to an ugly scene. Morphew and Edward Brooks, the first lieutenant, were again the ringleaders. They stood outside the tent and "used me with so much impudence and opprobrious language as never could have been believed to come out of the mouths of men." When Shelvocke's son George intervened to tell Morphew that he did not necessarily speak for everyone, he was promptly threatened by the mutineers. Shelvocke had been keeping the muskets near him for a practical reason. There was only a single flint for every gun, and he did not want the weapons damaged or neglected. Now he was obliged to hand the muskets over, and to his chagrin the men "had the pleasure of squandering away their time and powder and shot in firing at cats or anything else to waste the ammunition."

It took a real, outside threat to bring everyone to their senses.

On 15 August a large sailing vessel was sighted on the horizon, apparently heading for the island. There was widespread panic. No one recognized the vessel. She was certainly not the *Success* under Clipperton. Shelvocke suspected she was a Spanish ship, probably a merchant vessel. If her lookouts saw the castaways there, her captain would turn away without anchoring and report to the authorities on the mainland that there were strangers on the island. Inevitably the Spanish authorities in Chile would send an armed force to investigate, and the castaways would be in peril of being captured and perhaps condemned to death as pirates.

Shelvocke acted decisively. Before the strange sail came any closer, he ordered all the fires to be doused. The sight of smoke rising from the beach would have been a disaster. He also gave instructions to tie up all the Indians and the Negroes. His fear was that the foreign vessel might be becalmed near the island, and one of them might risk swimming out to the ship and giving the alarm.

The *Speedwell*'s crew watched anxiously from their vantage points to see whether the strange sail would approach closer. The ship had only to pass across the mouth of Cumberland Bay for her lookouts to see the most telltale evidence of human occupation—the skeleton of the rescue boat sitting on its blocks on the edge of the beach. It was unmissable.

Slowly the strange vessel moved across the horizon while Shelvocke tried to work out the course she was making. It was some time before he could be certain that the vessel was still keeping well offshore and would be too far away for her watchmen to notice any details on the island.

When the danger was passed and everyone had relaxed, Shelvocke took the chance to reassert his authority. During the scare many of the mutineers had abandoned their independence and obeyed his instructions. Now he appealed to them to continue to work together. But they bluntly told him that they had carried out his orders only because it was in their own interests. Worse, the next morning the mutineers called another general council to consider the question of destroying the half-built escape boat. Some of them argued that the boat represented a constant danger. It was far too conspicuous from the sea, and might attract the attention of the Spaniards. These sailors wanted to burn the half-built boat where she lay, and instead build two smaller vessels in some out-of-the-way creek where the hulls could be camouflaged. Shelvocke argued vigorously against such a reckless scheme. He pointed out that if they burned the boat, there was not enough surplus timber to complete the substitutes, and the boat building tools which Popplestone the armorer had made, were nearly worn out. In the end the carpenter and his mates who had actually done the boat building work quashed the proposal. They were understandably opposed to the idea that their months of labor should go up in flames. It was typical, said Shelvocke, that the boat burning scheme was put forward by the men who "had never done an hour's work since we had been cast away but had been on the contrary the first movers in perverting the minds of the rest and were, in return for my indefatigable pains to serve them, come to insult me and those few who had been my assistants on the strand."

This disaffected group now proposed, out of spite, that First Lieutenant Brooks should be promoted to captain and take command. Fortunately the bosun's faction overruled them. To add to Shelvocke's gloom, it became clear that the carpenter felt that some disaffected mutineer might set fire to the boat, whatever had been decided at the meeting. In the same night the carpenter quietly sent word to Shelvocke that he wanted to be paid the money he had been promised for completing the boat, even though the boat was not finished. Otherwise Shelvocke "should not see his face again." Once more Shelvocke was forced to pay up.

The arguments over the fate of the half-built boat marked the low tide of morale on the island. From now on there was a gradual return to cooperation between the main body of the castaways, as they began to realize that they would have to work together if they were ever to leave the island. It was First Lieutenant Brooks who made the first move toward a reconciliation. He re-appeared at Shelvocke's tent and asked if he could again take his meals with the captain and his associates. Brooks still remained on very good terms with Morphew the rebel leader, but he was now willing to take a hand with the boat building. His open cooperation encouraged other volunteers to join the team on the beach, and progress on the boat speeded up.

The construction had now reached a critical stage. The carpenter and his team had completed the skeleton of the boat. Keel, bow, and stern pieces and all the frames stood in place, and the moment had come to begin planking. This was when the castaways felt most severely the lack of suitable boat building timber on the island. None of the native trees could provide the carpenter with the length and width of planking he required. Instead he had to send men to prise deck boards from the wreck of the *Speedwell*, and attempt to reshape those into hull planks. But the salvaged deck boards were poor material. They were stiff and dry from long exposure to the sun—almost impossible to coax into new shapes. The carpenter tried his skill in applying fire and steam to make the salvaged wood pliable. When his assistants struggled to bend the planks against the frames and fix them in place, the timbers "split and flew like glass." Shelvocke began to lose heart. By now he was working alongside the men on the boat and "had substantial reasons to believe that all our labor had been in vain." He felt they might have to give up the boat altogether and "quietly sit down with the disagreeable hopes of being taken off by some Spanish ship some time or other, and after all our troubles be led to a prison to reflect on our misfortunes."

Section by section, the carpenter and his team persevered. They kept working at the shape and fit they needed, using the makeshift tools and stubborn timber. It took them "constant labour and a variety of contrivances, [until] we patch'd her up in such a manner that I dare say the like was never seen, and I may safely affirm that such a bottom never swam on the surface of the sea before."

Now that the escape boat was nearly planked up, Shelvocke turned his attention to laying in a stock of food for the forthcoming voyage of deliverance. From the *Speedwell*'s stores they had kept the emergency ration of one cask of beef and five or six bushels of cassava flour. But this was nothing like sufficient food for the number of men the boat was expected to carry. The rations would last no more than four or five days, enough to bring them directly to the coast of Chile, where they would have to force a landing and hope to seize more supplies. Shelvocke wanted to keep his options open. It would be better if the boat could stay at sea, proceeding along the mainland coast until they found an undefended target, or even intercept a Spanish ship off guard and loaded with supplies.

But without salt the men found it impossible to cure the fish and seal meat that ships normally carried away from the island as "sea stock." They made various experiments to preserve their catch, but nothing succeeded until they discovered a way to conserve the flesh of conger eel. First they removed the eel's backbone, then dipped the meat in seawater and afterward hung up the strips of flesh in the thick smoke of a fire. This combination of pickling and smoking conserved the conger eel meat sufficiently for their purpose.

In camp there was an increasing expectation that the plan of evacuation would succeed. The cooper checked and sealed water casks; the sailmaker's team recut and sewed the *Speedwell*'s old canvas to make a fresh suit of sails, and the bosun's team picked apart her old ropes, spun and relaid the yarn, and spliced rigging for the new vessel. Lieutenant Brooks was now so fully committed to the escape plan that he went out to the *Speedwell*'s hulk to see what else might be usefully recovered. The wreck was now largely underwater, but Brooks was a trained diver, the only one among the crew. He succeeded in locating two pieces of a large church candlestick "which was part of the Gentlemen Owners plate" and—more important—a small gun that had been mounted on the *Speedwell*'s quarterdeck as part of her armament. Brooks managed to get a line attached to the gun and, with the help of a float, buoyed the weapon to the surface and brought it ashore to be fitted to the escape vessel.

The final and most problematic stage of the boat building had now arrived: the caulking of the hull. This was when lengths of fiber, stripped from old rope or made up from twists of cloth or even vegetable matter, would have to be pushed into the crevices between the planks to make the hull watertight. Shelvocke had low expectations. He knew that the earlier work had been very awkward and the tools makeshift, and the workmen were not professional shipwrights. It was impossible that the hull would be tight. The workmen tried caulking the hull as best they could, then poured water into the boat to check the result. He was not surprised that a cry went up: " 'A Sieve! A Sieve!' " Water was gushing from dozens of leaks in the hull. It required the last reserves of optimism for the workmen to return to the tedious chore of locating and plugging each leak, one by one, until the hull seemed watertight. As a precaution Shelvocke asked the cooper whether he had sufficient materials to make every man a wooden bucket to bail with.

The next spring tide, the best moment to attempt to float their vessel off the beach, was on 5 October. It was over four months since the loss of the *Speedwell*. The cooper had his water barrels on hand to be filled with fresh water from the stream that trickled out through the boulders near the building site, and the eel fishermen had outdone themselves. They had prepared a massive supply of 2,300 smoked conger eels, each weighing about a pound, with sixty gallons of seal oil to fry them in.

The launch team assembled on the beach, and the keel blocks were knocked away. The hull should have settled down on the chocks placed to receive her, but there was one last, heart-stopping hitch. The hull came down awkwardly, and the chocks shifted. The stern dropped heavily onto the shingle. For a moment Shelvocke feared that the boat was irretrievably stuck and that all was lost. It was the same black disappointment that Robinson Crusoe felt when he found that after months of labor carving a dugout canoe from a large tree trunk, his vessel was too awkwardly placed and heavy to get into the water.

But Shelvocke's vessel was not stuck as fast as he had feared. The carpenter had built the boat with her bow toward the sea, and by lacing a cradle of ropes and tackles around her stern, the launch team were able to break the inertia. Before the tide had retreated, the castaways succeeded in dragging their creation into water enough to make her float. For an anchor they had only a rope attached to a heavy boulder, and remembering how the *Speedwell* had been driven ashore in that same bay, they knew they should not delay for an instant. The fresh water and stores were loaded that same day, and by next morning she was ready to set sail. Shelvocke was immensely proud of what he saw as his masterpiece: "She had two masts and was about 20 tons burthen, and to my great satisfaction, [we] found that one pump, constantly working kept her free [of water in the bilges]."

A hundred and thirty-seven days of miseries, mishaps, mutinies, bribes, and intermittent labor had produced the means of escape for the castaways. With a fine dramatic sense Shelvocke named her—*Recovery*.

The small boat was an extraordinary sight. More than forty men were crammed together so tightly that they had to lie on the bundles of smoked eels and "being in no method of keeping themselves clean, all our senses were as much offended as possible." To add to the squalor, they had with them four hogs which had been kept alive on Juan Fernandez by being fed putrid seal carcasses. To drink, the men sucked fresh water from the water butts through a musket barrel passed from hand to hand. Food was rationed to one eel per man per day, and there were frequent quarrels over extra scraps.

This noxious crew of ruffians prowled the coastal shipping route of Peru in search of a better vessel. After several thwarted attacks, they succeeded in capturing a ship four times larger than their own—the two-hundred-ton merchantman *Jesu Maria*. The Spanish captain offered to raise a sixteen-thousand-dollar ransom if he could retain his ship, but—for once—Shelvocke turned down the cash. He transferred his men and booty to the captured prize, and left the unlucky Spaniards to find their way to port aboard the frail *Recovery*. Meanwhile he sailed off in his new command which, with his flair for words, he renamed *Happy Return*. To the surprise of both captains he encountered his former commander, John Clipperton, cruising in the *Success* off the coast of Central America. The last time they had seen one another was two years earlier in the English Channel. It was a frosty meeting. Clipperton demanded that Shelvocke and his crew hand over the owners' share of plunder, but it had already been distributed under the Jamaica discipline. Shelvocke refused, and he and Clipperton sailed in company only briefly.

Shelvocke and his band next captured a valuable prize, the three-hundred-ton *Sacra Familia,* only to learn that peace had been declared between Spain and England and therefore their letter of marque was invalid. Undeterred, they made off with their catch and soon afterward took another Spanish ship, *La Concepcion.* This time Shelvocke used the excuse that he had been attacked first. He claimed that he had approached the Spanish ship to ask for a pilot, and had been fired on when he hoisted the English flag. Naturally he had to fire back, and the encounter ended with Shelvocke's men boarding and ransacking the *Concepcion* of more than one hundred thousand dollars in coin. They released the prisoners only after they had agreed to sign a document to say that Shelvocke had acted in self-defense.

Shelvocke now wisely made his exit from the South Sea. He took the *Sacra Familia* across the Pacific to China, where he sold her in Canton for cash to be divided among the crew. But he seems to have hoodwinked them by entering into a fraudulent arrangement with the Chinese customs officials. The *Sacra Familia* was sold for £700 but her customs dues had been officially calculated at £2000. The gross disparity between what Shelvocke claimed he paid the Chinese in customs dues and the real value of the vessel would indicate that part of the customs money found its way back into Shelvocke's own pocket. Without a ship and with a personal profit of at least seven thousand pounds, he landed back in England on 30 July 1722, accompanied by his son George. He had been away three years and seven months. Of the original 106 men who had sailed out from Plymouth aboard the *Speedwell* only 33 were left.

When Shelvocke called on his former mentor, Edward Hughes, he was arrested. Hughes was acting on information received from Betagh, who had come home almost a year earlier and denounced Shelvocke as a fraudster. Hughes, an investor in the original endeavor, was determined to bring Shelvocke before the courts to extract his share of any plunder. At the same time the Spanish ambassador demanded Shelvocke be tried for piracy. Shelvocke slipped adroitly through their fingers. He was acquitted of the piracy charge through lack of evidence, and while

Hughes's court case was pending, Shelvocke escaped from the King's Bench Prison, "probably through bribery," according to his official biography. He vanished. Betagh believed that Shelvocke fled abroad with his ill-gotten gains, escaping before a writ could be served on him with a penalty of eight thousand pounds if he fled the kingdom. Yet less than two years later Shelvocke coolly surfaced again. He presented a copy of his journal to the Admiralty, and soon afterward published his story as a successful book, which Betagh furiously denounced as "the most absurd false narrative that was ever deliver'd to the publick." It opened with a brazen dedication to the Board of the Admiralty. Shelvocke also put his son George on the first rung of a respectable career in government service. When Captain George Shelvocke died in 1742 at the age of sixty-six, his son had risen to become secretary to the General Post Office. Thus, the old sea officer was able to spend his last days at his son's official residence, a substantial townhouse, where the retired sailor and self-promoting adventurer was, by all appearances, a reputable elderly citizen.

Rascal, humbug, and knave, George Shelvocke was nevertheless the only Juan Fernandez castaway who succeeded in getting himself and his companions off the island by their own efforts. His version of events on the island is not the "just History of Fact" which Defoe claims, tongue in cheek for Robinson Crusoe's story. Every paragraph of Shelvocke's narrative betrays vanity, self-interest, and mendacity. Yet he was the driving force who created the *Recovery*, and it was a remarkable achievement. Sadly, Robert Davenport, the surly carpenter, and John Popplestone, the hard-working multitalented armorer, both died on the transpacific passage to China, so neither got to enjoy the "dividend"—£880 for Davenport, and £660 for Popplestone—they were awarded from the capture of the *Concepcion*. Shelvocke, by contrast, led a charmed life. He may have protested loudly about his tribulations on Juan Fernandez, pleading that he was insulted by his men, half-starved, and the victim of one plot after another, but he actually enjoyed some of his time there. It is clear that he was very closely involved in the building of the *Recovery*, and took great pride in the little ship. His description of the building process, stage by stage, is by a man who knew a great deal about boat building. Almost as an aside, he mentions that there came a time when he was working alongside the carpenter and his team. A reduced diet and hard work, he proudly states, meant that he "became one of the strongest and most active men on the island, from being very corpulent and almost crippled with Gout." His stay on Juan Fernandez did him good.

Not everyone had Shelvocke's confidence in the *Recovery*. When the little ship was about to set out on her perilous passage toward the mainland, Shelvocke contacted the gang of a dozen renegades who had been skulking in the bush. But none of them would risk going aboard the overcrowded vessel. They declared that "they were not yet prepared for the other world" and chose to stay on the island. They were joined by "the like number of Blacks and Indians," who had no choice. They were discarded so as to leave more room aboard the escape vessel.

These two dozen men were the last known maroons to be living on Juan Fernandez during Daniel Defoe's lifetime. Their tenure on the island was brief. That summer the Spaniards must have come and removed them, because a Dutch squadron visited the island the next year and found the place again deserted. The Dutch revictualed at the island and sailed away, leaving one man buried there. He fell to his death while climbing in the mountains. The tragedy recalled Shelvocke's memories of the alarming hours of darkness—and Robinson Crusoe's gloomy thoughts and night time fears—when "nothing can be conceived more dismally solemn than to hear the silence of the still night destroyed by the surf of the sea beating against the shore, together with the violent roaring of the sea lions repeated all around by the echoes of deep vallies, the incessant howling of the seals." To these dismal noises, wrote Shelvocke, must be added "the sudden precipitate rumbling of trees down steep descents; for there is hardly a gust of wind stirring that does not tear up a great many trees by the roots, which have but a slight hold on the earth especially near the brinks of precipices. All these, or any of these frightful noises would be sufficient to prevent the repose of any who had not been fore some time inured to it."

Today, the sounds of the island provide a link with the days of the maroons. The thrash and suck of the waves on the rocky shore, the incessant uproar of the seal colonies, the rustle of the wind through the brushwood on the higher slopes, and a great empty echoing of the wind across the high ridges are the same sounds they heard. The movements of cloud shadows on the slopes, the colors of the vegetation, the vast prospect of the ocean in every direction are the sights they saw every day they lived there. Yet the timelessness of these links leaves a feeling that the brief visits of the maroons and castaways are paltry events in the long history of the island. They have left no physical trace. The island flicked off its puny visitors like a large animal shivering its skin to remove a tiny insect. Indeed, Juan Fernandez Island constantly is shedding its skin. The mantle of volcanic soil is forever sliding and slipping down toward the ocean edge. It carries away the particles and remnants of human occupation. The pace of erosion is visible. Gullies appear overnight in the soil; a signpost hammered into the soil grows taller each month as the soil around it is blown or washed away, a waterpipe laid in the soil is exposed six inches above the ground within three or four years. There is a slow but constant erasing of human endeavor.

Only names survive. "Crusoe's Cave" and "Selkirk's Lookout" are there to evoke the past. So too are the ultimate accolades—the names Isla Robinson Crusoe and Isla Alejandro Selkirk. But there is no mention of the true castaways—Shelvocke and the crew of the wrecked *Speedwell*.

Nor is there a memorial to remind the visitor that the island was home to another maroon who was as real as Selkirk, and almost as famous as Robinson Crusoe—Man Friday.

Man Friday and Crusoe finally leave their island.

Chapter III
MOSKITO MAN

The *Batchelor's Delight* found Man Friday on a Sunday. It was 23 March 1684. The model for Defoe's native hero had been on Juan Fernandez, marooned and solitary, for more than three years. Yet he was remarkably nonchalant when the landing party from the *Batchelor's Delight* stepped ashore and ended his long solitude. He greeted the piratical crew as if he had been expecting them, and he had a meal ready—three goats cooked with some white leaves of cabbage palm. It was as though they had come to the island with the express intention of finding him, and he thanked them graciously. In a sense, he was right to do so.

Man Friday's story is in the fourth chapter of the richly bound volume that the ex-buccaneer William Dampier, the pilot of the vessel that rescued Alexander Selkirk, holds, spine toward the artist, in his portrait by Thomas Murray. When Murray painted the picture, the book was an obvious prop. Dampier's *A New Voyage round the World* had recently been published, and so great was demand that three editions were printed in the first year, 1697. Its far-traveled author was the talk of London society. Dampier's true-life descriptions of firsthand adventure, travel, and geography was so exotic that it was natural that Defoe, twenty-two years later, would take inspiration from Dampier's absorbing tale. Defoe's concept of Man Friday was to be shaped by events that Dampier witnessed, beginning on the shores of the Caribbean in the spring of 1680.

A flotilla of seven small ships was anchored in the lee of Golden Island, a tiny island on the Caribbean side of the Isthmus of Panama close to Cape Tiburon. The anchorage, a few miles north of what is now the border between Colombia and Panama, was a favorite rendezvous for pirates or, as their contemporary and unofficial historian, A. O. Exquemelin, called them more genteelly, "buccaneers." Three hundred thirty-one heavily armed pirates had disembarked, ready for a route march into the rain forest. The standard equipment each man carried was a "fuzee, pistol and hanger"; that is, a musket, a hand gun, and a short sword or cutlass suspended from the belt. Many wore "snapsacks" on their backs to carry their spare clothing, gunpowder, and shot. The ships' cooks had made three or four "doughboys," small loaves of bread, for each man as his marching rations. For water they anticipated drinking from the numerous streams draining the mist-covered mountains that lay ahead of them.

The intention was to launch a hit-and-run raid on the Spanish mining town of Santa Maria, which lay on the far slope of the continental divide that runs down the narrow waist of Central America. If they did not find enough loot in Santa Maria, they would continue on to the Pacific shore and strike at an even more ambitious target, the city of Panama. The raiders made little pretense of having the correct privateering documents to legitimize such an assault. Their "commissions," as one of their leaders put it, would best be read by the light of the muzzle flashes from their guns.

The raiders formed up in six companies, each company approximating the crew of the ship that had brought them. In the vanguard was Captain Bartholomew Sharpe. He had recently been ill and was still feeling very faint and weak; he had contributed forty men to the expedition. Their marching flag was red with a bunch of green and white ribbons. Next came Captain Richard Sawkins with thirty-five men forming up behind a red pennant striped with yellow. Captain Peter Harris's ship had the largest crew, 107 men. Those who had been picked to go on the raid marched as two companies, each with a green flag. Behind them came the man elected as overall commander of the enterprise, Captain John Coxon. His war band was reinforced with volunteers from two of the smallest ships, whose captains were staying behind to look after the invasion fleet. The sixth company followed a red banner striped with yellow. On this background Captain Edmund Cook had emblazoned his personal emblem—a hand and a sword.

The colorful quasi-military array masked the fact that the expedition was little more than a smash-and-grab raid by a gang of amphibious brigands. "Gold was the bait that tempted a Merry Pack of Boys of us" was how one ruffian jauntily described their motives. Their rule was to be the "Jamaica discipline": All decisions were to be made by vote of a general council; the men would elect or dismiss their leaders; and they would divide any booty equally and immediately.

Several members of the column had no vote nor any share in the booty. They were the prisoners and slaves, mostly Indian or black. They were treated as pack animals to portage the extra munitions and supplies. Nor did the Indian auxiliaries have any votes. The local Indian tribe, the Kuna, had suggested the attack on Santa Maria and Panama, and only the Kuna were capable of conducting the expedition through the difficult tangle of muddy footpaths leading up over the central cordillera and down the far slope to the South Sea. But very few of the Kuna spoke English. This was a disadvantage when the entire business of the expedition was conducted in English, the votes of the general council were called in English, and the raiders themselves were proud of their Englishness. Two more pirate captains had promised to provide men for the project, but had backed out at the last moment because, as one of the desperadoes scathingly wrote, their crews were "all French and not willing to go to Panama."

There was one conspicuous exception to this barrier of racial, linguistic, and chauvinistic discrimination. Scattered throughout the raiding column was a handful of Indians who spoke enough English to make themselves understood, and some were fluent. They had been promised, and would be paid, a full share of any booty. The English pirates were careful that no one should cheat these Indians. It was a level of respect the buccaneers gave to no one else, in a situation where double dealing and chicanery in dividing up the spoils was normal. Most remarkable of all, the Indians were also absolved from the rule that forbade any person to leave the expedition without the permission of the general council. They could come and go as they pleased, and no one would dream of stopping them. The English gave these Indians nicknames; the man who was to be the model for Man Friday was called Will.

These brothers-in-arms to the English pirates were Miskito Indians. They were "esteemed and coveted by all Privateers," according to Dampier. When a Miskito man volunteered to sail on a visiting ship, his offer was quickly accepted, and "It is very rare to find Privateers destitute of one or more of them." However, the Miskitos preferred to join a ship where "the Commander or most of the men are English"; for they "do not love the French, and the Spaniards they hate mortally." What made the important presence of the Miskitos among the English buccaneers even more remarkable was that there were so few of them. In their homeland, a swampy strip of Caribbean coast in today's Honduras and Nicaragua, the entire Miskito nation numbered less than two thousand individuals.

Miskito men solved a logistical problem that faced the buccaneers—how to feed such a large number of sailors. Dampier claimed that just two Miskito men could catch enough food for a hundred men. The secret lay in their technique. Most seafarers, of course, knew how to fish with hook and line and how to set nets. But this required time and patience, and a knowledge of where to find the fish. Even then the results were uncertain. The "Moskito Men" took fish quite differently, and their method was effective wherever their travels brought them. A Miskito launched his small dugout canoe from the deck of the ship and paddled off, standing upright in the narrow and unstable boat, "which our men could not go in without danger of oversetting." With phenomenally good eyesight, he scanned the water for movement. The instant he saw a target, he flung the barbed trident, his "fish gig," and very seldom missed. So the buccaneers called their Miskitos their "strikers" and never ceased to marvel at their accuracy. "They are very ingenious at throwing . . . any manner of Dart, being bred to it from their Infancy" Dampier wrote, "for the Children imitating their Parents, never go abroad without a Lance in their Hands, which they throw at any Object till use hath made them masters of the Art." Trainee Miskitos were so deft that as a game, two Miskito youths would take up their positions facing one another "at a fair mark." One would then fire arrows at the other. His opponent was expected to flick away the oncoming arrows using a small, thin stick arrow no thicker than a ramrod. "When they are grown to be Men," concluded Dampier, "they will guard themselves from Arrows, tho' they come very thick at them, provided two do not happen to come at once."

A Miskito striker seldom took the clumsy white men in his canoe when he was fishing, and he resented any interference. If irritated, the Miskitos were known to make their hungry shipmates pay the price. They "purposely strike their Harpoons and Turtle Irons aside or so glance them as to kill nothing."

The spearfishing skill of the Miskitos was so important to the English that when the time came to careen the ship, they brought their vessels to places on the coast where their strikers could hunt the prey that provided the most flesh. The most productive catch were manatees or sea cows and sea turtles, the latter being "the best meat in the world." For each species the Miskito carried special throwing spears—the turtle spear was tipped with a "peg," a short stubby point capable of penetrating the turtle's thick shell, whereas the manatee lance had a longer point and was more like a harpoon.

There is no description of what "Will the Moskito" looked like, though Dampier describes a typical Miskito as "tall, well made, lusty, strong." He had a long narrow face with a dark copper complexion, and long black hair. His expression was "stern and hard favoured," and he was a good man to have on your side in a fight, as he would not flinch when the battle was going badly. The Miskito "think that the white men with whom they are, know better than they do when it is best to fight, and let the disadvantage of their party be never so great, they will never yield or give back while any of their party stands." At home the Miskito had a more sinister reputation. They regularly deployed their weapons and fighting prowess to raid their neighbors' settlements, seizing slaves and tribute, and they conducted an unremitting guerrilla war against the Spaniards. Their dexterity and aim with the harpoon made them natural marksmen with firearms, and their buccaneer name Moskito may have been acquired, not from a comparison with stinging insects, but as a derivation from the word musket which they used so accurately.

Self-confidence, curiosity, and adaptability made the Miskito natural travelers. On visits to English settlements they bought and wore European clothes and took "delight to go neat and tight." But the moment they came home they reverted to their native dress, "wearing only a small piece of Linnen tied about their Wastes, hanging down to their knees." In their homeland they liked nothing better than "to settle near the Sea, or by some River, for the sake of striking Fish, their beloved employment."

The buccaneer raiding column took a fortnight to walk through the jungle from the "North Sea" to the "South Sea," from the Caribbean to the Pacific. It was a labyrinthine journey, even with six Kuna guides to show them the way. On one dismal day they had to wade the same river between fifty and sixty times. When the Kuna finally obtained canoes, the buccaneers found that there were so many shallows and rapids that they had to dismount from the dugouts and drag them over the rocks, and got drenched in the process. Kuna villages along the track gave them food, so they were not hungry, but the attack on Santa Maria was a disappointment. Captain Sawkins led the charge, and when the buccaneers burst inside the palisade they found that the Spaniards had been forewarned. The Spanish officials had shipped out all the gold they had obtained from sifting the gold-rich alluvial deposits in the region, and Santa Maria's strongroom was empty. The raiders decided to press on, hoping to seize Panama.

Their audacity was breathtaking. They emerged from the mouth of the river and paddled out on to the Pacific in a swarm of dugout canoes. They were equipped only with their muskets and cutlasses. Their targets were usually unarmed merchant ships, yet they also tackled full-sized sea-going vessels equipped with cannon. They suppressed the cannon fire by shooting the deck gunners, an extraordinary feat from a small open boat. Then they boarded and captured their targets. Soon they had acquired a small flotilla in which they ranged up and down the coast, spreading terror and fighting a series of running battles with Spanish patrols.

Their boldness was matched by equally disastrous mismanagement. Under Jamaica discipline there were quarrels, reversals of earlier decisions, and feuds. A rapid turnover of commanders was exacerbated by a high mortality rate. The bold Captain Sawkins, hero of Santa Maria, led one charge too many and was killed; Captain Peter Harris died of wounds after a tussle with a Spanish guard ship; and Captain Coxon, feeling slighted, withdrew from the expedition and led fifty men back across the mountains to the Caribbean. He was to have a spectacular career as a pirate and finish up, according to rumor, living among the Miskitos on the Honduran coast. Captain Bartholomew Sharpe, having recovered from his fever, was voted to overall command after Sawkins was killed, though by December the expedition he was in charge of had been severely reduced by death, desertion, and capture to less than half their original number, though it still included Dampier and "Will the Moskito." At that stage the expedition decided to withdraw and spend Christmas at that favorite place for recuperation: the island of Juan Fernandez.

The buccaneers were still loitering at the island, undecided as to their next move, when a group of their men in one of the ship's smaller boats appeared from the shore, frantically rowing toward their ship's anchorage and firing their muskets to attract attention. They had been hunting wild goats in the heights of the island, and from their vantage point had seen sails approaching. They feared that this was a Spanish flotilla coming to check up on the known buccaneer hideout. Half an hour later the visitors were identified as three Spanish warships. Another confused embarkation took place as the buccaneers hoisted sail and fled. Unfortunately they left one man behind. This time the maroon was one of their highly prized Indian comrades. Will the Moskito had been hunting goats in the interior of the island, and no one was able to warn him that the ship was leaving. Will was left to fend for himself. Unlike Selkirk, he was a genuine maroon and had not asked to be left behind. So he had to make do with what he happened to have with him at the time—his musket, a flask of powder and some shot, and a hunting knife.

Will's reaction to his predicament was very different from Selkirk's passive response.

He took matters in stride. He began by taking his food from the seal rookery, though he was not fond of the taste of seal meat. Later he only killed the seals and sea lions so that he could slice their hides into thin strips and make fishing lines for himself. For shelter he erected a typical Miskito hunting camp—a small hut of branches and thatch—about half a mile from the sea. He lined this shelter with goatskins for warmth and to keep out the rain. Inside his hut he built a barbecue. This was not for cooking meat, but the original "barbecu," a low frame of sticks about two feet high which the Miskitos and other Caribbean Indians used as a sleeping couch to keep them off the damp ground and away from insects. This bed he also covered with goatskins.

In his account of Will's adventures, Dampier recounts that Will's main enterprise was to destroy his musket. As soon as he had expended all the powder and shot, he started on the task of turning the now-useless weapon into more functional equipment. He began by cutting notches into the blade of his hunting knife until he had converted it into a makeshift hacksaw. With this tool he proceeded to "saw the barrel of his gun into small pieces." Next he tempered a section of the barrel in the fire, "having learned to do that among the English." Against this tempered metal he struck the flint salvaged from the gun, and so made himself fire whenever he wanted. Now he took the pieces of gun barrel and began to make himself "Harpoons, Lances, Hooks and a Long Knife." He heated each piece in the fire, and "the hot pieces of iron he would hammer out and bend as he pleased with Stones." Once he had achieved the rough shape, he did the finishing work using his jagged knife, then retempered the metal to extra hardness, and finally added a sharp edge by grinding the metal against rocks. "All this may seem strange to those that are not acquainted with the sagacity of the Indians," Dampier comments, "but it is no more that these Moskito Men are accustomed to in their own country, where they make their own Fishing and Striking Instruments without either Forge or Anvil, tho they spend a good deal of their time about them."

Time was a commodity that Will the Moskito had in abundance. Like Selkirk, he was only disturbed by the occasional visit by the Spaniards. But whereas Selkirk was seen only by chance when a Spanish landing party came ashore, the Spaniards deliberately came looking for any stragglers from Captain Sharpe's gang. They suspected that Will was somewhere on the island, but had no more luck than anyone else. The Miskito hunter was too agile and wary to be caught.

The *Batchelor's Delight,* which came over the horizon in the late autumn of 1684, three years after Will's marooning, was a former Danish merchant ship. The pirates who captured her off the African coast had converted her into a sea raider, and sailed round Cape Horn to begin another raid on the Spanish. Astonishingly, several men aboard her, including Dampier, had been with Captain Sharpe when they beat a hasty retreat from Juan Fernandez and left Will to his fate. Now they were curious to see what might have become of their former companion.

The *Batchelor's Delight* carried its own Miskito striker. His shipmates called him Robin and he made sure he was in the ship's boat when it was rowed to the beach where Will stood waiting. Will's clothes had long since fallen to pieces, and he was dressed only in a loincloth made of goatskin. As soon as the ship's boat touched the beach, Robin leaped out and ran pell-mell toward Will. When he came close, he threw himself facedown on the ground. Will stooped over, and helped him back on his feet. Then the two men threw their arms around one another and embraced. Now it was Will's turn to throw himself flat on the ground before his fellow tribesman, and be raised back to his feet. Again the two men locked in a close hug. Dampier and the other pirates looked on in wonder: "We stood with pleasure to behold the surprize, and tenderness, and solemnity of this interview which was exceedingly affectionate on both sides. And when their Ceremonies of Civility were over, drew near." It was an exuberant reunion. One by one the pirates who had known Will previously embraced him and congratulated him on his survival.

With this touching scene, Will the Moskito vanishes from the pirate record as an historical figure. He sailed away on the *Batchelor's Delight* and participated in her piratical cruise. Whether he was still aboard her when she returned to the Caribbean four years later is not known. It is equally possible that he left the ship in the Pacific and accompanied a group of the English pirates who joined up with a force of French buccaneers to make an extraordinary reverse trek overland across Honduras. They came down the Rio Coco, which flows into the sea in the Miskito territory on the Caribbean shore. If he did, Will probably brought home his booty and was able to settle down on the Miskito Coast at some place "near the Sea, or by some River, for the sake of striking Fish, his beloved employment."

Nicaragua's Costa de Mosquitos is still marked on modern maps, partly because such a large and vacant space is a tempting place to write a label. The four-hundred-mile-long swathe of coastal lagoon, swamp, woodland, and savanna bordering the Caribbean is virtually empty. There are no mountains for the map makers to identify, only a half dozen rivers, a thin straggle of roads, and just two towns, Puerto Cabezas and Bluefields. Human settlement is almost entirely confined to the coast. There the people are so widely separated that the cartographers have room, if they wish, to write in the names of villages and hamlets which would never be remarked in a more populous part of the world. The names are relics from a wild past. The Moskito Coast begins in the south at Bluefields, a ramshackle seaport in Nicaragua named after a Dutch buccaneer who made it a practice to careen his vessel here and which became, for a brief time, the world's biggest banana shipping port. From there the Coast runs almost due north, past Haulover, where a portage led to Pearl Lagoon; Set Net, where the turtle fishing was good; Little Sandy Bay; another Haulover with another portage; and Big Sandy Bay. Then the Coast angles abruptly to the west, and into Honduras. The corner was named Cabo Gracias a Dios by Christopher Columbus, who wished to give thanks to God for finally being able to clear its maze of dangerous shoals and continue on his explorations.

Cabo Gracias a Dios, as I first saw it from the sea in June 1999, is unremarkable. There are merely a few bushes and a clump of trees on the low, flat horizon where the turbid sea meets a thin slope of sandy shore. Here lies the boundary between Nicaragua and Honduras, but there is no one living in the district to respect the claim, and no border post. At night there are no shore lights, only darkness. There is not even a coastal highway. The only figure to be seen here is the occasional pedestrian walking along the shoreline from one invisible hamlet to the next.

The final section of the Coast within Honduras is the department of Gracias a Dios, but everyone calls it La Mosquitia. Here I went to begin my search for Man Friday's heritage. It was a mistake. A string of Miskito villages occupies the soggy spit of land between the sea and the coastal lagoons, and the people speak the Miskito language. But they do not regard themselves as true keepers of Miskito culture. If I wanted to find Miskito living in their traditional manner, they told me, I would have to go deeper into the bayou lands, to Big Sandy Bay, and that was down the coast, in Nicaragua. I had come to the wrong country.

This was not a problem, at least for the Miskitos. A guide was found to escort me to Big Sandy Bay. Safel was tall, gaunt, and utterly casual and a vagabond. He lived and worked in Puerto Lempira, the scruffy Honduran port town nearest to the border. For a fee, he was ready to take me to Nicaragua if I would just wait half an hour. He had been sanding down the fiberglass hull of a boat, and his clothes were a mess. We walked through the muddy, unpaved streets of Puerto Lempira to the little wooden two-room shack on stilts on the outskirts of town that was his home. He went inside for no more than five minutes, and reappeared. He had changed his shirt for a slightly cleaner one, his jeans were less torn, and he carried a cheap sports bag. His boots, I noticed, were still powdered with fiberglass dust.

Safel claimed to speak English, but his command of the language was more halting than my knowledge of Spanish. I had brought no map of the area, as I had not expected to enter Nicaragua. So for the next seven days I was never quite sure of what would happen, nor where exactly we were going. Neither, as it turned out, was Safel.

I was certain of one thing: I did not want to waste any time loitering in Puerto Lempira. The town is notorious as the former base of the CIA-funded instructors who trained Contra troops during the protracted and vicious guerrilla war against the Sandinistas across the border in Nicaragua. The instructors were long since gone, but the place still teeters on the brink of being a sad no man's land. The streets are empty. The low, jerry-built houses are forlorn and neglected. It is the sort of place that when you arrive, your first thought is how soon can you leave. The only interesting moment was the lucky dip offered when I was disembarking from the small plane that brought me and a score of passengers to the gravel airstrip. Our air hostess was waiting at the bottom of the aircraft ladder, holding out a large brown paper bag like a supermarket paper sack. As the passengers filed past, they reached in and retrieved the items they had given to her when boarding the plane. At least five of the passengers took out hand guns.

Safel assured me that we could cross into Nicaragua at Leimus, a border post on the Rio Coco, which is also the border with Honduras. Unfortunately there was no regular transport to get to Leimus, but we could hire a pickup truck. The price for the journey was exorbitant, but there was only one vehicle and driver willing to make the run. Before we set out, I took the precaution of tracking down an official at the customs office and having my passport stamped to show that I had left Honduras. Safel and I then crammed into the pickup's cab and were rattled and shaken for three hours along an unsurfaced road that led inland. The land sloped very slightly upward as we drove across low, rolling barrens of sand, then ridges and flats of gravel where the rainwater in the puddles in the track ruts were rust red. Seen from only a few yards away, the country seemed like ideal pastureland. But it was an illusion. As you drew level, what looked like blades of grass turned into a thin groundcover of weeds. There was no livestock. Eventually we came into a wide, open area where pitch pines grew at random. The trunk of each tree was charred with the marks of a dozen brush fires as if a serial pyromaniac had been at work. The entire countryside was scorched raw and devoid of human life except when we came across an ancient timber lorry, mired down to its axles in the track, its gearbox broken. We gave the driver a lift to the log huts of a small timber camp, surrounded by barbed wire and tucked away among the trees. By then we were on the outskirts of Leimus.

A crooked wooden pole, hung across the track on two forked sticks, was the only sign that we had arrived. Our driver swerved around the barrier, took us another quarter mile, and stopped the vehicle. Fifty yards away across a ditch was a small shack with a metal bed frame on the porch. On the bed frame sat two men, watching us with complete disinterest. They were dressed in jeans and T-shirts and army boots. Their caps were marked "Policia" so I went across and arranged to have our names written in their logbook. I then returned to the pickup truck, and Safel and I were driven past four or five more shacks to the point where the road suddenly dropped down a steep mud slide to the edge of a broad, khaki-colored river. It dawned on me that this must be the frontier. The Rio Coco was at least eighty yards wide. I stood in the mud of the foreshore and looked across the water expecting to see a ferry. There was nothing. Puzzled, I looked up- and downstream. There was still nothing. I had low expectations of the place, but this was even less than I had anticipated. On the far bank there was not a shack, nor a jetty, nor even a dugout canoe hauled up in the ooze. The Nicaraguan side of the river was abandoned and utterly deserted.

A category 5 hurricane—the most severe classification—had destroyed the road on the Nicaraguan side eight months earlier. No one had bothered to repair the road. But that was not the underlying reason for the emptiness and desolation. Unwittingly, I had blundered into my first reminder of Man Friday's heritage.

"The Forgotten Indian War" sounds as though it happened in the seventeenth or perhaps the eighteenth century. In fact it took place between 1980 and 1990, and was a subset from a proxy war between superpowers. The main combatants were Sandinista troops of the Marxist revolution, which overthrew the corrupt regime of General Anastasio Somoza, dictator of Nicaragua. The Sandinistas were supported by the Soviet Union. Opposing them were fifteen thousand former members of the right-wing National Guard, called *contras*. Most of them withdrew into Honduras, where they were secretly armed and trained by the United States. Caught in the middle, but increasingly associated with the *contras*, were Miskito war bands. The Miskitos and the Sandinistas fought "the Forgotten Indian War" for control of what had once been a Miskito reserve, the territory stretching inland from the Miskito Coast with its strategic northern frontier on the Rio Coco. The Sandinistas forcibly relocated Miskitos who lived along the river. Many chose to flee into Honduras. Eight years after the war ended, very few had returned. Those who did come back had every reason to loathe "the Spanish," as they called the Spanish-speaking Hondurans who had in the meantime dispossessed them.

Obviously, Safel had not visited the river crossing at Leimus since the hurricane. There was no border crossing there. The pickup had already turned round and departed, so there was no way for us to return to Puerto Lempira. But Safel was unruffled. A single building overlooked the river from the Honduran bank. It was the old ferry café. Built on a bluff, it was constructed around a rickety skeleton of heavy timbers. The sides and floors were massive timber boards, warped in the sun and rain.

A balcony overlooked the river, and here Safel and I waited. Below us clouds of beautiful yellow butterflies circled and settled on the mud at the water's edge. Then they rose again, circled, and settled once more. They always settled among the dead leaves washed down by the current. When the butterflies closed their wings, they vanished in perfect mimicry of the dead vegetation.

A woman walked down the riverbank and washed some garments. Her wash basin was a fragment of a broken and swamped dugout. A smart jeep appeared, with three young Hondurans. Each wore a crisp white T-shirt, emblazoned with the insignia of a medical charity. They looked around, stayed five minutes, then drove away. A banner hung from a huge mango tree. It announced a mass inoculation program, but clearly there were no children to inoculate. My hopes rose when I heard the sound of an outboard engine. It was driving a massive dugout whose hull must have been at least forty feet long, which was proceeding downstream. But it was fully loaded with several passengers and a large heap of cargo hidden under a tarpaulin. The steersman did not even look up at Safel and me. He passed like a truck driver on an interstate and we were idle onlookers. Half an hour later two more dugouts appeared, coming upriver. These were much, much smaller and had no engine. Two men were paddling and a third stood in the bows and punted with a bamboo pole. They kept to the far bank, tucked under the bushes, to take advantage of the back eddies. Occasionally the standing man would haul on the fronds to help their progress. It took them forty-five minutes to labor past us and vanish upstream, still toiling slowly along against the current.

Finally, after a two-hour wait, a tiny canoe put out from the other bank. It contained a very small boy. He must have seen us waiting, and was coming across to negotiate the fare with Safel. The canoe was leaky and half full of water, and the boy did not look as if he had the strength to paddle back across the rapid current with two men on board. Climbing into his shabby canoe, Safel and I sat in three inches of bilgewater; there were no thwarts, and it was a slow and wobbly journey to the Nicaraguan shore. I was glad that my rucksack was waterproof.

We scrambled out on the far bank, and the boy disappeared with his money. Safel claimed that if we walked along the riverbank, we would soon come to a road that would take us inland. There was no road, only a one-room open-front store run by "Spanish," a Honduran couple. The woman behind the counter was a sullen beauty, dressed in purple slacks and a loose blouse. Seeing potential customers, she gave a welcoming smile. Her husband continued languidly pouring kerosene on a column of ants which was threatening to invade his premises. His stock hung from nails in the ceiling—children's cheap party clothes, camouflage hats, plastic hammocks. On the earthen floor were tubs of onions and cardboard boxes of six-inch nails. A gorgeous tame macaw on a tree stump added a wanton touch of color.

Once again Safel began to negotiate, and once again I had the feeling that I had no real idea what was happening. It turned out that there was only one outboard engine in the area, and it belonged to the shopkeeper. He demanded a huge fee to take us to the only place where a road met the river, three hours downriver. Fuel would be expensive, he said meaningfully. I was coming to appreciate that if you had the chance to exploit another person's need on the Rio Coco, you did so.

The wife closed the shutters of the shop, and disappeared. Her husband summoned a young lad to produce the dugout and the essential outboard motor. When the wife reappeared, it was clear that she was not going to miss the chance to visit town. She had changed into a frilled blouse, tight jeans, and new shoes. She had also done her hair and put on makeup, and she held a parasol. The effect was to obliterate any vestige of her natural attractiveness, and for the entire journey she sat in the center of the canoe, under her parasol and facing forward, her back turned toward her husband and rigid with disdain. The only time she turned around to face us was when we pulled over to the bank to drop off a Miskito family who had appeared at the last minute. A young man had come with his wife, a babe in arms, two small children, and several bundles. I was pleased to give them what I thought would be a free ride in the canoe I had hired for the journey. But when the family disembarked, halfway along our route, the shopkeeper wife held out her hand. The fare was pressed into the outstretched palm from a very slender roll of crumpled, torn bank notes.

Her husband sat glowering in the stern. He had not dressed up for the trip to town, and looked like a stage villain. He was stockily built, with a pockmarked complexion and long greasy hair curling down over the collar of a very dirty shirt. His baggy trousers were tucked into the top of short rubber boots, and his paunch oozed out over the belt, showing a deep belly button. He wore a permanent scowl between his heavy beard, a thick black mustache and the cap pulled low over his forehead. Only his pocket knife in its leather belt case was out of character. It should, at least, have been a machete.

The river journey was eerily detached and forlorn. We floated in the middle of the broad, ocher-brown flood, riding the powerful current and enveloped in the noise of the outboard engine. We saw no houses on either bank. The edge of the river was a line of reeds, a steep bush-covered bank, and then a glimpse of the upper branches of the forest trees. Above us the sky was overcast, dull, and oppressive. For long stretches the rain forest came right to the water's edge, and the branches of the massive trees overhung the racing water. Once, there was a heavy splash after the brief glimpse of an iguana tumbling through the air, as it lost its grip on a branch and fell.

Twice the engine was shut off, so the lad could clamber to the stern of the canoe, balancing fresh cans of petrol, and refuel. The second's worth of merciful silence was swiftly filled by a new wave of sound rolling in. There were whistles, sudden shrieks, echoes, and gurgles. They were the noises of the river and rain forest, and they lasted just as long as we sat in the silent canoe, still whirling rapidly downriver in the grip of the current. A massive tree had tumbled into the river and floated downstream until its roots caught in a submerged shoal. Now the forest giant lay at angle with its trunk beneath the water. The array of upper branches desperately waved up and down in the rush of water. The brown current boiled around the twigs, and the press of water raised a distinct surging hiss.

The overwhelming impression was of emptiness, and of isolation. Very occasionally, in the distance, appeared the small black silhouette of an Indian canoe, its occupant standing as he paddled from one bank to the other. It was like a Chinese ink drawing in slow motion. Always by the time we reached the spot, the canoe had vanished into the greenery of the riverbank, as though the sight had been a mirage. Once a mirage proved to be reality. Round a wide bend in the river appeared two inflatable boats traveling toward us at speed. The rubber boats were brand-new, very smart, and very expensive. The cowlings of their large outboard engines sparkled. On the black side of each dinghy a bright white patch was painted, and in the center of the patch was the insignia of the Red Cross. Sitting in each dinghy were three men. Each wore some sort of dark uniform and a bright orange life jacket, also new. The men had Red Cross insignias on their caps. They returned my curious gaze, passed us, continued upriver, and dwindled into the distance. Where were they going? Who had funded this incongruous exercise in philanthropy? Would they find anybody to help? It remained a complete mystery. Their crisp dress, the magnificent machinery, the shiny newness of all their kit made it look as if they had landed from another planet.

It was half an hour to dusk when our dugout reached its destination, a cluster of wooden shacks on the Nicaraguan riverbank. They extended out into the river on pilings and provided landing stages for a dozen or so dugouts made fast there. One shack had "Sandinistas Always!" painted defiantly on its boards. We had arrived at Waspam, the road head. For forty miles behind us upriver lay only desolation, as far as I was aware. Until the Sandinistas had razed their villages, more than sixty Miskito communities had lived along the river. In Dampier's time, this was "the River of Gold" and explorers grew excited at the glitter of golden spangles suspended in its waters. The spangles were delusory specks of shining mica, and brought disappointment. Now the Rio Coco had become a river of bitter ghosts.

Waspam was a single, sandy main street, half a dozen small shops, a couple of cantinas, and four churches. They stood in the irregular scatter of small houses that made up the residential suburb. The Catholic church was large, handsome, and gaily painted. The Moravian church was almost as large but very plain. The buildings of the Church of Christ and the Church of the Seventh-day Adventists were mere shacks. They were distinguishable by the slogans crudely painted on their walls and—from the Seventh-day Adventists—a continuous blare of prayer, hymns, and shouted exhortations relayed by a loudspeaker wired to the roof, which lasted far into the night.

Safel and I spent the night in Waspam's "hotel," well within earshot of the Adventists. Our rooms were unpainted plywood stalls erected on a half-finished rear extension to the building. In the night, when anyone walked past our doors the entire structure shook. As part of our bargain I had promised Safel as a bonus to keep him in cigarettes during our trip. Now I discovered that each evening I was also expected to pay an advance on wages so he could seek the services of a prostitute.

Water for an early-morning wash was from a rusty sixty-gallon drum. Then we took our place in the queue on the main street for the daily bus to Puerto Cabezas. Safel assured me that to get to Big Sandy Bay we must go first to Puerto Cabezas, and from there, "plenty of boats" went north along the coast to Big Sandy Bay. The bus was the result of more charity—a cast-off school bus from some far-distant high school in the United States, with its yellow paint still and no sign of subsequent mechanical maintenance. We staked our claim to seats and sat waiting in the crush for nearly two hours before the bus lumbered off on a five-hour journey to Puerto Cabezas. En route we saw no other vehicle traffic and stopped four times. Once was to pick up a passenger at the only settlement along the entire route, a village with perhaps thirty houses. The other three halts were where a heavy wire cable was cranked up and stretched across the road to stop the bus. Each time a squad of four or five soldiers emerged from their primitive bivouac beside the road. They were living under a tarpaulin stretched over sticks, and their jungle battle dress was shabby and unkempt. They looked seedy but also vaguely menacing as they demanded that everyone get out while they searched the bus. I was concerned that I had no stamp in my passport to show that I had entered Nicaragua legally. To my surprise they ignored me and Safel. Instead, there was some incomprehensible exchange of cash between the bus driver and the soldiers, and more money was extorted from a couple of passengers. Then we proceeded on our way.

My intention, already faint, to try to find an official and have my entry in Nicaragua formalized, vanished entirely when we reached Puerto Cabezas. There was no sign whatever of any official presence in its grim streets. It was the administrative capital of the region, yet even the government party headquarters had its windows boarded up. The municipal water supply had broken down, the electricity was erratic. Grass grew in cracks along the pavement, and plaster had fallen in great chunks from the facades of buildings. The Forgotten Indian War had ended in a stalemate, the Sandinistas were no longer in power, and the debt-ridden central government of Nicaragua had problems closer to home. Puerto Cabezas and the province had been left in limbo. Barbed-wire entanglements and privately hired armed guards surrounded the town's only two factories, a small sawmill and a fish freezing plant. The region had become, as one observer put it, *tierra sin lei,* land without law.

Safel took me to the so-called port, created by a single venerable wooden jetty built out into the sea. Several of the heavy planks of its deck were missing. There was not one crane, nor a merchant ship. The only vessels tied up to it were a dozen rusty fishing boats. Safel pointed to one of them and proudly told me that it was owned by his brother-in-law. To me they looked like death traps.

After some inquiries at the foot of the pier, Safel produced a man who owned a boat for hire. It was, he said, a "speed boat." The owner could have been first cousin to the villain who had brought us down the Rio Coco. He was another "Spanish" with the same cutthroat look, the same baggy trousers tucked into his boots, and this time he took care to let me see that he had a gun tucked in his belt, inside his shirt. By now I had concluded that the only people who owned "speedboats" with powerful outboard engines were the *contrabandistas*. And in Puerto Cabezas the smugglers made their money transporting and trading drugs. It was little wonder that their hire rates were so high.

Safel explained to the smuggler that I needed to rent a boat for a journey along the coast. Clearly it was not an unusual request, and the boat owner looked me up and down, judging my potential as a client. When would I like to travel? As soon as possible, I answered. A satisfied look. A client in a hurry was a client who would pay handsomely. Yes, he was willing to take me. He could be ready that same afternoon and would load enough fuel if I would tell him where I wanted to go. To Sandy Bay, I replied (locally, "Sandy Bay" by itself means Big Sandy Bay). It was as if the pier had tilted beneath his feet. His expression changed. "No!" he muttered. "Not Sandy Bay." He turned on his heel and walked off.

I wondered what was so horrible in Sandy Bay that it would deter an armed narco-trafficker.

It took another twenty-four hours for Safel finally to locate someone willing to take me on the journey. Significantly, he had a skin so black that no one could have mistaken him for a "Spanish." He imposed a condition for taking Safel and me to Sandy Bay: we would not stay there overnight. Two weeks earlier a narco-trafficker had taken his boat into Sandy Bay. He had been shot and his body dumped on the beach. No one could say exactly why. One story was that he had tried to sell "at too low a price"; another was that he was working for a drug cartel that did not have a trading agreement with the Miskitos of Sandy Bay. But both stories agreed that the dead man's disadvantage was that he was a "Spanish"—pale-skinned and associated with the detested Spanish speakers who came from the towns.

The ride to Sandy Bay was purgatory. First we had to wade in water chest deep out into the sea to reach a small, open boat that was kept on a mooring well away from the town jetty. A drum of fuel was floated out and hoisted aboard. Then "Shine," our boatman, produced a bottle of rum and it was passed around until it was empty and rolling, clinking in the scuppers as we hammered against the brisk breeze and chop for three comfortless hours. Out to sea, there was nothing to be seen except a pair of slovenly shrimp boats—"poachers from Honduras" explained Shine, who had worked in the Cayman Islands and spoke excellent English. The shrimp boats were surrounded with a hover of terns and other gulls waiting for scraps, and above them were the sharp black outlines of the frigate birds, the food stealers waiting to rob the gulls. On the landward side, the Moskito Coast had the same "dreary aspect of an endless white stretch of surf with an even line of green behind" that Charles Bell, a timber trader, had described to the Royal Geographical Society in 1862. He had lived on the Moskito Coast for eighteen years, and said that the only way the Indians could identify any location along the coast was "by certain odd shaped trees. Or patches of tall cabbage palms which grow at the rivers' mouths."

Then came the first encouraging sight: well out to sea appeared a small triangular sail. A boat was heading toward us, sailing downwind, and she was so small that the hull was lost among the waves. Her skipper must have seen our speeding motorboat because the distant sail swung across as the little craft changed course to steer closer. Five minutes later the boat was passing no more than half a mile a way, and I could see she was crammed with passengers, mostly women and children, all seated low in the hull and well wrapped in plastic sheeting to keep off the spray. A couple of young men, naked to the waist, stood clinging to the mast and balanced lithely as they returned my curious inspection. They were aboard a true sailing vessel, about 30 feet long and six feet in the beam, fine at bow and stern, and with no place whatever for any engine. "Miskito from Sandy Bay" said Shine. They were on a shopping trip to Puerto Cabezas, swaying to the motion of the sea, often hidden by the wave crests, and totally unconcerned and as casual as if they had been on a bus. It brought to mind a comment by a French buccaneer, Ravenau de Lussan, a contemporary of Will the Moskito's. De Lussan had come down the Rio Coco and met the Miskitos off Sandy

Bay. They are, he wrote, "the most courageous in the world at braving the perils of the sea. . . . They go out to sea in small boats that the average sailor would scorn, in these they remain three or four days at a stretch as unconcerned, despite the weather, as if they were part of the boat."

An hour later Shine was looking tense. He had turned the bow of the launch toward the shoreline and we were rapidly approaching the broad line of surf that lay between us and the land. Clearly this was our run-in for Sandy Bay. Safel, who had spent the journey drinking rum and smoking cigarettes, now took over. He stood up in the bow, his back toward Shine, and carefully watched the waves. Shine did not take his eyes off him. Casually Safel flicked his hand to the left. Shine turned the boat that way. Immediately Safel held up his hand in a gesture calling for delay. Shine straightened the boat and cut back the engine speed. We were on the outer edge of the whitewater. The sea foamed ahead of us, the waves breaking right under our bows. With the wind and more waves pushing from behind, we were drifting inevitably down on the bar. I could not see a gap or passage. The bar was broader than I had expected. Safel dropped his hand. Shine opened the throttle and the boat shot forward. Even at that speed we had to ride the backs of five rollers, lurching forward then sagging back as the waves rolled under us, and the crests reached up and slopped into the boat. In the trough of the second wave I felt the engine propeller guard thump on the sand. A little more than halfway across the bar Safel gestured urgently to the right, and Shine steered the boat into the dog leg of the channel. Safel sat down. As far as he was concerned, the danger was past.

We had gone from one watery world to another. One moment there was jolt and hiss of the cresting waves under us and the deeper rumble of the sea. Now we were gliding along on a still, flat surface. We had entered the short, broad river that links the lagoon system of Sandy Bay to the Caribbean Sea. The water on which we floated, I learned later, was ambivalent. At some seasons of the year it was the sea, salty and full of marine creatures. At other times it was a freshwater lake, dependent on the rains, and home to a entirely different group of fish and birds. On this shifting boundary between salt and fresh water and at home on both, lived the Miskitos of Sandy Bay.

There was no landing place as yet. On each side a thick tangle of mangrove roots was the advance footing for a great green and black wall of forest. Shine opened the throttle of the outboard engine and we raced up the channel between the mangrove forests. He intended our visit to Sandy Bay to be as brief as possible; he wanted to be gone by nightfall.

We emerged in a mile-wide lagoon. On the far bank stood a line of a dozen houses, the first of the nine villages that make up the community of Big Sandy Bay. After the squalor and neglect of Puerto Cabezas, the buildings were a happy surprise. They were substantial bungalows, standing high off the ground on pillars. Some of them were made of concrete and had corrugated iron roofs, but many were built of more traditional wooden boards standing on timber posts. They were well cared for and neat. Several houses were positively immaculate with bright new paint and hanging potted plants. Others were double-fronted and boasted porticoes. Each house stood in a generous open space of luxuriant green sward, on which grazed sleek ponies. Behind the houses extended a handsome parkland of mature palm, mango, cashew, lime, orange, and breadfruit trees. Along the waterfront coconut palms leaned forward in graceful curves. There were no advertising hoardings with peeling posters, no unsightly wires strung from house to house, no television aerials, nor rusting abandoned vehicles, because no road reached Sandy Bay. Instead, neat dugout canoes were drawn up in a line at the water's edge, and three sailing boats—sisters to the crowded sailboat I had seen at sea—were moored picturesquely off the waterfront. The only noise was the shouts of the children. The place was neat and clean and swept. This place, the object of the narco-traffickers' phobia, looked like a hideaway tourist resort.

Safel told Shine to take us straight to the village and to wait in the boat, while he and I splashed ashore through the tea-colored water of the lagoon. On closer inspection the impression of a neat, calm prosperous community was enhanced. Even the dead leaves from the fruit trees had been swept up into neat piles, ready for burning. We found two men near one of the houses and Safel explained that I had come only for a brief visit, and was interested in the survival of Miskito traditions, particularly concerning boats and the techniques of hunting fish. All the fishermen were away on the sea, we were told, but there was a brand-new sailboat in the next creek. It was not yet launched. We were welcome to go and look at it.

For a couple of hours I photographed the boat and chatted with the builder, who seemed puzzled that anyone should be interested in his work. Meanwhile, Shine refueled and fidgeted. He was so keen to be leaving Sandy Bay that he offered to take Safel and me back into Honduras by boat. It was, he said, only a few miles to the border.

This was too good a chance to miss—even though we risked being intercepted by a coast guard patrol, for this route is forbidden—and Shine set out at high speed. Instead of taking the river back to the sea, he swerved into the maze of channels that braided through the mangrove swamps. For the next hour we did not see another boat, a single house, or a human. The only sign that anyone had passed that way before us was a fresh scar where a chainsaw had cut back an overhanging branch that threatened to block the channel. Occasionally we had to crouch down when branches brushed across the top of our boat, threatening to sweep us into the water. I was treated to what anywhere else would have been a private water-borne tour of a carefully guarded wildlife preserve. Everywhere we saw herons, fish eagles, cormorants, ibis, alligators, egrets, pelicans, and huge butterflies. How Shine picked the correct channels was impossible to guess, but clearly he had been here before, and it was equally clear that no one used these channels except as smuggling routes.

Finally we burst out of the forest and were on the edge of the sea again and crossing back into the salt water. Then we ran up the coast toward Cabo Gracias a Dios and the Honduran border. Here Safel and Shine quarreled as they tried to pick out the entrance to the next lagoon.

Eventually Safel won the argument, and again we bumped in over a shoal marked by the bleached skeletons of great trees locked in the sand. Now that we were in Honduras Shine wanted us off the boat as fast as possible. If the Honduran authorities caught him, he said, they would steal his precious outboard motor. For the second time on our trip Safel and I were dumped on a muddy and uninhabited shore. Shine gave us a wave, and then gunned his motor as he sped back into Nicaragua.

It took two more days to get back to Safel's home in Puerto Lempira. Much of the time we were wading up to our thighs in swamp water, or squelching through mud, as we followed a footpath that led from one Miskito village to the next. The people gave us food and hammocks for the night. Back in Puerto Lempira Safel casually strolled off, and I went again to the police to have my passport stamped to show that I had reentered Honduras. No one questioned why there was nothing in my passport to show where I had been in the meantime. Apparently I had vanished into thin air.

Captain Nathaniel Uring was shipwrecked on the treacherous shoals of Cabo Gracias a Dios in early November 1711, within a month of Alexander Selkirk's return to London. The story of the mishaps and survival of the English sea captain, cast away among Man Friday's people, is a match for the fictional adventures of Robinson Crusoe. A merchant seaman since the age of fourteen, when his father, a sailor-turned-shopkeeper, sent him to London to learn the rudiments of practical navigation, Uring was immensely experienced in the ways of the sea and the sudden turns of fortune in maritime commerce. When he came to grief on the Moskito Coast, Uring was only twenty-nine years old, yet he had already been captured on three occasions by French privateers, ransomed or released, survived a bout of smallpox and a shipboard fire, made two trips to the Guinea coast in the slave trade, been impressed into the Royal Navy for wartime duty, and worked for five years as the skipper of packet ships carrying mail across the Atlantic between England and the West Indies. The voyage previous to the one on which he was wrecked bore a strange likeness to the smuggling venture that Defoe imagined as the prelude to Crusoe's misfortune. Crusoe is on a trip to bring slaves illegally into Brazil when he is shipwrecked. Nathaniel Uring successfully carried out a similar plan early in 1711 when he smuggled 150 slaves from Jamaica to an out-of-the-way anchorage at Monkey Cay, close to Portobello, on the Caribbean coast of the isthmus. There he met merchants from Panama who had ridden across the isthmus disguised as peasants and carrying their money hidden in jars of cornmeal loaded on mules.

That same year Uring was hired as the captain of a small sloop sailing to the Moskito Coast on a slightly less dubious venture. This time his clients were the roughnecks who went to the Caribbean coast of Central America to make a quick profit by cutting down logwood. The Spanish authorities regarded them as thieves and poachers, but had no means of policing the creeks and backwaters of the Bay of Honduras and Bay of Campeche, west of the Yucatan, where logwood, *Haematoxylon campechianum*, grows wild. The tree itself is unspectacular. It has crooked branches, a straggly appearance, and a contorted trunk that looks as if it is twisted and fused together from several stems. But cut a large splinter of the heartwood and steep it in water, and the water turns a deep crimson, the color of blood. The red tint from logwood was so valuable to the textile industry that the dyers in London paid as much as one hundred pounds a ton for "bloodwood." The owner of Uring's sloop could make as much profit from a single shipment of logwood as from a year of hauling general cargo.

The logwood cutters had a brutish reputation. Many were fugitives from the law. They lived singly or in small groups widely scattered along the coast or on the banks of the rivers and lagoons. Their homes were small shacks thatched with palm leaves and furnished, like Will the Moskito's hut on Juan Fernandez, with nothing more than a "barbecu" sleeping frame. Over this they erected a crude wooden scaffold from which they hung sheets of a coarse linen known as ozinbrigs. It was their primitive mosquito net. Without these "pavilions," as they called them, the clouds of insects would have made their lives unbearable. In the rainy season, according to Dampier, who had spent time as a logwood cutter himself, the cabins flooded, and the men "step from their beds into the water perhaps two foot deep, and continue standing in the wet all day, till they go to bed again." For one day each week they would hunt wild cattle in the savannas to stock the larder. Dampier describes how the custom was to hack the dead cow into quarters, remove all the bones, and then "each Man makes a hole in the middle of his Quarter, just big enough for his head to go thro," then puts it on like a Frock and trudgeth home." If the burden was too heavy and "he chances to tire, he cuts off some of it, and flings it away."

In the dry season the cutters worked in small teams, felling the logwood trees, chipping off the outer skin, and sawing the heartwood into billets small enough to be carried on their backs to the collection points. It was appallingly hard work in the muggy heat, but "the Logwood cutters are generally sturdy strong fellows and will carry Burthens of three or four hundred weight." When a tree trunk was too big to be cut up easily, "we blew it up with gun powder." Getting the trimmed logs to the beach in the rainy season was easier. The small back channels filled, and the tree trunks could be floated.

The lives of the logwood cutters were so isolated and lonely that they too were dubbed "marooners." The high point of their forsaken and sodden year was the arrival of someone like Uring to collect their valuable timber crop. The visiting ship anchored offshore and waited for the half-savage logwood cutters to paddle out in their canoes in search of the cargo they most craved—rum. This was a crucial moment in the negotiations. The visitor should be generous, Dampier advised, and hand out rum punch freely to everyone who arrived. Then the logwood cutters would pay for their own drinks on the following days and ask a fair price for their timber. But if the visiting trader was stingy, he would be sold the junk from the stockpile. The logwood cutters kept a store of substandard logs ready to sell to such skinflints. They "cheat them with hollow Wood filled with dirt in the middle and both ends plugged up with a piece of the same drove in hard, and then sawed off so neatly that it's hard to find out the Deceit."

Uring's sloop had already called at Bluefields to take on fresh water and was heading north along the Moskito Coast when "the Wind began to freshen, with a small drisling rain." Since the days of Columbus, the coast had kept its evil reputation for its numerous offshore shoals and reefs, so Uring was following another trading vessel whose captain knew the route and was acting as his guide. But in the drizzle the lead vessel soon vanished from sight, and though Uring lit signal flares, he was unable to reestablish contact. Uring had no firsthand experience of the coast, and though he had some "draughts," or charts, of the area, they were unreliable. Foreseeing just such a difficulty, he had asked the owners of the sloop to provide him with a pilot who knew the coast. But with visibility deteriorating and the wind backing into the northwest and increasing, Uring decided to play it safe. He turned the sloop about, ordered his men to bring down the mainsail and jib, and hove to under a single small headsail, intending to ride out the bad weather. The wind increased to a storm.

At nine or ten in the night the sloop's bowsprit snapped. It fell into the sea under the lee bow. The crew tried to rescue the spar and haul it inboard, but found it impossible. The gale had raised a "very great sea," and the sloop was plunging and laboring in the large waves. Uring feared that the loose bowsprit slamming against the hull could impale his ship and sink her. He ordered the spar to be cut away, and a hawser brought forward and rigged as an emergency stay to hold up the mast while the foresail was reefed and reset. But the wind was so strong that almost as soon as the foresail was up, it had to be taken down again for fear of tearing the mast out of the ship. The vessel was now drifting at the mercy of the wind and waves.

An hour later the crew had a bad fright. In the darkness they saw white water close at hand. Worried that his sloop was driving on a shoal, Uring ordered a sounding to be taken and the lead was heaved.

Strangely, the depth was found to be fourteen fathoms, more than eighty feet. Again Uring ordered the foresail to be hoisted in the hopes of getting some control of the vessel, and he asked the pilot whether, judging by the depth, he knew where they were. But the pilot was useless. He was "a poor elderly fellow" who "knew nothing of the Matter." Uring kept the leadsman hard at work, taking repeated soundings, and was relieved when the soundings showed very little shoaling. This "gave me hopes that we were not in so much danger as I before feared." Better, the wind had eased slightly and it was possible to hoist the double-reefed mainsail and take down the foresail. The little sloop now lay closer to the wind, and was not being driven to leeward so rapidly.

Ominously, the leadsman began to report that the depths were steadily decreasing "to Thirteen Fathom, and so to Twelve, and then Eleven, and about Three a Clock we had but Ten and quickly after Nine Fathom." Uring was well aware that they were in a very bad situation—close to a shore fringed with reefs and shoals, in darkness and heavy weather, and without any idea of their actual position. He looked again at his charts, which "laid down several Ledges of Rocks and Shoals. And expected nothing less than to be thrown on some of them every moment where we could expect nothing but immediate Death."

When dawn broke, the leadsman reported the depth had decreased to eight fathoms and was still decreasing. Daylight also showed that the little sloop was alarmingly close to a long, low horizon, which marked the Moskito shore. Again Uring was forced to risk setting the foresail again and trying to work away from the land. He asked the pilot whether he recognized where they were, now that it was daylight. But the old man "confessed he did not, and having no one onboard acquainted in those seas except himself, we were entirely at a loss."

From the deck Uring could see what looked like the entrance to a river or lagoon, but he was wary. "I had thoughts of venturing, but considered it was a shoal coast, and that it was the highest probability there was not water enough for the vessel, and if there was not, and she should touch the Ground, she would quickly be in pieces." He decided it would be wiser to claw along the coast, hoping to find an island behind which to take shelter.

After some miles the pilot announced, at last, that he recognized "a remarkable tuft of trees" on the land. He knew the sloop's position. They were close, he said, to Cabo Gracias a Dios. If the sloop could keep her course and edge her way around the cape, they would find shelter in its lee. He assured Uring that it was a safe passage "where he had been several times" and had five fathoms of water.

Uring took his advice. For a short interval it seemed that his ship would extricate herself from danger. The depth stayed at five fathoms, but then suddenly the bottom shoaled again, and at the same moment the pilot lost his nerve. He was no longer sure that the clump of trees marked Cabo Gracias a Dios. Then he changed his mind, and said it did. As he was dithering, a shudder passed through the hull as the ship ran onto a rocky shoal and came to a halt. She then "gave but a few Thumps before the Main-Mast jumped out of its step."

Uring kept a cool head. He directed his men to cut away the mainmast before it damaged the ship. But there was only one ax aboard, and the work took an agonizingly long time. Next, knowing that the sloop was hard aground, Uring organized the crew to chop a gap in the rail around the edge of the deck so that the sloop's tender, a large, heavy canoe, could be launched over the side for use as a lifeboat. Without the mast block and tackle to help them, it was all the crew could manage to manhandle the canoe from its place on deck. But "everyone outdid themselves" and eventually succeeded in sliding the canoe into the water. The entire crew of sixteen men, including the elderly pilot and the ship's boy, jumped down into the lifeboat. In their haste to get clear before the hulk began to break up, they took with them only some firearms "a little gunpowder, some small shot, an axe and an iron pot."

The sloop had struck an offshore reef, so now they were faced with rowing the canoe across six miles of open water to get to land. As the sailors approached the shore, their courage failed. They saw that the gale had kicked up a heavy swell, and a broad expanse of whitewater was breaking on the long, straight slope of the beach. It was such a daunting sight with "the Break of the Sea so high and at such a distance" that the crew "were very much afraid of the Canow's over-setting." To add to their plight, the sun had gone down by the time they were ready to attempt a landing.

By the light of the moon they waited and watched for a quiet interval between the larger crests. Then came a moment "after the Breach of the Great Seas," when Uring shouted to his men to row with all their strength for the shore.

Rather to their surprise, the canoe stayed upright, and despite "the Sea breaking over us several times," they pitched up safely on the strand "by the providence of God." Jumping out of the canoe, they dragged it up the open beach and out of the reach of the surf, and took stock of their situation.

In the moonlight they could see the line of trees that marked the edge of the coastal forest. They were "wet and sadly fatigued," and urgently needed shelter. Hoping to find firewood and timber to build a hut, they left the canoe and began trudging up the slope of the beach, only to discover that they were mired in the typical feature of the Moskito Coast: the long, stagnant marsh that lies trapped behind the beach. "We came quickly into a Morass and were up to the mid-Leg, and sometimes up to the Knees in Mud and Water." Blundering through the slough, the castaways discovered that "it was full of long cutting Grass intermixed with Briars which tore our legs in several places." They advanced for more than a mile "in this miserable way" before they found themselves, scratched and bleeding, among the trees. There "by the help of a Pistol and some Gunpowder we made a Fire and dried our cloaths."

The next priority was to build some shelter. They "cut down some small trees with which, and the Branches of others we set up a little Hut to shelter ourselves from the rain in which we designed to rest ourselves after Two Days and a Night's Fatigue." Exhausted, they lay down to get some rest.

They had overlooked the scourge of the swampy coast—mosquitoes.

There were "millions of *Muschetos,*" wrote Uring, "and other biting flies about us. So that neither Mouth, Nose, Eyes or any Part of us was free from them; and wherever they could come at our Skin, they bit and stung us most intollerably." The torment from the clouds of insects was so bad that the castaways were unable to sleep for the rest of the night "though we were tired to Death."

Itching and irritable, Uring and his companions made their way back to the beach at first light, and looked out to sea, hoping to see the wreck of their vessel stuck on the reef. But there was nothing. They had become unwilling "marooners."

Despondently they began to explore their surroundings to see what they could find to eat. Their only food was the single piece of dried beef they had brought with them in the canoe. It weighed about six pounds, and would not last sixteen men for no more than two or three days at most. After four hours of searching, one of the men returned carrying a bunch of unripe plantains. He had found them in an abandoned plantation. It was a hopeful sign that someone, probably native people, occasionally visited the area. The searchers had also seen plants growing near the plantation which they recognized as "sweet cassava." They dug up the roots. Unlike "poison cassava," whose roots must be cut up and beaten until all the poison juice is squeezed out, then dried and turned into flour for making cassava bread, "sweet cassava" can be eaten immediately. The sailors peeled off the skin of the roots, which were the size and shape of long parsnips, and boiled or roasted the vegetables. They tasted "something like a potatoe tho' not so good."

The next day Uring handed out the guns, shot, and gunpowder and divided his men into hunting groups. They were to shoot "such creatures as probably we might find in that country, to prevent our being starved if we found no Inhabitants." Also they were to keep a sharp lookout for any more signs of the natives who had planted the cassava. Uring took a gun and, going by a separate track, was angry with himself when he fired at, but failed to hit, a "Tyger Cat" in a tree. It must have been a big animal, possibly a jaguar, because he noted regretfully that his target "would have been sufficient to have made us a plentiful meal" if his aim had been better. When he got back to the camp, he found that the other hunters had shot several large fishing hawks, and "notwithstanding they were very tough and fishy, we eat them very heartily."

There were more fishing hawks on the menu on the next day, the third since the shipwreck. The birds were already in the cooking pot when the last of the hunters came into camp, carrying a large chunk of fresh beef. They had met a wild cow in the forest and shot the beast. Unfortunately, soon afterward they saw three more cows and realized that the animal they had killed was not wild at all, but tame.

Sure enough, they were eating the beef when a Miskito Indian appeared. Speaking broken English, he informed them that they had just shot a cow belonging to the local Miskito chief, who called himself Captain Hobby, and that the chief would be most displeased when he heard the news. Captain Hobby and his people were in a camp sixteen or eighteen miles to the south. The Miskito also told the castaways that the fresh wreck of a vessel was lying in the shallows only a few miles down the coast. The hulk lay without mast nor people aboard, so to the castaways it sounded as if it was the wreck of their sloop. Uring hurriedly apologized for shooting the tame cow and suggested going to Captain Hobby's camp. On the way, they would visit the wreck and see if anything could be salvaged.

By now the seas had become calm enough for the canoe to be relaunched. With some of the castaways in the canoe and the others walking along the beach, they headed southeast accompanied by the helpful Miskito. After walking all day, the sailors pulled the canoe back onto the beach and turned her upside down. Some of the party crawled under the canoe to sleep while others lay down on the beach to rest. Those under the canoe soon learned their error. The mosquitos attacked so ferociously that they quickly shifted to join their companions in the open air, where "the Wind blew most of [the mosquitoes] away." That to Uring's chagrin, two of his men deserted, carrying away "my Fowling Piece and a Musquet, with a good part of our Powder and Shot." He never mentioned them again.

By noon the next day the little party had reached the wreck. It was their sloop. The hulk was lying close enough in to shore for them to wade out and check to see whether they could salvage anything. They found that the hull had been stripped bare.

Their Miskito guide now suggested that he would go with some sailors in the canoe down the coast and into the mouth of the Black River. There they would rendezvous with the rest of the party at Captain Hobby's camp, which Uring and the remainder of the group could reach by walking overland.

Uring arrived in camp to find the Miskitos gloriously drunk. They had ransacked the wreck for her cargo of rum and carried home the windfall and were celebrating. "I found most of them very happy," he noted. "Some of them were so drunk they could not speak, others mighty drunk singing very heavily, and some about half gone, carousing over their drunken Brethren." The tipsy Miskitos welcomed the castaways with open arms. A couple of Miskitos were sufficiently sober to lead the sailors to the cache where the Indians had stacked some of the supplies from the wreck. The ravenous sailors started cooking themselves a meal and when the canoe party arrived, "the sober Indians were very courteous and gave us some of our own Rum and Sugar, with which we made some punch and cheared our Spirits." In this atmosphere of mutual celebration, the Miskitos generously "let us know where they had hid some of our rum. From whence we took a small Cask and put it in our canoe."

There was still the matter of the dead cow to settle. Uring was nervous of the outcome. He did not expect "Captain" Hobby to take kindly to one of his cattle being shot by strangers. Judging by his title he was a middle ranking chief. The Miskitos had adopted various English titles for their own hierarchy. Their most senior chief was the "king" at Sandy Bay, and various "captains" were scattered along the coast. Later there would also be a governor, a general and even an admiral. Fortunately,

Captain Hobby was in too good a humor from the windfall of the shipwreck to be very resentful about the lost cow. He behaved "very civilly" and though he "he made a heavy Complaint for the Loss" he accepted Uring's explanation that it was a genuine mistake and "that our People [would not have] killed it if they had not believed it had been wild." He "was very friendly, seeming sorry for our Misfortune."

Captain Hobby was much more concerned about the health of his mother. She had drunk so much rum "that she speechless lay for three days." He asked Uring "what he should so to save his Mother's Life?" and Uring replied that "time would throw it off, and she would be well again." He had already noticed how the Miskitos had great powers of recovery from a drinking bout. They would drink vast quantities of rum, then lie down in the grass at dusk "scattered about like so many sheep and goats" and completely oblivious to the clouds of insects hovering over them. Next morning they "got upon their legs, shaked themselves, and seemed as well as our true Scots in England, when they have been very drunk overnight; who if you ask them how they do next day, say they are neither sick nor sorry."

Clearly the rugged Miskito way of life had prepared "Will the Moskito" for his long stay on Juan Fernandez as a maroon until the *Batchelor's Delight* brought his compatriot Robin leaping ashore to embrace him. One of Will's shipmates, the buccaneer Basil Ringrose, who had been with Captain Sharpe's raiders, marveled how robust, yet carefree, the Miskitos could be. Some, he said, were mere "vagabonds." They wandered the riverbanks and beaches and, when tired, lay down on the ground and slept comfortably with nothing more than a large leaf to screen them against the wind and rain. If there were mosquitoes, they "dig a hole in the sand . . . and then cover themselves therewith." Others, he said, were so relaxed that they "lie all day in their Amacks which are a kind of moving beds . . . and when they are pressed with Hunger, they go afishing in their Boats at which they are also very skilful, and when they have taken any, they eat them, and go not any more until Hunger returns upon them again." The place where these blithe natives congregated, according to Ringrose, was "about ten or a dozen leagues to the windward of Cape Grace a Dios." Here, in the region now known as Sandy Bay, the Miskito live "in those places they call Sambay and Sanibay."

For a second time I stood on the rickety wooden pier at Puerto Cabezas. It was four months since my brief reconnaissance trip to Sandy Bay with Safel the footloose Miskito. Now my companion was very different. Kendra was thirty years old, tall, serious-looking with a very pale skin and brown eyes. When her dark hair was pulled back, her face with its high forehead, neat features, and narrow chin took on a pixy shape, and then—if something had caught her interest—her whole expression lit up like that of an alert forest creature, a pine marten perhaps, hearing a distant twig snap. At that moment you realized Kendra's deliberately quiet exterior hid a questing intelligence which—betrayed by the faint twitch of a smile—was matched by a sense of humor always at the ready. Kendra was Canadian, a doctoral student of geography, and this was her first visit to Puerto Cabezas. She approached one of the group of idlers standing on the pier. "Can you tell me if there is any boat going up to Sandy Bay," she inquired politely, knowing full well what the effect would be. Once again I saw someone react as if Puerto Cabezas pier had tilted beneath his feet. Last time it had been a drug runner appalled at the notion of going to Sandy Bay. This time it was because Kendra had asked the question speaking fluent Miskitu.

I had located Kendra on the Internet. A flurry of reports about La Mosquitia appeared in late 1998, when Hurricane Mitch with its two-hundred-mile-an-hour winds raked Nicaragua and Honduras. Among the volunteers organizing outside help for the indigenous people was Kendra. I contacted her by e-mail, asked whether she spoke the Miskito language, and if so, would she be available to accompany me as an interpreter. She was diffident. She was not sure whether her language skills were sufficient. She had learned to speak Miskitu—she pointed out that the convention was to spell the language with a final *u* instead of an *o*—

while doing field research among a related group of Indians, the Tawakha, in Honduras. She had lived in a remote Tawakha village for twenty-two months. The Tawakha were former victims of Miskito slave raids and though they spoke their own language, they also spoke Miskitu and still supplied dugout canoes to their former overlords. Fortunately Kendra was curious to learn just how the Miskito lived today and she agreed to accompany me to Nicaragua.

Kendra need not have worried about her language skills. A Miskito mother in one village we later visited ran home to fetch her two children and bring them before Kendra. "Listen to this pale woman!" She admonished them, "You must study hard to learn our language so you can speak it one day as well as her!"

Puerto Cabezas, I had learned by now, was notorious in the narcotics trade. The Nicaragua guidebook cautions visitors not to go alone to the beach, where drug deals are frequent. And if Puerto Cabezas was bad, then Sandy Bay was worse—"Sandy Bay is supposedly the drug capital of the coast and has no places to stay" was the warning.

When Kendra and I returned to the pier at midnight to secure a place aboard a small motorboat due to leave for Sandy Bay at three o'clock next morning, she asked the driver of the shabby taxi whether much had changed in the town since the end of the "Indian War." He shrugged. The town was better now, he said. Five years ago the place was really lawless. People were being killed in the street in drunken brawls, in fights over drug deals or from drug overdoses, or from "crazy sickness," when they simply ran amuck. It was quieter now—and he paused— though a woman was killed with a knife in this street two or three hours ago.

The wind was blowing too hard from the north for the little motor boat to leave, so we spent the rest of the night in a row of Miskitos sleeping on the deck boards of the pier like so many corpses. From time to time a Miskito would crawl over in the darkness and whisper to Kendra, just to make sure that the rumor was true. She really did speak their language.

At dawn there was a sudden flurry of activity. A file of young men appeared in the half-light. With them were wives and girl friends carrying small packages of food and bundles of spare clothing which they handed over as they embraced the menfolk and said farewell. The men were all in their teens or early twenties, and they walked along the pier with a certain swagger. Each carried a large wooden paddle and a thin iron rod about four feet long. The point was turned over into a sharp hook. The implement reminded me immediately of the fishgig, and the men recalled the strikers from the days of Will the Moskito.

They passed us and began to climb aboard one of the rundown fishing boats moored at the end of the pier. The vessel was in calamitous condition. The wooden hull was scuffed and battered. The vent pipe spewed black diesel fumes when the ancient engine rattled into life. Deck gear, such as it was, was broken or jammed. The wheelhouse windows had cracks repaired with bandages of plastic tape. Nothing had been painted or greased or maintained. Stacked on deck like paper cups were small canoes, perhaps twenty of them. A few more canoes were piled up on the roof of the wheelhouse. The canoes were very crude—most were little more than bean pods unskillfully made of fiberglass. Ranks of scuffed and dented aluminum air bottles lay stuffed into a huge metal rack, and an ancient air compressor had been bolted to the deck and was leaking dirty oil. There was no safety equipment and there was no crew accommodation, either, for the thirty to forty young men clambering aboard.

They were a sad descent from the skilled Miskito strikers whom Dampier had so admired. The young men were embarking on a twelve-day trip to the offshore shoals and banks. The fishing company in Puerto Cabezas supplied each diver with a canoe, twelve bottles of compressed air a day, a regulator, and a face mask if he did not have one of his own. The diver had to bring along a helper, usually a younger brother or a cousin. Each day while the fishing boat was on the banks, the two-man team was dropped overboard with a canoe. They would paddle off to a likely spot where the diver descended to the sea floor and swam from rock to rock searching for lobsters. He used the long thin hooked spike to prize the animals out from crevices and crannies. Above him, his companion followed the line of air bubbles, paddling so as to be on hand when the exhausted diver was forced back to the surface with his catch. The normal regime was to use up four bottles of compressed air, then take a fifteen-minute rest. If the mother ship was close enough, the two men paddled back to their ship, climbed aboard, and ate some food. Then it was back into the canoe, more paddling, and more diving until another four air bottles were empty. Another rest break of a quarter of an hour, and it was time to use up the last four bottles of air. The lobsters were collected at depths between 100 and 130 feet, and even taking turns to dive, the two men were working far beyond the accepted limits for safety and their health. Finally the team returned to deliver their catch, eat, and lie down on the open deck to rest while the air compressor shuddered and pounded through the night, recharging the air bottles for the next day of drudgery. If the weather was cold or rainy, the divers were allowed to lie on wooden pallets in the hold. Next morning they were sent overboard again.

Acute unemployment in Puerto Cabezas drove the system. Lobster diving was the only legal way for the divers to earn cash. But the pay packets were meager. The boat owners deducted for the air bottles, for the food, for the loan of the canoe, then paid a miserly rate for the lobsters. The owners also advanced money to the divers before a trip, and when the boat returned to port the diver often found he had not paid off the debt, and was obliged to go to sea on the next lobster run. Much of the catch was destined for "surf 'n' turf" platters in restaurant chains in the United States, where the clientele had no idea of the true cost.

Occasionally a diver drowned. His canoe man lost sight of his bubble track, or he surfaced so exhausted that his colleague failed to reach him before he slipped back under the sea. Divers were slowly poisoned by the foul air they inhaled from the bottles, toxic with exhaust fumes from compressors. The divers were not supplied with depth meters to show how deep they were diving, nor gauges to show how much air was left in the bottles. They had to guess. They received no formal instruction about the need for a controlled ascent to the surface, and at the rate of twelve bottles of air per day they were already operating beyond safe physical limits. Inevitably diver after diver suffered from nitrogen sickness, the bends. Sometimes the onset was swift—a diver would suddenly be writhing in agony on the deck of the fishing boat as nitrogen bubbled in his blood. Much more often it was a cumulative effect with creeping joint failure leading to lower-limb paralysis. There was no treatment and no cure. The nearest fully equipped compression chamber for treating the bends was in Honduras—for the use of sports divers on sunshine holidays.

At first some of the Miskitos believed the diving sickness was the curse of the *liwa mair*. In Miskito lore the *liwa mair* is a pale-skinned mermaid who lurks in the depths of the sea. To see her brings disaster. The divers began to wear good luck charms to ward off the curse. The true reasons became better understood when the divers were obliged to dive deeper and deeper to find the dwindling lobster stock. By the time Kendra and I arrived, many of the younger Miskitos were refusing to dive. Others—the brash, the heedless, and those forced by necessity to do so—sometimes turned to drugs to mask growing physical pain. It is a grim repetition of the days when the Spaniards first came to the Caribbean. They forced the native peoples to dive for pearls. The wretched natives would come to the surface with ears and noses bleeding, and be sent down again and again to gather the pearl harvest. Within fifty years, entire tribes had been wiped out, and the oyster beds were destined for terminal ruin. Nicaragua's modern lobster harvest has been as heartless, on what some might call the Cripple Coast.

Miskito mothers tossed their babies and toddlers casually off the pier. They were caught in midair by the young man loading the little motorboat lurching in the swell far below. It was ten in the morning and the north wind had at last dropped enough for us to leave for Sandy Bay. None of the passengers was exasperated by the delay. The Miskitos knew that it was foolish to challenge a headwind. The same wind had just brought another engineless Miskito sailboat from the Miskito Cays, the scattering of low sandbars twenty-five miles offshore. The four-man crew brought the little boat into the lee of the pier and threw us a line. I peered down. Laid out in the bilges were seven large turtles, alive and lying on their backs. The sailors were bringing them to market in Bilwi, as the Miskitos call Puerto Cabezas, preferring their Indian name. Of all meat the Miskitos prefer turtle meat, and it amounts to a craving. As they furled the sails, the sailors casually walked up and down the boat, stepping on the turtles like so many boulders. The turtles lay passive, their heads scarcely moving, flippers slowly waving, as if they were puzzled. Once the boat was secure, the sailors manhandled the heavy animals, each weighing between 90 and 130 pounds, up and over the edge of the boat and tipped them into the water with a massive splash. The turtles sank, then floated to the surface, blinking. One of the sailors jumped into a small row boat, grabbed the rope that tied the turtles into a chain, and rowed for the beach towing the heavy animals behind him like a line of elephants in a circus ring.

By an hour we missed an event that entertained the whole of the dock community. Three Miskito women had gone from the beach in a dugout to collect a quantity of marijuana found floating in the sea by one of the fishing boats. They were paddling back ashore in a dugout when the waves capsized their boat. The women and their cargo were thrown into the water. Every onlooker knew exactly what was in the canoe, and there was a joyful stampede into the waves. People waded into the water to collect their share of the windfall, grabbing up the loose packets of marijuana floating on the surface. "Of course the policemen joined in," we were told. "They were just as happy to have their share." Our informant had been butchering the turtles on the beach, and traded lumps of turtle meat for his joints.

Kendra and I were on our way to Sandy Bay by then. The motorboat journey was much more sedate than my earlier trip with Shine and Safel. The Miskito women crammed far into the stern of the open boat with their small children to avoid the spray. One husband sat so far aft that he was perched precariously on the head of the rudder, well out over the water. In one hand he held a small infant, in the other a cigarette. For five hours he sat there, and I watched in fascination each time his arm grew so tired that he switched burdens and juggled the baby from one hand to the other over the sea.

The helmsman of the ferry was surprisingly clumsy as we negotiated the dangers of the bar at the entrance to Sandy Bay. He failed to reduce speed on the crest of a large wave, and for a moment the motorboat surfed along on the top of the wave, out of control and yawing from side to side. The boat could have rolled over if a grizzled Miskito man, a passenger who had been sitting quietly beside the helmsman, had not quickly stood up, stepped to the wheel, and taken control. He straightened up the boat and reduced the speed, and we surged safely into calm water.

His name was Marco. He and Kendra chatted quietly in Miskitu, and by the time the ferry had worked its way up the mangrove channels and out into the lagoon of Sandy Bay, we had found ourselves a guide.

Marco was fifty years old and had been born in Sandy Bay. He was a veteran of the "Indian War" and lived in dignified poverty with wife and five children. Once his family had been prosperous, and his grandfather had run a small shop. But Marco's father had died young, and Marco had been brought up by uncles. The arrival of Sandinista troops during the Indian War accelerated what had been a slow decline for the village. "They came and burned our houses. They killed our people," he said simply. Marco and his family fled to Honduras with thousands of other Miskitos and had spent ten years in exile there. Ironically, these ten years were among the best of his life. For two years he was a soldier, and was taken secretly for military training in the United States. When the war ended, he returned home to Sandy Bay and was trying to rebuild his life on a very slender foundation. He was very capable. He could hunt and fish and manage a sailboat, but he was too old to dive for lobsters and he did not care to take the risk. Physically he was slender and wiry, with thick graying hair cut short, and his narrow face and watchful eyes made him look like a wise gray fox. He used hand gestures when he spoke, and they were fluid and elegant, and what he had to say was worth listening to. His troubles and travels had given him a great breadth of general knowledge and he exuded reliability. He was so gentle and courteous that it came as a shock whenever his quiet voice and manner sharpened to a harsh edge. This was when he talked about the "Spanish," as he called the Hispanic Nicaraguans. He detested them. They had no business in the Miskito lands, and they should stay away. A "Spanish" had come to Sandy Bay recently. It was not clear what the visitor wanted, but the people of Sandy Bay suspected that he was trafficking in drugs. They asked him to leave. He refused. "What happened?" asked Kendra. "He was killed," Marco replied flatly.

The boat passengers dispersed to their homes carrying the news that a white woman had arrived who spoke their language, and Kendra's fluency in Miskitu became major gossip. Within a day the whole of Sandy Bay seemed to have heard the astonishing news. Children came running to double-check the phenomenon, and report back to their parents. Marco, feeling that his home was too humble, had led us to a more prosperous household, explained who we were, and asked if we could stay. A few sentences from Kendra in Miskitu and the woman of the house opened her eyes wide with delight, and we had found a home in Sandy Bay as long as we wanted to stay.

Up close, the legendary "drug capital of the coast" was as attractive as I had remembered. The balconied and porticoed houses beside the lagoon were as handsome. Cattle and ponies still cropped the springy turf under the mango and breadfruit trees. The fallen leaves, coconut husks, and household rubbish was swept into neat piles, ready for burning. There was a freshly painted church of the Moravians, a Protestant sect that had sent missionaries to the Miskitos for 150 years. Now the pastor of Sandy Bay was a Miskito, as was usually the case elsewhere on the Coast; he was dapper in white shirt and smart business suit. Sandy Bay had no road, no piped water, no drains, though it did have electricity from a generator, a very recent gift from the government of Taiwan. But Sandy Bay was out of television transmission range, so even when there was fuel for the generator, the houses on stilts did not yet pulse to a neon blue-white. More often they were lit by hurricane lamps. Seemingly scattered at random in the parkland, the houses were in fact arranged in family clusters. Night traffic was the moving beams of torches carried by children as they went from house to house. The network of footpaths criss-crossing the settlement was so well known to the children that more often they were just small shadows flitting past in the darkness.

Activity began half an hour before dawn, as with most waterside people. There was a light tap on the window and Marco's voice asked if we were ready to leave. He led us to a boat hidden in the reeds. It was a smart, open, fiber-glass skiff with a brand-new engine; Siriaku, its owner, was to take us to the Moskito Cays. When Siriaku appeared in the half-light, he did not reply to our greeting, but silently untied the boat, as if ignoring us. He was heavy-set, with the powerful shoulders and hands of a middle-weight boxer, and a massive, big-boned face with high cheekbones and long jet-black hair. Siriaku's ancestors must have come from the "wild Indian" tribes, for he looked much more like a North American Indian than any other Miskito we ever met. The Miskito complexions could be anything from a dark coffee color to Marco's brownish-black, but Siriaku was a copper-brown. When Siriaku spoke—which he did rarely—it was in a profoundly deep bass rumble. Only when you looked at him and he glanced away did you realize that this hulking man was not malevolent. He was acutely shy.

The Moskito Cays were the place to learn to what extent the Miskitos were still the "boldest people in the world for exposing themselves to the Perils of the Sea," as the French buccaneer Ravenau de Lussan had claimed.

To a passing mariner, the cays are merely four small, low islands twenty-five miles out to sea from Sandy Bay. There is nothing special about them. The islands are clothed with the usual dark-green mix of mangrove and thorny shrub. They have springs of fresh water but the sand flies are so viciously fierce are that no one would live there for more than a few days at a time. Except as sea marks there is nothing remarkable about them. But the Miskitos have a mental image of a different world. To them the four islands are only the surface features of a vast submerged shelf of rocks, shoals, sand bars, coral heads, and reefs which they visualize as clearly as if they were able to see through the opaque seawater. The Miskitos carry a mental map of a submarine hunting ground where they stalk their favorite food: turtle. It was in the hunt for turtles that the Miskito strikers honed their extraordinary skill.

Siriaku steered his boat down the bayou from Sandy Bay, across the bar, and headed straight out to sea. Within minutes the flat Moskito shore was only a low, featureless shading on the horizon behind us. The position of the sun gave an indication of the direction we were heading, and so did the wind, which was blowing steadily out of the northeast. But there was nothing to indicate our precise position. Siriaku did not have a compass, and there was no instrument to show how far or fast we were traveling. He sat impassively by the outboard engine. The water was a dense yellow-green. It could have been two, twenty, or two hundred feet deep. Yet from time to time, Siriaku changed course. He swerved the boat from one line to another, as though he was driving down a twisting highway. Occasionally Marco stood up and scanned the water ahead. The two men were helped by the angle and pattern of the wavelets. They were telltales of hidden sand bars and reefs. But in the main, we were picking our way from one safe channel to the next according to the mental chart that the two men carried in their heads.

After about half an hour Marco muttered, then pointed to something off the port bow. Far, far in the distance a tiny spike broke the horizon. The mast of a small sailing boat. Siriaku said nothing. He had spotted it some time earlier.

Marco asked if I would like to go closer. He said it would be people fishing for turtles.

Ten minutes later we hove to about thirty feet from a small open sailboat that swooped and pitched in the waves. It was exactly the same sort of craft that we had seen used as a sailing ferry. Her sail was lying in a heap along the boom. Two young men pulled raggedly at long oars to keep the bow into the wind and the boat in the same position. In the narrow bow stood the captain. He was a thin, wiry Miskito dressed in tattered trousers and a singlet. He was hauling in a wide-mesh net hand over hand, straining against the weight. White polystyrene floats, slightly smaller than footballs, came in with the net. They were tangled and trapped in the mesh. Whatever had been caught had been twisting and turning and wrapping the net into a spiral. A pale patch began to show just beneath the waves. It was the belly shell of a turtle, the color of Jersey cream. Then the head and front flippers broke suddenly into view. The great oval eyes were open, their large pupils clearly visible. The crooked flippers waved upward, like the last gesture of a drowning man. The hooked mouth opened and closed as the animal gulped for air.

The Miskito captain maneuvered the heavy animal, still in the water, aft until it was amidships. The two young men dropped the oars and left their benches to lean far over the side, arms in the water up to the elbows, and grab hold of the net. It took the strength of all three men to heave the creature up out of the sea. It offered no resistance except for one brief lunging flurry as it first broke the surface. Then it was balanced on the edge of the boat, lying on its back with its four flippers waving and the short stubby tail, the shape of a wasp's sting, curling in spasms. With a final heave they slid the animal into the boat and down into the bilges.

The fishermen would have set a turtle net on the previous afternoon, Marco explained. They place it beside the hole in the rock where the turtle sleeps. During the night the turtle has to emerge from the hole every three or four hours and come to the surface to breathe. On the way up or back down to the sleeping hole, there is a chance that the creature will become entangled in the net, particularly when there is little moonlight and the animal fails to see the waiting mesh. In the morning the fishermen sail out from their houses on the cays and check to see if they have caught anything.

To Marco there was nothing to it. This was humdrum fishing. A good turtleman had to judge which was the most likely sleeping hole, that was all. Whether or not a turtle actually swam into the net was a matter of chance. Neither Marco nor Siriaku gave a thought to the extraordinary knowledge that was implied. The shoals around the Moskito Cays extend across an area of four hundred square miles, the size of Hong Kong. Occasionally the edge of a reef emerges at low tide, but it is lost again from view within hours. Otherwise there are no buoys, no shore marks nor visible signs of any description to indicate to a sailor his position. Yet in this area, as featureless as the flattest and emptiest desert, the Miskito turtlemen know the underwater terrain precisely. They have names for zones, for banks, and for particular rocks and coral heads. They know, often to within a few feet, the location of an individual rock and the side on which there is a hole or an overhang where a turtle would spend the night asleep. How the Miskitos are able to navigate to these spots under sail, allowing for current and drift and leeway, and still arrive with pinpoint accuracy, and without using a plumb line or an echo sounder, and then drop their nets in the place is an astonishing feat of seamanship. They take it for granted.

We left the turtle fishermen to their work, and Siriaku chose his new direction without a moment's hesitation. Fifteen minutes later we could see two or three small shacks on the horizon. They stood three feet above the surface of the sea on thick mangrove branches driven as pilings into the ridge of a hidden sand bank, and they might as well have been houseboats. Marco had brought us there because he thought I might want to meet "the American."

The American turned out to be English. His speech retained a soft Oxfordshire burr. Norman was in his late fifties or early sixties, and wore only long, loose shorts and red flip-flop sandals. With his paunch, short, straw-yellow beard, spectacles, and a skin sunburned to a pinkish shade, he could have been an English tourist on a Mediterranean beach. He was not. William Dampier would have called him—a man living and working in self-exile among the Indians of the Moskito coast—a "marooner."

Norman had spent years in the employment of the Export Division of the Ford Motor Company in England and California, until the moment came, as he put it, "to make a change of life." He became a buyer of lobster tails from the Miskitos. Now he lived for up to six months a year on an isolated wooden platform on top of a sand bank, fifteen miles from the mainland. In the hurricane season or when the isolation became too overbearing, he returned to his girl friend in Puerto Cabezas. He made an occasional trip to Managua to renew his British passport. His lobster station was three platforms linked side by side. On them stood three open- sided shacks. Two served as dormitories for the Miskito lobstermen, and the third was his home. It was a tin-roofed shed with a length of cotton sheeting hanging as a screen to divide his iron sleeping cot and lumpy mattress from his desk. There he lived with two young Miskito assistants and—a cautionary sign—two guard dogs. During our visit the two dogs leaped into the sea to cool off. They paddled round and round until they were exhausted and Norman gave a nod and one of the Miskito lads hoisted them back aboard the platform.

A venerable air compressor, a pile of air bottles, and four drums of fuel were the working gear. The Miskito divers came in their canoes to the cay to refill their air bottles. This was a free service and Norman's lure. The Miskitos found it convenient to sell their catch to Norman and he would stow it in a large storage container filled with ice brought weekly from the mainland until there was enough lobster catch to take to the freezer plant in Puerto Cabezas. On the day of our visit Norman could not have left the platform if he had wanted to. The Miskito divers had all left. They had gone to watch a baseball match on the mainland. The only boats tied to the platform were a swamped dugout and a damaged fiber-glass bean-pod boat, which looked as if it was salvage. Norman knew little about the Miskito divers who came to his platform, except that most of them were from one particular village, Dakura, on the coast. They came and went according to their own whims. They brought turtle meat to his platform, and he enjoyed eating turtle for breakfast. He did not speak Miskitu, and he had never inquired into

Miskito culture. It did not interest him. He was concerned more with the price of lobster tails, the cost of ice, the price of fuel, the price the freezer plant would pay him, and the slowness of renewing his passport. Norman was undemanding, sedentary, and thankful to have escaped the business treadmill when his life had been so stressful, he said, that he had smoked four or five packs of cigarettes a day. Now he suffered from emphysema but still smoked at least a pack a day, though he stuck to using tobacco and not the marijuana the Miskito divers smoked "until you could scarcely enter the room for the smoke." He communicated with the Moskito with signs, basic Spanish, and goodwill. Only five miles to the west was one of the above-water cays. Its mangroves were clearly visible. But he hardly ever went there—his marooner's world was a forty-by-ninety-foot rectangle of wooden boards.

Siriaku took us on to where the Sandy Bay men had built their stilt homes. A dozen sheds stood in the lee of the largest island of the Moskito Cays group. Most were roofed with palm fronds, and their decks all stood a few feet above the surface of the sea on the usual arrangement of mangrove posts. Several of the structures were deserted and empty, the thatch in tatters. The Miskitos came and went in nomadic style, occupying the houses when they wanted, returning to the mainland as they wished. Every hut that was occupied had at least one boat tied up at the platform. The majority were fiberglass skiffs like the one Siriaku owned. The others were single-masted sailboats, all of identical design. These were for shallow-water lobster diving, for fishing and for turtling.

Marco now brought us to the hut of two turtle captains. The most northerly of the stilt huts, it was the best maintained. It had a corrugated-iron roof, wooden walls bleached to a pock-marked gray, and was open to the front. It could have been a suburban two-car garage standing on legs in the ocean. A huge woman who must have weighed 180 pounds ruled the hut. The deck quivered when Jemina walked across the boards. She organized the supplies of food that arrived, prepared meals on a charcoal hearth on the apron where the boats tied up, and made sure that the plastic barrels held enough fresh water. The fresh water and firewood came from the mosquito-infested cays. Jemina also supervised the weighing of lobster tails. During the afternoon small motor skiffs arrived and tied up at the platform, and the young Miskitos handed in their catch. The lobster tails were meticulously weighed, one at a time, first in grams on a table scale, and then in ounces on a hanging scale. The fishermen looked on attentively. They were paid in cash, then diplomatically huddled in the tiny "office" partitioned off in plywood to share a marijuana cigarette. The lobster tails waited in a tub of "soda salt"—a solution of sodium bisulfate which prevented the flesh from turning soft—until a middleman in a larger motor skiff appeared. The vessel was fitted with a fiber-glass holding box, and the middleman bought all the lobster tails, then headed off to make his rounds of the other huts.

In the mid-afternoon, too, a string of bean-pod boats came past. A small motor boat was towing them home to their shacks. Nine little bean pods were strung out in a line, each with a young Miskito lad in it, lying back as if relaxing in his bath. They were coming back from diving in the shallows for lobsters. They looked like a class of junior dinghy sailors being towed back to the yacht club at the end of a lesson.

The turtlemen arrived last. Their two sailboats came racing in from the northwest as if this were the main regatta. The afternoon had turned bright and sunny, and the water sparkled with tropical intensity. The two boats swept along, their sails set to taut perfection. They were using weatherboards. A long plank projected out from the side of each boat. Right at the end of the plank sat a crewman, his weight counterbalancing the press of the sails. As the boat tacked, the weatherboard man skipped back aboard and the plank was pulled inboard; then, as the bow came about through the wind and the boat found its new course, the plank shot out like a thin tongue to the other side, and the weatherboard man nonchalantly scrambled out to this new position. The two boats came bustling up to the platform, and the sails came flapping down as their momentum carried them to the precise spot. Their crews, four men to each boat, were as tattered as corsairs. They were dressed in a multicolored selection of cutoff trousers, T-shirts, bandannas, caps, and turbans. One young man wore a flapping gray cloak knotted over his shoulders to keep off the sun. With scarcely a glance at the visitors, they stepped nimbly onto the platform and handed to Jemina two splendid fish they had caught for supper. Their main catch stayed in their boats. Lying in the bilges like lumps of ballast were half a dozen large green turtles.

There was lighthearted camaraderie on the platform. With turtlemen, lobster divers, and visitors, we were now fifteen people on a small space. Yet no one jostled. However hungry, people waited their turn for food as it was prepared on the tiny hearth, or took it in turns to take a glass of water from the freshwater butts. There was a leak in one of the sailboats, and its weatherboard was slid into position so that the captain could stand on it, heeling the boat far over, while a crewman stood in the sea and pounded strips of cloth into the crack to seal the hull. The conversation, Kendra told me, was mostly professional, interspersed with banter and teasing over minor incidents in their day's work. One boat had gone to this place and checked their net but there had been no turtle. Another had been to such-and-such a coral head, and it was the same. But the net had shifted a little, so perhaps it should have been more heavily weighted. Someone else had seen a turtle swimming in this place. One skipper thought he would change his nets to a different sector the following day. Listening, I could pick out the English words in their vocabularies—"jib," "gill net," "fishpot," "saila," and the balance board was a "wederbord."

That night we all lay down on the planks to sleep. There were so many of us in the small space that we lay in a tangle, legs criss-crossed. Under us the wavelets muttered against the mangrove pilings, and the entire platform quivered gently.

The turtlemen left for work while the stars were still visible. There was the rattle and slap of canvas, and the sails rose against the night sky. The boats unhitched their lines and dropped back into the darkness. No one spoke. There was the creak of timber, the rub of a line running as the sails were sheeted home, and the clatter of canvas abruptly quieted as the boats gathered way and vanished. It would take them two hours to sail to the precise locations where they had set their nets the previous day.

The two captains had informed Siriaku where they would be headed, and after breakfast he took us directly to the place—on a featureless open sea—where the two sailboats were hunting from net to net. Again, their boat handling was wholly adroit. Each sailboat was tacking and spinning and coming up on a net. There it came to a halt as simply as a driver parks a car and sets the hand brake. The skipper left the helm and strolled casually the length of the boat. If the polystyrene buoys were submerged, it was a good sign. Maybe a turtle was trapped. Standing in the bow he cast a small hook on a line and snagged the net, then pulled it aboard. If the net was empty, the crew reset it or stacked it in the bilge ready to set again at another spot. The two boats darted back and forth across the surface of the sea like eager gun dogs. It was no more than thirty seconds from the standing start when the boat was hove to under slack sails and the men were checking the net to the moment when the sails were taut and the boat was going at full speed. Three more turtles were collected that morning.

They brought the turtles to the "klar." This was a small stockade made of mangrove branches hammered into the crest of the sand bar fifty yards from the "workplace," as they called their stilt house. The klar served as a corral where they could keep the turtles in a couple of feet of water until they were ready to be taken to market. If the turtles needed feeding, someone could cut a branch of mangrove and throw it over the fence. The turtles grazed on the leaves like cattle.

A generation earlier turtlemen came regularly from the Cayman Islands and Jamaica to catch turtles on the Moskito Cays. They took them by the thousands upon thousands, and hauled them off to the canning plants in Bluefields and Florida. The cays are the largest pastures of underwater sea grass in the Western Hemisphere, and the flocks of turtles feeding on the weeds seemed as limitless as the herds of buffalo on the Great Plains. But the international demand for canned turtle and turtle soup eventually demolished the population, until the trade was banned, and the factory in Bluefields closed in 1977. Then the 'Forgotten Indian War' helped restore the balance. The Miskitos stayed away from the cays because the Sandinista air force strafed their boats from the air, and the number of turtles increased. Now the Miskito men were catching turtles only for themselves, as their traditional food, and the number of turtles caught every year was fairly constant.

Lunch was a turtle feast. A 120-pound turtle was hoisted from the bilge of the boat and dragged upside down to the edge of the apron. Siriaku took a machete and with the point of the blade tickled the animal under the chin so that it stretched its neck. There was a swipe as fast as an eyeblink, and the reptilian head flew off to one side, its jaws still snapping. Siriaku inserted the machete's blade into the joint between upper and lower shells, and sawed around the full circumference as if opening a giant can. He levered up the belly shell, turned it over, and laid it on one side. It became an oval serving dish.

The turtle was clearly a herbivore. Large loops of dark gray gut were similar to a cow's main intestine. The shoulder blades, curiously, were like those of a sheep. The animal produced almost two thirds of its weight in firm dark red meat, after Siriaku carefully cut out the "rank," two patches of meat on the flanks, which he said would taint the flesh if they were not removed. He methodically carved the muscle tissue into pieces, put the flippers aside for making soup, and saved every edible morsel in the upturned belly shell. The windpipe and guts went for fish bait, and finally he tossed the offal to the spiral of men-of-war birds and red boobies which had taken up their station downwind of the platform. The gelatinous lining of the upper and lower shells, greenish above, yellowish below, would be scraped off and eaten later. This was calapash and calipee, the main ingredient in turtle soup, which had sustained the foreign trade in turtles.

Jemina produced turtle hamburgers—she called them "ballmeat." They looked, cooked, and tasted like the finest beef.

Dampier and Captain Uring would have not have recognized the handy sailboats which I so admired and which the Miskitos handled so well. The Miskitos had copied them from the Cayman Islanders. (In fact, the most prolific boatbuilder was a Cayman Islander long settled in Sandy Bay.) The Cayman islanders called it a catboat, though it did not resemble its North American namesake, and the Miskitos insisted on calling them dories, the same word that Uring had heard when he was shipwrecked on the coast. But the true Miskito dory was a large dugout canoe. When Kendra asked why the Miskitos had given up using their sea-going dugouts in favor of catboats, she was informed that the dugouts were too big and clumsy, their carving wasted a vast amount of wood, and they required enormous strength to paddle. Compared to catboats, they were "krap."

On our way back to Sandy Bay, a motor skiff painted in military camouflage pattern intercepted us. Aboard was an armed Nicaraguan army corporal. He came from the lone stilt hut that flew a Nicaraguan flag on a pole and showed a radio aerial. This was the official outpost of Nicaraguan authority on the cays, and the soldier was suspicious and aggressive. He hectored Siriaku in Spanish, while the two teenage Miskito militiamen who drove the skiff for him looked embarrassed. Marco, sitting next to me, began to get very edgy and tense. For him the presence of a Nicaraguan army man on the Miskito Cays was an outrage. The corporal wanted to know who we were. Siriaku sat passive, and answered the questions in his deep rumbling voice, speaking in Spanish. The corporal then turned on Kendra and me and truculently demanded to know our business. Kendra replied with her customary tact, also in Spanish, and we handed across our passports for inspection. The corporal leafed through them, and there was an uncomfortable moment as we sat, wondering what he would decide. Then Kendra spoke to the Miskito militia lads in Miskitu, and the corporal glanced up from his reading, obviously startled. Clearly he did not know what was being said, and suddenly he seemed very alone and isolated. He moderated his bullying tone, and told Siriaku to accompany him to the militia post. Siriaku returned after a quarter hour. The corporal had demanded a "license fee" for allowing the carriage of passengers, but nothing else. Marco told us that the Sandinista troops had landed on the cays during the Indian War and, in their ignorance, had set up camp there. "The sandflies made sure they really suffered. They were very, very sorry they came."

Uring and his men at Captain Hobby's camp got little sleep. They continued to be "grievously pestered" by the biting insects, and were anxious to be on the move again. They set out with eight of the men in Uring's canoe, and the rest of the party in a canoe lent to them by the obliging Captain Hobby.

Uring's plan was to backtrack on their previous route, heading for an anchorage at Trujillo. There he hoped to find a logwood trading ship that would pick them up. As they paddled past the point where they had been shipwrecked, the elderly pilot recognized his earlier error. The "remarkable tuft of trees" he had seen grew not on Cabo Gracias a Dios but on another cape twenty miles farther northwest. Its name was False Cape. Glumly Uring noted that the name indicated that "some other People had been deceived in it as well as my Pilot."

By day the castaways paddled and rowed along as close to the beach as possible. Each night they dropped a light grapnel to anchor themselves away from the mosquito-infested shore. Then they boiled up a pot of food on a crude hearth they rigged up in the bilges. They ate "Hasty Pudding," balls of duff made of flour and water and flavored with shreds of beef. Afterward they lay down in the boat to rest. But Uring's canoe was very leaky. Uring found "it was impossible for me to sleep in her bottom, where the water washed continually from side to side." He laid one of the paddles across the canoe for his legs to rest on, repositioned a thwart under the small of his back, and then lay with his head in the

stern. "I leave anyone to judge," he added, "whether I had not a very un-
pleasant time of it."

Three or four days of this tedious progress brought the travelers to
the mouth of the Plantane River. There, to the sailors' relief, they saw
the English flag flying from staff. It marked the site of a marooners'
camp. Eight or ten English marooners were living there with their
women, slaves, and children. The women were Indians, some of them
living as wives of the marooners, others as slaves. Uring remarked how
feckless was their way of life: the marooners simply waited until their
food ran out, then either went hunting or sent their negro and Indian
slaves to paddle nearly fifty miles upriver against the current to a place
where they could gather plantains from abandoned Indian plantations.
The round trip took four or five days, depending on the force of the current, yet the marooners did not take the trouble to raise their own crops,
and no one laid in any advance stock of supplies. Nevertheless they
treated Uring and his sailors generously. The marooners fed the castaways and gave them powder and shot. For the first time since he was
shipwrecked, Uring had a good night's sleep. He was given a four-foot-
high barbecue to sleep on, its platform covered with "a good quantity of
leaves . . . and a piece of old canvas" and he lay under the first "pavilion"
he had seen. The linen, he observed, "falls down on every side, which
tucks in all round, and serves not only for curtains, but also keeps out
the flies . . . nor is there hardly any living without it."

Uring was doggedly determined to find a rescue ship. The marooners
on the Plantane were not expecting a vessel to call there, so he decided
to push ahead to Trujillo, nearly eighty miles farther along the coast. It
proved to be the wrong decision. When the little party reached the
Trujillo anchorage a few days later, they found it empty. There was no
choice but to return to the Plantane River encampment, where they
could at least find food. But they faced a new difficulty: until now they
had been traveling west, with the northeast trades in their favor. Now as
they turned their canoe around and headed eastward once again, they

had to paddle and row against wind, waves, and the current. The return journey became a nightmare.

On the very first afternoon, dark clouds began to mass on the northern horizon. Fearing a storm like the one that had wrecked his sloop, Uring ran the canoe into the mouth of the nearest river to seek shelter. There was already a dangerous sea breaking on the bar, and waves swamped the canoe. Bailing furiously, the sailors succeeded in emptying out their vessel, and paddled far enough up the river to avoid the worst of the weather. There they spent that night at anchor, listening to the wind raging and the waves beating on the shore; in the morning they paddled farther upstream to find a place to make camp. They chose a spot on a small ridge where they erected a tent from the sails of the canoe. They picked the site because they thought it would be dry. But it rained again very heavily after dark, and they spent their night slapping at mosquitoes and listening to a rivulet of water running across the floor of their shelter.

In the morning the wind was still blowing too hard for them to think of venturing out to sea again and they were faced once again with the difficulty of foraging for food. They no longer cared what they ate. Scavenging along the riverbank one of the men grabbed for a large iguana that he saw on a branch. But the animal leaped into the river and escaped. A little distance farther on they came across a troupe of large black monkeys in the trees. The sailors promptly shot several of them and brought them back to the tent. They skinned and gutted the monkey carcasses, then laid them on the fire to roast. Monkey flesh had the "taste of ill-fed Pork" and was popular with the men, but Uring found "that it was several days before I could prevail with my self to taste them, they looking so like young Children broiled." His hunger eventually drove him to join in and he admitted that "it was not long before I got over the Prejudice and eat them as heartily as any of our Men."

For more than a week, the little group was bottled up in the mouth of the river, unable to go to sea. Their constant hunting rapidly depleted the food resources of the area. The troupes of black monkeys were frightened away, to be replaced by bands of white-faced monkeys who would "hang by the extreme part of their tails upon the branch of a tree, and swing themselves to reach another with their Paws, but will not quit the hold of one till they have sure hold with the other." They chattered and grimaced at the sailors who had entered their territory. But the white-faced monkeys were too small to provide much meat, and were so nimble that it was judged a waste of ammunition to try to shoot them for the pot. The mosquitoes, however, were as voracious as ever, and as the hunting declined, the sailors decided to abandon the forest camp and move back to the beach where the wind would keep away the insects.

They found they had exchanged one plague for another. The bites of the mosquitoes were replaced by the stings from hordes of sand flies, "which made our men grow so impatient that they raved, stormed, and swore like Bedlamites."

Desperate to get clear of the insects, the sailors took it upon themselves to try going to sea in the canoe again. They had now been twelve days onshore, and were reduced to eating the buds of the cabbage palm, the same plant that had sustained the visitors to Juan Fernandez. Uring himself was in no fit state to travel. His right thigh was grossly swollen and red and he was only able to crawl. He diagnosed the illness as the result of eating monkey meat or prolonged exhaustion, though it was probably caused by an insect bite that had turned septic. He asked his sailors to delay their departure until he was recovered and he warned them that the sea was still too rough to attempt getting out over the bar at the river mouth. They ignored him.

Uring knew that if he was left behind, he would die. So he dragged himself into the stern of the canoe, and devised a system of steering with the help of his bosun. The crew took their places at the oars and waited in the river mouth with the canoe pointing seaward. Judging the moment when there was a "a small intermission" between the larger waves, they began to row frantically. But the canoe was heavy and slow, and they were not clear of the breakers when the next series of cresting waves rolled down on them. Uring shouted at the men to row harder. The next incoming wave broke over the canoe and they lost their nerve. They were "frightened and confounded, and star'd like men amazed . . . crying out for the Lord to have Mercy upon them." The hesitation was fatal. The next wave broke clear over the boat, half filling it with water. The canoe canted over and slued. To save her from being rolled, Uring and the bosun managed to turn the canoe stern-on to the breakers. The next big wave that crashed over the boat swept her from stern to stem, this time filling her with water. The crew were so terrified that they sat stock still in their seats with the oars in their hands. This saved the little vessel from capsizing, and she was swept inshore, still the right way up, as wave after wave carried her back to land. Had the canoe capsized, Uring calculated, not one of them would have survived.

Sodden and shaken, the crew splashed ashore, hauled up the canoe, and swore that they would not try crossing the bar again. They would rather walk along the coast.

Uring tried to change their minds. The weather would improve, the sea would calm, and a trek along the swampy shoreline was foolhardy. He reminded them that the Moskito Coast was a wilderness; they would have to swim or ford dozens of rivers and streams; and they should be mindful of "the Risque they run of the wild beasts devouring them."

His sailors would not listen. Uring's earlier insistence on leaving the marooners on the Plantane River and going to Trujillo now seemed a gross error. The men had lost confidence in their captain, and they became a rabble. They were no better than "baptis'd Beasts," Uring lamented, and their obstinacy "showed me what wretched ungovernable Creatures Men are, when there is no Power or Laws to restrain them."

Without forethought, the straggle of mutineers set out on foot along the beach, with Uring hobbling along behind. The impromptu saltwater bath had greatly improved the condition of his swollen leg, and he found he could just about manage to keep up with the group until they came to their first major obstacle, the Romaine River. There the mutineers came to a halt. They had not anticipated the difficulty of the crossing. The Romaine was in flood and running strongly. Anyone who ventured on it risked being swept out to sea. There was also the danger of alligators. Halfheartedly the mutineers began to hack at the trees to make a raft. But they still had only the single ax and the work went so slowly that Uring saw his opportunity to persuade them to return to where they had left the canoe, and think out a more sensible rescue plan.

Try as he might, he still could not persuade them to risk another sally in the canoe. Even another attempt by land was now beyond the enthusiasm of most of the party. Finally Uring volunteered to make the overland journey himself if just one man volunteered to come with him. He calculated a small party stood a better chance of getting through to the marooners on the Plantane River, and bringing back help.

Two men and the ship's boy agreed to go with him, and they were escorted back to the bank of the Romaine. There they collected bamboos to make two small rafts, which they lashed together with fishing line. When the fishing line ran out, they used twisted strips of bark. Then the main party of castaways turned back, leaving the four travelers to paddle their improvised rafts upstream to the point where they could safely cross the river. For three hours they sat astride their little craft, legs dangling in the warm water as they paddled upriver. They stayed close to the bank, well out of the main current, and often pulled themselves along by grabbing on to overhanging branches. At times they had to dismount, then wade through the mud pushing their rafts in front of them. Toward dusk they picked "a fine green spot" on the bank and clambered out to make camp, receiving a sudden shock "when several large alligators flounced from thence into the water close by us." They were so tired that they soon fell asleep beside the fire they lit with the help of a "pistol and a little gunpowder" they had brought along "in a calabash which was close waxed up to prevent its being damaged with Water."

At daybreak they were back in the water, pushing, paddling, and hauling along their bamboo rafts and "often saw large alligators leap from among the bushes into the water just by us." When they reached the point where an island divided the main width of the river, Uring judged it was safe to attempt the crossing. It had taken six or seven hours to get that far, but their perseverance paid off. They slanted across the current on their bamboo floats, and reached the far bank in safety. Then they floated downstream to the river mouth where they could resume their coastal trek. Untying the bamboo poles, they retrieved the precious lengths of fishing line, knowing that they would need them again when they had to cross the rivers that lay ahead.

During the twelve hours it had taken to cross the Romaine river Uring had been in and out of the water so often and "the weather being ex-tream hot," he had worn only a shirt. Now he learned his error. "That leaving my thighs very often bare" he wrote, "the heat of the sun scorch-ing them made me frequently throw water on them to keep "em cool, not thinking of the consequence, but soon after we landed I found them extreamly sore, very red and blister'd in several places which grew very painful."

Badly sunburned, he ate his ration of "a little Morsel of Bread with an ounce of raw salt beef" and then the four travelers filled up their can-teens before setting off along the coast on foot. Their shoes were broken and loose. They floundered in the soft sand or slipped and tripped on the shingle. When they tried to walk on firmer ground on the back of the beach, the thorns and briars ripped them. At night they tried to get some rest around a campfire on the beach, only to be kept awake by the pain of their sunburn and the bites of the sand flies. On the second and third days they crossed several small rivers, either wading across "some up to knees, others to our middle, and others up to our chin." One of the men knew how to swim, so whenever they came to what looked like a deep river, he would plunge in first, and test its depth. If he could wade safely, the others would follow. If he found it too deep to wade, the others would again begin to look for loose logs and branches and tie them to-gether as floats. But such cooperation was rare. The two stronger men usually went ahead, and Uring and the lad limped along, struggling to keep up with them.

Their greatest disappointment came on the third day, when their advance along the beach was blocked by a steep headland covered in thorns and jungle. They turned inland, intending to circle around the back of the obstacle. They spent hours groping through the jungle, pulling themselves forward from tree to tree, then slithering down hanging on to vines, only to misjudge their progress. When they emerged on the beach, they found themselves "to our great Mortification . . . still on the same side [of the headland] and not far from the place where we entered the woods." They camped that night where they were, and next day tried to force their way directly through dense brush which covered the headland. But it was no use. "We retired, after tearing our cloaths, and losing some of our flesh." Finally they took the risk of clambering round the cliff face, hanging on like acrobats and "stepping from one hole in the sides of the rocks to another, and from one crag to another, holding by the ragged part of it with one hand and our spare cloaths with the other, and by Providence we got all well over; but had any of us made the least false step or slip, he must have fallen forty or fifty foot down into the sea, and perished immediately."

On the morning of the fourth day they found a fallen coconut which they opened for the milk and flesh; and a little farther on was a single palm which had grown from a coconut washed ashore by chance. The tree had a few half-grown fruit, which the castaways knocked down and ate greedily. They had finished the last of their bread and salt beef the previous day. That afternoon they came to an area where the mangroves extended so far into the sea that the men could not wade around the barrier. Instead they were obliged to "go through the scragged trees and bushes, being obliged to creep between the branches of some, and climb over others, which tore our cloaths and even our flesh in many places."

What kept them moving forward was the hope that they might stumble across some of the "marooners" thought to be living near Cape Camerone, on the near side of the Plantane River. Not until late on the fifth day of their excruciating trek did they know their ordeal might be coming to an end. They had reached a coastal lagoon and were walking along the sand spit that divided the lagoon from the sea. Soon they came to the channel that joined the lagoon to the sea, and one of the men waded across the channel to reconnoiter the far bank. He returned two hours later with "joyful news." He had found a human footprint.

On the morning of the sixth day since leaving their companions, they came across a clearly defined path leading from the beach into the woods. The ragged and half-starved castaways followed the track and it led them to a "hutt, and soon after to our great Comfort a White Man appeared." He was a marooner, Luke Haughton.

The first thing Uring asked for was "a dram." But Haughton had no alcohol left. He ordered his Indian "wife" to prepare food.

Haughton was a typical marooner of the Moskito Coast. He had taken part in several buccaneer campaigns, including the notoriously barbaric attack on the Mexican city of Vera Cruz in 1683, when several Spanish priests had been beheaded. He had been captured and served time in Spanish prisons in both Mexico and Peru. Somehow obtaining his freedom, Haughton then got into debt while running a Jamaican sugar drogher, a small cargo vessel, carrying sugar from the plantations to the Jamaican ports. He also had an affair with a married woman. To escape his creditors he ran away with his lover to the Moskito Coast and they set up house together. But then they quarreled and the woman went off, this time with a logwood cutter from Honduras. Haughton's current "family," as Uring called it, consisted of "two women and an Indian boy of above fifteen years of age." All three were slaves taken by Miskito raiding parties from neighboring tribes. One of the women belonged to Haughton, and she "used to sleep with him and dress his provisions." The other woman was the property of Haughton's marooner colleague, who was absent when Uring arrived. The young Indian lad did the general work around the camp, fetching and carrying and helping on hunting and fishing trips.

For such a rough-cut character, Haughton proved to be exceptionally charitable. He gave shelter and food to the castaways for as long as they wanted. He was also an excellent raconteur and he kept Uring entertained with tales of how he had done battle with the Spaniards and gone on slave raiding expeditions with the Miskitos. The only thing Haughton refused to do was go to the rescue of Uring's crew who had stayed behind. The journey along the coast was too hazardous, Haughton said. Later Uring learned that a lookout on a sloop passing along the coast had seen smoke from a signal fire lit by his crew. The captain of the sloop had guessed that the fire had been lit by shipwrecked sailors and he sent a boat to investigate. The rescuers brought off the emaciated survivors, all except the elderly pilot. He had been too weak to sustain the semistarvation and had died in the final camp. His death, Uring noted sourly, was "his reward for undertaking what he was incapable of," adding that his own crew "would have shot him long before I left them, if I had not prevented them."

At intervals Haughton disappeared from camp, usually to pay visits to other marooners along the coast. On the first occasion Uring discovered just how difficult it was for an inexperienced stranger to survive in the swamplands and savannas. Haughton had made it look so easy to wander off casually into the woodlands, carrying a gun, and come back every time with a wild pig or a monkey or a deer for the pot. But when Uring tried hunting he got so badly lost in the woodlands that he only found his way home by climbing a tree and locating the river where he had parked his canoe. He promised himself never again to venture far from camp on his own. Next he tried fishing in the river. But even with the help of the Indian slave lad he caught only a few fish. He and his companions would have gone hungry but for a Miskito who happened to drop by. When he heard that Uring and his companions were short of food, he asked if he could borrow a musket. He disappeared, and an hour later came back with a large fawn, which he cleaned and cooked for them. The Miskito came from a small Indian camp nearby, and until Haughton returned a week later, the Miskito "were so kind as to bring us something or other to eat every day."

Uring was becoming more and more bored with the isolated, monotonous way of life. To keep himself busy, he asked Haughton for paper,

and set about making a chart of the Moskito Coast. He mixed gunpowder and water to make ink, and cut a quill from the feathers of jungle
fowl. With homemade dividers and a wooden ruler he drew the shoreline to scale, and added all the coastal features he could derive from
Haughton's extensive knowledge as well as his own travels. His own
odyssey in the sloop and by canoe and on foot he marked with a dotted
line. His "draught of the Bay of Honduras . . . and the coast of the
Mushetos," he observed with some pride, "is a pretty good one."

A day or two after Uring had finished his chart the neighboring
Miskito called on Haughton and invited him and Uring to his camp.
Haughton warned Uring that he would be expected to drink mishlaw,
the Miskitos' favorite alcohol. There were two types of mishlaw,
Haughton explained. One was made by fermenting chunks of ripe plantain in plain water. The other was a mishlaw made with pieces of sweet
cassava steeped in much the same way, except that the cassava pieces
were first boiled, then "chewed by their young women that have the
cleanest mouths" to speed up fermentation and then spat into the brew.

The Miskito camp had two or three families living together, some sixteen or eighteen people in all. When their guests arrived, the Miskito
men were swinging contentedly in their hammocks waiting for the
women to finish broiling mullet on the campfire. Gourds of mishlaw
were handed round. Uring was dismayed by the way the women dipped
the gourds into the tub of fermenting alcohol stew, then picked out the
lumps and "with their hands squeeze the plantains and water together,
till it comes to a pulp, the liquor running between their fingers, taking
out the strings and mixing it well together till it is of such a Thinness fit
to drink." He overcame his squeamishness and accepted a calabash of
the thin gruel when Haughton assured him that it was only plantain
mixed with water. Knowing that his hosts would be offended if he did
not finish his calabash, Uring drank the entire contents. Glancing down
into the dregs he saw the unmistakable strands of sweet cassava, and
knew that he must have swallowed some of the saliva-fermented alcohol. When he accused Haughton of deceiving him, the ex-buccaneer

burst out laughing, as did all the Miskitos who were waiting for Uring to be taken in by the joke.

Uring learned a good deal about the Miskitos from his visit, as well as from Haughton, who had adopted many of the native customs. "They take no care for Tomorrow," Uring observed. Like his buccaneer host, the Indians would stir themselves to go hunting only when all their food supplies had run out and they were driven by hunger. The night before a hunt the menfolk would discuss "which way they shall hunt next day." At two or three o'clock in the morning the Miskito hunters quietly "get into their canows without saying a word to each other, and paddle so far up the river as they think proper." There they came ashore and by daybreak would be in position in the woods. When a herd of wild pigs ran into the ambush, the Indians formed a circle around their prey, and closed in. Helped by their dogs, they blocked all attempts of the pigs to escape, and usually succeeded in spearing or shooting several animals. These they carried back to the camp and shared out equally. Even Uring and Haughton received two pigs for themselves.

Like most foreign observers, Uring was impressed by Miskito dexterity "at throwing the Launce, Fisgig or Harpone, or any manner of Dart, and shooting exceedingly well a Bow and Arrow as well as with small Arms." They obtained their firearms, he noted, from English traders who arrived from Jamaica. Before the arms dealers arrived, the Miskitos would go in a expedition of canoes out to the Moskito Cays. There they would catch hawksbill turtles, remove the shells, and have them ready to barter them with Jamaican men for "Guns, Powder and Shot, Hatchets, Axes and iron Pots." The Miskito youths had their own sideline in monkeys and parrots, which they exchanged for "Beads, Knives, and other Trifles."

Uring met enough Miskitos to notice that they did not all look the same. The men were "generally a tall, well-shap'd, raw-bon'd strong People, nimble and active." Most had copper-colored skin and long black straight hair. Others—like Captain Hobby—had much darker skins and "bushy curled hair." Uring learned that Captain Hobby looked part

African because he and others like him were the descendants from "a Ship with Negroes [that] by Accident was cast away on the Coast." Those who escaped drowning "mixed among the Native *Muscheto* People who intermarried with them, and begot a race of Mulattoes." In effect, the Miskito were a nation descended, in part, from castaways, and this may have accounted for their hospitality toward those who arrived among them in distress or weary of life at sea. Forty years before William Dampier watched two Miskitos, William and Robin, greet each other on Juan Fernandez, a Dutch buccaneer described how a Miskito host greeted guests who arrived at his hut near Sandy Bay. Walking out from his dwelling to greet his Miskito guests, the host "falls down upon the ground, lying flat on his face, in which posture he remains without any motion as if he were dead." His guests took him up, set him on his feet and escorted him to the doorway of his hut. There too they "use the same ceremony, falling on the ground . . . but he lifts them up one by one, and giving them his hand conducts them to his cottage, where he causes them to sit."

Uring lost track of time during his stay with Haughton. It was "between two and three months" after he first arrived that he was startled awake by what sounded like the boom of a cannon fired from out at sea. Although it was pitch dark and only two or three o'clock in the morning, he roused Haughton and told him that it must be signal gun fired from a sloop passing along the coast. It could even be a ship searching for him. Haughton told him that the noise might equally be the sound of a large tree falling in the forest, and, anyhow, he would have to wait till daylight to investigate. Uring was by now so "heartily tired with this manner of life" that he was up before dawn, eager to hurry down to the beach. At daybreak, after packing his few possessions and his new chart and "having made my best compliments" to Haughton for his kindness, he set out with all speed. To his disappointment, there was no ship waiting in the offing.

Undeterred, he turned eastward and began walking along the beach heading for the Plantane River. The larger marooner settlement was a more likely port of call for a visiting ship. This time his trek along the beach was less fraught. The Miskitos knew who he was, so when he came to a broad river, a young Miskito promptly ferried him across in a dugout. A Miskito woman gave him a roast plantain for his traveling supplies. After a long hot walk of twenty miles, Uring finally reached the marooner settlement on the Plantane River. To his acute disappointment there was no visiting ship there either. And the settlement was partially deserted.

The main body of the Plantane marooners had gone off to Sandy Bay to join a Miskito slaving raid.

"The Manner of these Expeditions are thus," explained Uring. "When [the Miskitos] have concluded what Number of Men is proper for their Design, they furnish themselves with a sufficient number of Canows, Dories and Pitpans." The pitpan, he said, was "something like a wort cooler"—the trough for fermenting beer mash. A pitpan drew only four inches of water and could nose into the smallest backwater, carrying the raiders far into the interior. As guides the Miskito took along trustworthy slaves captured on previous raids. They knew where to find settlements of "wild Indians." A Miskito raiding flotilla might travel as far as two hundred miles along the coast before turning into the mouth of the river leading to their victims. Leaving behind their larger canoes, the raiders then paddled and poled the pitpans some forty or fifty miles upriver until they reached the target settlement. With the same technique they used for catching wild pig, the raiders landed from their pitpans, quietly surrounded the village in the darkness, and attacked at dawn. Sometimes they managed to capture every living soul in the community. If the alarm was raised so the surprise was spoiled, the Miskitos seized the women and children. These they took down to the coast and sold off to the visiting Jamaican traders. "I have seen many of those poor Wretches sold there [in Jamaica] which have had so pitiful a Look it would soften the most obdurate Heart." However, he thought that the women who finished up as wives to the marooners "live tolerably well."

Uring noted that the Miskitos regarded the Spaniards as "their mortal enemies, and kill them wherever they meet 'em," and he admired their warlike spirit. He calculated that the largest army the Miskitos could assemble was only eight hundred men. Yet they had defeated a large canoe-borne Spanish expedition sent against them two years earlier. Rather than wait to be attacked, the Miskitos assembled their own war fleet, and went to meet the invaders as they paddled along the coast. Hiding within a river mouth, the Miskitos sent a small fast scouting canoe to sea as a decoy. The Spaniards caught sight of the canoe, chased it, and were drawn offshore. Behind them the Miskito flotilla emerged from the river mouth and forced the Spaniards, cut off from land, to give battle. The Miskito killed every one of the invaders except for a negro who was spared when he claimed to be a prisoner of the Spaniards. Later he escaped and carried back the news of the disaster.

Uring left the Moskito Coast ten days later. A trading sloop appeared off the Plantane River bar and hoisted an English flag. She was loaded with logwood and heading for Jamaica, but her master was such a poor navigator that he had lost his way. The crewmen who came ashore in a canoe were equally inept. They capsized on the river bar, and had to swim for their lives. The waiting marooners gathered up their oars, rescued the upturned canoe, pulled the sailors ashore, and learned that the vessel needed provisions. Uring took the chance to offer his services as an experienced navigator in return for a free passage to Jamaica.

Uring never lost his interest in the Miskitos, though it had been such a "troublesome, fatiguing and painful voyage" which cast him away in their homeland. In four more years of plying the Caribbean as a merchant seaman, he often met individual Miskito strikers aboard English ships, and he was in Jamaica when two hundred Miskito warriors were shipped in as mercenaries to fight for the British colonial government. Their pay was forty shillings a month and a pair of shoes, and their task was to track down runaway slaves living in the interior of the island. With a touch of pride Uring reported that the Miskitos "performed the Service they were employed in very well, and were sent home again well pleased." Later he also heard that there was a project for transporting the entire Miskito people to live in Jamaica. The idea was to give them land and offer them English citizenship. But whether the scheme was put into effect, he did not know, though he suspected that the Miskitos would not take up the offer, because they "did not like to quit their own Country" and "they have always maintained their Liberty."

Kendra employed an eloquent range of gestures, facial expressions, and other stratagems during her Miskitu conversations. To glean information, she might raise a quizzical eyebrow, turn the corners of her mouth up and down like a cartoon drawing to express her feelings, or put on the air of an innocent, a comedienne, or a coconspirator. She knew just when to pause, offering the interviewee a gap to fill with a reply. If a statement seemed exaggerated, Kendra tilted back her head, half-closed her eyes, and looked doubtful, and gave her informant a chance to correct what had just been said. And when an informant was in full flow, Kendra would coo encouragement with an admiring and carefully modulated "aoooaw" "aoooaw," the sound a Miskito makes when listening with approval. After Kendra had talked with the Miskito men, she would drift away. She was en route to the cookhouse. From the women she picked up the gossip.

We had puzzles to solve. Why were some Miskito houses so much more substantial than others, obviously having cost a lot of money? How could Siriaku afford a smart fiber-glass skiff and a brand new motor? Who paid for the expensive gold necklaces worn by many of the young Miskito girls or the dentistry that gave their elders a gleam of gold teeth? How could anyone afford such high-priced items in an economy whose cash came from the sale of lobster tails, and where most people lived on a diet of rice, cassava, yucca, and turtle meat? Very soon Kendra had found an entirely new meaning for what it now means to be a Miskito "striker": the wealthy people were those who had made "a lucky strike."

A lucky strike was the accidental discovery of a bale of narcotics. These "strikes" were astonishingly frequent. They might happen at least once a week in the right season of June and July and then again in November and December. A single really big strike might net more than forty pounds of drugs. The strikes occurred at sea or on land. The crew of a turtle boat pulled up a bale of drugs caught in their net; a ferryman spotted a bundle of drugs bobbing in the waves; a beachcomber came across a carton washed up on the strand. The packaging was usually intact. Black rubber sheeting kept out the seawater, and inside the bales, the narcotics—marijuana or cocaine—was divided into smaller plastic-wrapped packets, usually of one kilo in weight. These packets often bore trade symbols. Cocaine in packs stenciled with the icon of a bicycle, for example, was of better quality than those marked with the outline of a football. Where this extraordinary manna came from was unclear. It had begun in the late 1980s. Some said that the narco-traffickers stashed the drugs on the cays to be picked up later; others that high-speed smuggling boats dumped the bundles overboard when the authorities were in hot pursuit. If a boat was caught and had no drugs aboard, there was no evidence for the prosecution. Another explanation was that the bales of drugs were simply the slops. They were failed pickups dropped by aircraft to waiting boats or bales mishandled during transfer from boat to boat out at sea. The Moskito Coast lies beside the most lucrative trade route in the modern world—the narcotics conduits from South America to the United States. The analogy with the era of Will the Moskito was clear. Formerly the galleons had sailed past the coast laden with the highest-value cargoes of that time, bullion and gems. Now the main narcotics trade followed much the same track. Across a span of three centuries the Miskito lived off the crumbs from that table.

Making a lucky strike was winning the lottery. When the news spread, people would call at the home of the lucky striker and ask for a handout or a loan. It was like the days when the Miskitos salvaged a cargo of rum from Captain Uring's shipwreck, and shared that lucky strike and held a party. The Miskitos in Sandy Bay still distributed the proceeds from a bonanza. If the haul was marijuana, it was easy for the finders to share or trade the resin and leaf. If the lucky strike was cocaine, then the division was more complex. The first cut was set aside for the police and militia. Then smaller divisions were allocated to help older people, for the sick, and for mothers with large families who had no one to support them. The finders had a portion which they divided among themselves. A part of the revenue found its way to the Church.

The Miskitos barely knew what cocaine was when the lucky strikes first began to appear on the beaches. They sampled the drug, and a number of Miskitos became addicts. Eight of them, including young women, died since then. Others moved to live in Bilwi, where narcotics were bought and sold commercially. Now only a few of the Sandy Bay Miskito used cocaine regularly, and there was a clinic for drug treatment and antidrug education. But nearly everyone smoked marijuana quite openly. Alcohol, by contrast, was permitted only for discreet private use. Its public sale in Sandy Bay was prohibited.

Drug traffickers came to Sandy Bay to purchase in bulk when they heard there had been a large lucky strike. But the Miskitos soon learned that they got a better price if they took the cocaine to Bilwi and sold it there. There was always the possibility that the men, suddenly rich in town, would squander their cash on drink and gambling and prostitutes, or be robbed. If the women acted as the couriers, they drove a shrewder bargain and then spent the cash more wisely on their families. This was how the children got their gold necklaces and teeth or an education. Siriaku had been canny. He had invested his share of a twenty-five-kilo lucky strike of cocaine—five kilos—in a fine, 40-horsepower outboard motor and new boat. The substantial family house in which we were staying had been built from the proceeds of three different strikes. Unlucky Marco had only made one tiny lucky strike in all his life—a kilo of marijuana floating in the sea.

Occasionally the Miskitos smuggled the drugs onward themselves, usually into Honduras. There was little risk if the proper procedures were observed in the "land without law." The basic precaution was to advise the police and militia when and where the drug run would be made—and arrange for them to get their share. But the system was not foolproof. A young Miskito lost his life when the smugglers ran into a police boat. The smugglers had already paid a bribe of six kilos of cocaine, but there was confusion in the darkness. They were not recognized. Shots were fired on both sides, and the Miskito got killed. After this tragedy many favored the tried-and-tested scam of arranging for the police to make a raid and recover a quantity of drugs. The raid was greeted with great fanfare, but in fact the drug haul was only a small part of the original lucky strike.

Kendra was receiving only puzzled glances when she asked whether any Miskito of Sandy Bay had been wrecked or cast away, perhaps on the cays, and had had to fend for himself. No Miskito could disappear for long in that predicament, she was told. His family and colleagues would notice his absence and go looking for him. He would very soon be found. A boat rarely got wrecked while working on the cays. They were dismasted or capsized, but the crew scrambled back aboard, baled out the water, and came home under jury rig. "If the mast snaps, you take a machete, cut the pole short, and stick it back in its hole" was how one veteran skipper put it. The danger zone was the bar at the river mouth. Celtan Lopez, fifty-three years old now, had lost two boats there. Starting at the age of thirteen he had worked his way up from boat cook and bailer to weatherboard man to jib handler, and finally to skipper. Yet even the most experienced helmsman sometimes misjudged the wild ride through the waves in heavy weather. The north wind had destroyed him on both occasions. Fifteen-foot-high waves tumbled his boat when he was coming back from the cays with a big load of turtles. His vessel was smashed to splinters, and the cargo of turtles disappeared. Both times the crew swam ashore and no lives were lost. He built a replacement boat, and went back to fishing. "I do not learn," he commented ruefully.

Serenio, Celtan's eighty-three-year-old father, had his own version of how Miskitos could survive. The entire community of Sandy Bay had been marooned for four years. A great hurricane had raged in from the sea in 1935 and destroyed everything—the houses, the crops, the coconut and mango trees, the cassava fields. The land was flooded, and nothing would grow in the soil. "It was as though everything had burned." Worse, all the large sea-going dories were wrecked or blown away. The community was left with two small dugouts, and no means of reaching the outside world. For those four years they saw no one, no outsiders. Many Miskitos died. The Sandy Bay community dwindled to less than two hundred inhabitants. They survived by gathering shellfish along the shoreline, plucking mussels from the mangrove roots, digging into the estuary mud for edible crustaceans, and waiting for the crops of yucca and the newly planted coconuts to begin to bear fruit again. Even after they carved replacement dories large enough to be paddled down the coast to Bilwi, they had nothing to take with them to sell or barter so that they could bring back flour and salt and cloth. They had to make their own salt by boiling seawater over fires of driftwood. "Wood, there was always plenty of that," said Serenio. "It was cooking pots that we lacked."

Serenio and Celtan remembered striking—harpooning—turtles before the Cayman Islanders showed them how to use nets. The strikers hunted in pairs from a small *cayuco*, a dugout. One paddled very, very quietly and the other stood, watching the surface of the sea, ready to throw the lance. Iron was too costly so the striker whittled "the peg," the three-inch point, from supa wood. It was as heavy as metal and pierced a turtle shell as cleanly. With a peg made from any other wood, the lance was likely to slide off the carapace harmlessly—even if it had hit fair and square—and you heard the quick slithering screech as the throw was wasted. Striking turtles by daylight was possible for one month during the year, March. That was the time when the turtles were so gorged on sea grass that they came to the surface and rested on the waves with "their eyes closed as if they were sort of drunk or crazy." Only then could the striker get close enough. Otherwise the strikers hunted at night, paddling slowly near the underwater sleeping places and listening for the *phooo . . . phoooo* of a turtle breathing. Then the striker had to be lightning fast. Once struck, even the biggest turtles, females weighing over 140 pounds, tired in less than ten minutes. The hunter hauled the turtle into the *cayuco,* pulled out the peg, and plugged the hole in the shell with a twist of cloth or tree bark or soft wood. If he closed the hole properly and kept out the air, the turtle would survive in the klar—the enclosure where they kept them alive in the seawater—as if nothing had happened.

Serenio was adamant that he was never afraid of the spectral *liwa mair.* Other sailors had seen her. She had long, blond hair and her eyes blinked rapidly as if weak in the light. But he was a Christian, and evil spirits never bothered Christians. He admitted that when he reached his fishing spot and after he rolled up the canoe sail, he stood up with a machete in his hand and whirled it around his head in the air. That kept the evil spirits away. The mermaid *liwa mair* was not the cause of the sickness of the air bottle divers. It was the *liwa* of the lobsters, their guardian spirit, punishing them for taking too many lobsters.

Marco produced an old harpoon. It had a rusty "fish peg" on the end, with small barbs on it, and was made from a triangular metal file sharpened to a point. He took it with us as we paddled through the backwaters and showed us how to spear crabs among the tangle of mangrove roots. He made demonstration lobs, tossing the harpoon into the waves as we walked the beaches where the lucky strikes were made. But he could think of nobody in Sandy Bay who was still an active striker in the old style. He had heard that there was at least one striker farther south along the coast, working out of Tasbapauni, the "village of the red earth." But maybe he had retired, or it was just a rumor.

Kendra and I set out for Tasbapauni and on the way stayed overnight at the village of Pearl Lagoon, Laguna de Perlas. The village was an interchange for *pangas*, the motor boats that use the maze of waterways to link the southern Miskito villages. Waiting for a *panga*, we went for a stroll and I spotted a nine-foot-long harpoon propped against a fisherman's hut. Its peg was honed and bright. But the owner had the bloodshot eyes and grayish skin tone of a confirmed drunk, and he was settling down on his porch with a bottle of Ron Plata, the cheapest grade of rum. Kendra asked whether he would be going out fishing next morning, and he mumbled that he did not know. It depended on the weather, how well he slept, and how much food was in the house. He was already too deep in drink to be coherent. We walked on, disappointed. Fifty yards farther on, the village butcher was out in the street, standing under a broad mango tree and cutting up a turtle on a chopping board. A line of women waited patiently with metal bowls. Dogs circled for scraps, and the butcher's assistant was knee deep in the lagoon, wading out to the *klar*, where twenty captive turtles bumped against one another for space, like exhibits in an overcrowded aquarium. We were watching the butcher when there was a discreet cough behind us, and a burly, thick-set man inquired, in richly accented Caribbean English, if we were looking for a striker. He had a netting sack of yellow vegetable peppers on his shoulder, and he was going from door to door "peddling peppers," as he put it. He had heard we wanted to know about "strikin'."

Charles Archibald had learned "strikin'" when he was seventeen years old. His grandfather had taught him in the days before there were nets. That was forty-seven years ago. The two of them would go out in a small canoe, first with Charles as the "skipper," paddling and steering, and his grandfather with the "staff." Later it was Charles who made the strikes. Between 7 and 10 A.M. they could strike enough fish—tarpon, jack fish, mullet, jewfish—to fill the canoe. "You have to know what you is about." A single mero fish could weigh upwards of three hundred pounds, and every fish required its own technique—the high-angle throw dropping down on flat fish, the low throw with an almost flat trajectory for "narrow fish" like mullet, which were the most difficult of all to strike. In April they would go out on "the blue sea" to strike turtle during "pair-up time," the mating season. Then the male and female were so busy with each other that they didn't notice the approaching canoe. Between June and August, the rainy season, the hunters prowled the mouths of the swollen rivers which flooded into Laguna de Perlas. If they were lucky they encountered manatees—"manantee," as Charles called them—which had come into the lagoon to feed on the sea grass beds. Manatees were hard to spot. They barely put their nostrils above the water to breathe, hardly made a sound, and in the murky flood waters you could not see the body. You had to guess where to throw the staff with its special, stout peg. If you made the mistake of using the thin fish peg, it would bend and break in the manatee's thick hide. The biggest manatee that Charles had ever struck had weighted 320 pounds, and the last one he had taken was back in 1958. Now it was forbidden to hunt manatees, as he was aware, for they were protected. Similarly, there was a now a closed season, the *veda,* when hunting turtles was banned. This was not the reason there were so few strikers left. The reason was the gill net. The netsmen had stripped Laguna de Perlas of prey. Yet given clear water and a high sun Charles still went out to gather food for his family. He could see into the depths. "I like to strike. I love to strike!" he said.

Charles was a darker, heavier-set version of Marco, our guide to Sandy Bay. He projected the same air of long-acquired competence, and there was no mistaking that he was a boatman. He had the massive, work-worn hands, heavily muscled forearms, and rolling gait of the seaman. He would have made an ideal foretopman or bosun on a square-rigger. His laugh was deep and throaty, and when he spoke, the wrinkles around his deep-set eyes and broad mouth were always on the point of forming a good-humored smile. Even when his face was relaxed, his expression was that of a man who relished life.

Charles showed up next morning in a dugout canoe paddled by his teenage nephew, another Marco. He had come to give us a demonstration of strikin' and carried his nine-foot "staff." It was tipped with the same style of barbed fish peg that we had seen in Sandy Bay. He suggested that we go for sting ray in the lagoon. Marco would handle the dugout, and Kendra and I could ride alongside in a small *panga* belonging to Charles Archibald's friend Joe, and watch.

The little dugout makes a slightly bizarre picture with a great rip in its lurid yellow sail stitched from plastic sheet, Marco in a green T-shirt printed with an Adidas advertising slogan, and Charles Archibald dressed in a moth-eaten, sweatstained shirt and trousers rolled up to the knees. The day is bright and sunny with patches of cumulus cloud, giving Charles enough visibility to see the fish. When they reach a patch of shallow water about a few feet deep, our striker rolls up the sail and places it in the bilge. He hands Marco a bamboo pole and indicates that he should punt. Charles then hops up on the thwart of the canoe. It is like a circus trick. Marco is already standing up in order to punt; the slim canoe is as tippy as a floating log, and there is sixty-four-year-old Charles balancing like an acrobat on the canoe seat to gain a few more inches of height as he peers down into the water. As Dampier had said, the Miskito strikers were reluctant to allow any of the buccaneers to go spearfishing with them in such a wobbly contraption.

Out of the corner of my eye I see a black shadow whiz past. It is a sting ray racing across the shallows. Its shape flickers hazily against the yellow sand. Startled by the approaching canoe, it has leapt up from the lagoon floor and is rippling away at maximum speed, hugging the sand in a panicky zigzag. Charles Archibald has seen it too. He points urgently in the direction it had disappeared. Marco obediently punts the dugout in that direction. The sting ray must have doubled back, for a moment later Charles makes his strike. He had been standing in the classic stance of the javelin thrower, the leading arm outstretched and pointing at his target, the right arm, holding the harpoon, cocked back over his shoulder. Most harpoons have a line attached to the boat that uncoils as the harpoon flies through the air. But the Miskito fish gig is designed differently; it is self-contained. A wooden reel stuck on the back end of the shaft holds the retrieval line and also acts like a floating marker. Now Charles flings the weapon, and the shaft, peg, and reel all hurtle through the air. The harpoon strikes the water and disappears, but then the wooden reel detaches and comes surging back to the surface, twirling. It is a successful strike. The unseen fish is ripping off the line as it tries to escape, and the floating reel spins. Charles helps Marcus punt the dugout canoe rapidly to where he can lean over and grab the floating reel and line. Marcus picks up the harpoon shaft, which by now has also floated to the surface. Muscles bulging on his forearms, Charles hauls steadily on the line, gathering in the catch. As the fish comes closer to the canoe, the angle of the line grows steeper. It is vertical in the water, and taut as wire. Charles pulls in another two feet of line, then pauses carefully. Out of the water suddenly springs an evil-looking snake. It is thin as a lash, and dances back and forth maniacally. It whips in every direction, deliberately seeking a target. Occasionally it slaps into the side of the canoe, only an inch or two from Charles's body. It is the stinging whiptail of the ray. Carefully Charles leans aside, never taking his eye from the poisonous tail as he reaches down into the canoe and picks up a cutlass. He waits his moment, with a backhand chop slices off the deadly tail, and lifts the now-harmless fish into the canoe. It is less than three minutes since he first spotted the sting ray. The fish is three feet across, and could feed a family for two days. Charles pulls out the harpoon peg, picks up the ray, and tosses it back into the water to swim away. "The tail will grow again," he says.

I wonder whether this was a fluke, a lucky strike. So when Charles asks if I would like to see it again, I say yes. In the next twenty minutes he spots, stalks, and boats four more sting rays. He has achieved five hits out of six throws. He hits the final ray clear through the eye.

My quest for a Miskito striker is over. It is time for Kendra and me to leave. As we arrive at Bilwi's airport to catch our flight, Marco, our guide from Sandy Bay, staggers into view. He is hugely and harmlessly drunk. Every pore of his body reeks of rum and beer. He had found his way from town where he has been carousing away his wages, and out to the airport to say good-bye. He brushes unsteadily past the security guards and bears down on us. Then he throws his arms around each one of us in turn, buries his head in the curve between neck and shoulder, and gives a long, deep, shuddering, sniffing snuffle. It is the *kia walaia*, the traditional Miskito sign of greeting, affection, and farewell. *Kia walaia*, Kendra later tells me, translates as "to smell, to understand." I imagine that it was the embrace that Will and Robin exchanged on the island of Juan Fernandez on the day when the *Batchelor's Delight* brought Man Friday's long solitude to an end.

Crusoe spends his first night in a tree.

Chapter IV
PAINTED MAN

If a forest is the best place to hide a leaf, a library is the easiest place to mislay a book, and the worst place to try to find it again. As a result the "lost list" tantalized Defoe experts for a quarter of a century.

The "lost list" was a catalogue. The only clue to its existence was an advertisement that appeared in the London press six months after Defoe's death, in 1731. A London bookseller, Olive Payne, placed the advertisement to announce that he would be selling off Defoe's personal collection of books. In his advertisement Olive Payne informed the public that they could pick up a free copy of his auction catalogue at any one of eight booksellers' shops prior to the auction and see exactly what was in the "curious Collection of Books" going on sale.

The first scholar to spot the advertisement in the course of his research on Defoe and to realize that it could hold clues to Defoe's own literary taste was his mid-Victorian biographer, William Lee. He reasoned that if a copy of the catalogue could be found, it would reveal what books Defoe had read—books that might have influenced his writing. But had a copy of Payne's catalogue survived? If so, where was it? Lee and other literary sleuths hunted diligently. But they found nothing. William Lee reported sadly that he "had searched in vain for the Catalogue, and fear that a copy does not exist."

Twenty-six years later, in 1895, another Defoe scholar, George Aitken, observed in the learned journal *Athenaeum* how "others have echoed Mr. Lee's regret at the loss of the Catalogue." With a scholar's reproving tone Aitken scolded those experts who, not finding the list, had "indulged in speculations, based upon Defoe's own works, respecting the books he must have read."

Then George Aitken dropped his bombshell. "The missing Catalogue," he announced, "has . . . been lying all these years in the British Museum." Payne's catalogue would have been found much earlier, he observed tartly, if "there had been a cross-reference under "Defoe" to "Catalogues."

Aitken's treasure trove has fifty-three pages. At the start of his catalogue Olive Payne states that he is offering the books of "the ingenious Daniel De Foe, Gent., lately deceased." The auctioneer promises that the books "will begin to be sold very cheap (the lowest price marked in each book)." The sale is to begin on Monday, 15^t November 1731, "and to continue daily until all are sold." With typical auctioneer's puff, Payne adds: "N.B. The books are in very good condition, mostly well bound, gilt and lettered."

The discovery of the catalogue raised a new problem for scholars. Olive Payne had sold off two private libraries at the same time. One book collection had belonged to Daniel Defoe, the other to "the Reverend and Learned Philip Farewell, D.D., late Fellow of Trinity College, Cambridge." Unfortunately, Payne did not bother to note on his list which books had belonged to which of his two deceased clients. This oversight sparked a fierce debate among the scholars of Defoe's work, a debate that continues to this day. Some argue that there is no way of knowing which books really belonged to Defoe; others that it is reasonable to ascribe the books on theology, divinity, canon law, and classical literature to the Cambridge don and divine. The books on history, travel, geography, and the "several hundred curious Tracts on Parliamentary Affairs, politics, husbandry, trade, voyages, natural history, mines, minerals etc" surely had attracted Defoe's jackdaw mind. Among them are a Spanish-English dictionary, Raleigh's *History of the World* ("a very fine copy"), *History of the West Indies,* by the humanitarian Spanish cleric Bartholomé de Las Casas, and a volume of the political writings of Richard Steele, the essayist who said he interviewed Alexander Selkirk after his return from Juan Fernandez.

Four of the books reveal Defoe's fascination with tales of buccaneers, pirates, and privateers, both before and after he dreamed up the adventures of Robinson Crusoe. On his shelves was a copy of Betagh's *Voyage round the World* describing his troubles with the knavish Captain Shelvocke, as well as an *Account of the Proceedings in relation to Captain Kidd,* who was hanged for piracy at Execution Dock in 1701. Defoe also owned the 1699 edition of *The Buccaneers of America*, by A. O. Exquemelin. The volume contains a firsthand narrative of the raid by Bartholomew Sharpe and his "Merry Boys" into the Pacific and mentions how Will the Moskito was stranded on Juan Fernandez Island. Also in Defoe's library was a copy of another major "castaway story": *A new Voyage and Description of The Isthmus of America* tells how a buccaneer surgeon, Lionel Wafer, was marooned and lost not on some lonely island but in the green depths of the Central American forest.

Captain Simon Rowe of His Majesty's Ship *Dumbarton,* cruising off Chesapeake Bay in June 1688, was well pleased: he had arrested four pirates and impounded their spoils, nearly a quarter ton. Captain Rowe's squadron commander, Admiral Sir Robert Holmes, had struck a most unusual—and lucrative—arrangement with his sovereign, King James II. In return for suppressing piracy in the Caribbean and adjacent waters, Sir Robert was allowed to keep all the profits from the sale of vessels, valuables, and other property that his agents and officers confiscated from anyone shown to have engaged in piratical acts. Captain Rowe could reasonably expect that part of the value of that quarter ton of pirate loot would eventually find its way into his own pockets.

Captain Rowe had no doubt that the four persons he had caught were pirates. They had been arrested, if not red-handed, at least with damning evidence in their possession. Their sea chests were stuffed with an incriminating assortment of silverware—plates, dishes, basins, and cups. Many items were broken or dented and looked as if they had been pillaged from church altars. There were lengths of silver lace, strips of silk ribbon, and several bags plump with dollars and pieces of eight, all Spanish coins. The suspects might as well have had "pirate" branded on their foreheads.

Naturally the four rogues were denying everything. They hardly knew one another, they said, but happened to be traveling together. They were honest citizens, not pirates. They had acquired their motley selection of valuables by hard work and legitimate trade. They admitted knowing privateersmen, had even sailed with them on occasion. But they had never committed any acts of violence themselves or stooped to commit larceny on the high seas. They were honest men who had bartered the silver utensils from their former shipmates, with no idea that it might be plunder. They had earned the pieces of eight and the other Spanish coins in lawful trade with the Spanish. One of the four rascals even had the impudence to protest that five hundred of his pieces of eight—they were in a bag clearly marked with his initials—were a bequest from a friend. Of course, that friend was now conveniently dead and could not be questioned.

The four suspects dropped juicily into the captain's clutch when the *Dumbarton* intercepted them rowing a small boat surreptitiously along the backwaters of the Chesapeake. The place was a known retreat for outlaws, and that is precisely why Captain Rowe had taken his patrol vessel nosing in there. Captain Rowe now planned on turning the prisoners and their treasure over to the civil authorities in Virginia. They would take a precise inventory of all the confiscated goods—including the quantity of "fowle lynnen" found in one sea chest. He expected the Virginia courts to impound the treasure and cross-examine the miscreants to establish their guilt. Doubtless their lame alibis would collapse in court. If any of the gang were found to have committed murder during their piracies, then they would be hanged. One of the four men, the only black man, was likely to turn King's evidence. His name was Peter Cloise, and whether he was slave, servant, or collaborator was not clear.

But he was the one pulling at the oars when the *Dumbarton* caught them. The three white men had just been sitting there taking their ease.

Captain Rowe would have been incredulous to know that he would never get his cut of the spoils, later valued at £2,316 19s. He was not yet aware that he had arrested, by sheer luck, one of the most slippery of all pirate-privateersmen: Edward Davis, ex-captain of the *Batchelor's Delight*, the ship that had rescued Will the Moskito from Juan Fernandez.

By a remarkable coincidence, the two other white men in the captured rowboat were also former castaways of a sort. One of them, the glib fellow offering the cock-and-bull story about a dead man's legacy of five hundred pieces of eight, was to have a hand in shaping both American and European history. He was also the most literate of the group. When the three white prisoners signed their petitions of innocence, the former captain of the *Batchelor's Delight* wrote only the letter E, the first letter of his Christian name. The second suspect, John Hingson, managed a mere squiggle as his "mark." But the third signed his full name with a flourish: Lionel Delawafer.

Lionel Wafer, or Delawafer, or Wasser, as he variously called himself, was a buccaneer surgeon. It was a job that paid well. Privateers, buccaneers, and pirates needed surgeons to tend them just as much as they needed Miskito strikers to feed them. Battle injuries were an obvious occupational hazard of their trade. A badly wounded privateer was unlikely to last long if he did not get prompt medical attention. Even minor injuries could fester and lead to complications, particularly in the tropics. There was also the risk of contracting fevers and venereal disease or picking up such unwelcome parasites as the fiery serpent. A waterborne parasitic worm, the fiery serpent, or guinea worm, enters the human stomach as a microscopic larva, then penetrates the gut and takes up residence in the host's subcutaneous tissue. There, the white female worm, though only two millimeters in diameter, feeds and can grow to a length of three feet in a year. When the creature is ready to lay her own larvae, she burrows up to the surface of her victim's flesh.

Usually the first sign her host notices of the parasite's presence is the appearance of a painful boil or pustule on the feet or legs. When the boil bursts, the worm's head appears. William Dampier was infected with a guinea worm and describes how, when the head of the parasite came out of his leg, he "roll'd it up on a small stick" and every morning and evening "strained it out gently about two inches at a time, not without some pain, till at length I had got out about two foot." Dampier warned that, if roughly handled, the worm breaks. The broken part stays inside the human body and may mortify.

Faced with such diverse challenges, the ideal medical attendant for a pirate crew needed steady hands and a pragmatic approach to treating his patients. Formal medical qualifications were less useful than a roving disposition, a set of well-honed surgical instruments, and a knowledge of practical pharmacology.

Lionel Wafer met this prescription very well. He had gone to sea in his teens "in the Service," as he put it, of a surgeon aboard an East Indiaman bound for Java and Sumatra to pick up a cargo of pepper. Of all commercial shipping, the East Indiamen had the best record for providing medical facilities. This was due to the efforts of John Woodall, the "father of sea surgery." For thirty years he had been surgeon-general to the East India Company and had been responsible for "ordering and appointing fit and able Surgeons and Surgeons Mates for their ships and services, as also the fitting and furnishing of their surgeon's chest with medicines instruments and other appurtenances thereto." Woodall had become so tired of writing out, again and again, the list of instructions for each surgeon that he had published a manual on the subject. It was the first medical text ever written for surgeons at sea. Woodall had been dead for thirty-five years when young Wafer first shipped out, but Woodall's manual, *The Surgions Mate,* was to be found on every East Indiaman. The manual was comprehensive. It listed the instruments and medicines to stock the ship's medical chest, had instructions on how to treat wounds and medical emergencies, including how to cut off limbs, discussed the causes and treatment of scurvy, and finished up with a section on the chemistry of the day, alchemy.

Young Wafer found he liked seafaring. Barely a month after getting back to England from his two-year East India voyage, he signed on again. This time he sailed as the servant to a surgeon on a packet ship bound for the West Indies. Wafer's "chief inducement" to make this trip was to visit his brother, who was the manager at a sugar estate in Jamaica. So when Captain Buckenham delivered his cargo and mail to Jamaica and decided to continue onward to the Campeche coast of the Yucatan for a load of logwood, Wafer chose to stay behind in Jamaica. It was as well that he did. He later heard that Captain Buckenham was arrested by the Spanish as a poacher and taken to Mexico. There he was seen working as a baker's delivery man with "a Log chained to his Leg and a Basket at his Back, crying Bread about the streets." Wafer had clearly been paying close attention to what went on in the ship's sick bay during his years as a surgeon's servant, and now with the help of his brother he set himself up as a practicing surgeon on his own account in Jamaica's chief harbor, Port Royal.

Port Royal was notorious. Built precariously on a sand spit that twelve years later would dissolve partially into the sea during an earthquake, its population of some six thousand included many who catered to the recreational tastes of privateersmen, smugglers, and seafaring low life of all sorts. It was claimed that two out of every ten buildings were "brothels, gaming houses, taverns and grog shops." It was home to a "walking plague" of prostitutes, the most famous being Mary Carleton, notably described as being "as common as a barber's chair: no sooner was one out, but another was in." When ships docked at Port Royal's wharves to unload, the crews went ashore to spend their pay, carouse, trade on their own account, look for new berths on other vessels, and gamble. Some of them went to find a surgeon for medical treatment. Their medical bills could be three times more expensive than in Boston, the only equivalent-sized English port in the Americas, because Port Royal—particularly when the crew of a buccaneer ship had come ashore—was sometimes awash with cash.

Lionel Wafer, still in his early twenties, found that he was not yet ready to settle down. He was more attracted by the prospect of travel and adventure than the daily chores of a seaport medical practice. He met two privateering captains who were recruiting crew in Port Royal and, in his deliberately vague phrase, "they took me along with them." Captains Cook and Lynch told Wafer that they were planning a voyage to Cartagena. This was their cover story. In fact they were setting off for the great buccaneer rendezvous on the coast of Central America where it would be voted to launch an overland raid on Panama. Thus it was that in the first week of April 1680 Lionel Wafer found himself landing—in the company of William Dampier and Will the Moskito—to join the "Pack of Merry Boys" as they disembarked near Golden Island, and Captain Edmund Cook raised his personal red and yellow banner with its badge of a hand and sword.

Wafer was not the only surgeon in the expedition. There were at least four others. Three would be captured by the Spanish in January the following year during a disastrous attack by the pirates on the Chilean town of Arica. The buccaneers fought their way into the main square but suffered such heavy casualties during the Spanish counterattack that they were forced to retreat. They left behind their wounded laid out on the floor of Arica's church—which they had already looted—and the three surgeons to tend them. The Spaniards retook the town and executed the wounded men, but spared the three surgeons on condition that they stay in the Spanish colony and practice medicine there. The fourth surgeon had already left the expedition within the first few weeks. He was surgeon to Captain Coxon's war band, and when his captain turned back with fifty of his men, he went with him. According to one disgruntled buccaneer, Coxon took not only his surgeon but also "the best of our medicines, unknown to the major part of us."

A medical chest stocked according to John Woodall's specifications was far too heavy and bulky for the expedition's porters to shoulder through the rain forest. It contained plasters, unguents, salts, natural oils, "chymical oils," syrups, elixirs, pastilles, spices, gums, simples, opiates, and laxatives. Only a limited selection of the drugs could be carried on the porters' backs or in the surgeons' knapsacks on the march over the isthmus to the South Sea. The logical choices of what to take included laudanum, a painkiller; Jesuit's bark, or quinine, against fever; and various ointments and salves such as ferric chloride—known as "soldier's ointment." The relevant surgical tools were specula for widening wounds and gashes; forceps for removing bullets and splinters; metal syringes for administering enemas—constipation being a chronic affliction of seafarers, according to Surgeon General Woodall; needles and thread; and an awesome array of scalpels, knives, and saws to cut bone and flesh, as well as cauterizing irons to seal the result.

Wafer spent a year with the rapidly dwindling band of "Merry Boys" and accompanied them as far south as their landing on the island of Juan Fernandez to spend Christmas. There he took part in the scrambled embarkation that left Will the Moskito stranded on the island. The Arica debacle came soon afterward, and the capture of the three other surgeons may have led Wafer to reconsider his own future. In April 1681 he elected to join a breakaway group, including William Dampier, who had decided they'd had enough of the South Sea adventure. They would leave their ship, the *Trinity*, then commanded by the untrustworthy Bartholomew Sharpe, and try to sneak back across the narrow waist of Central America and reach the Caribbean on foot, each man carrying his share of the plunder.

Their plan was desperate enough. The Spanish authorities were expecting the buccaneers to try just such an evasion. Every small town had been put on watch for gangs of buccaneers trying to slip past. Search parties had landed at various isolated points and checked for buccaneer hideaways. A squadron of three warships was on standby in the city of Panama, on the Pacific coast, waiting to put to sea the moment there was any sighting of buccaneers. The organizers of Wafer's breakaway group worried that some of their volunteers lacked stamina if the

Spanish came in hot pursuit. For one reason or another—age, poor health, lack of brawn—some of the group might not be able to keep up with the main party as it made the quick dash across the rugged terrain of the isthmus. "We knew," wrote Dampier, "that the Spaniards would soon be after us, and one Man falling into their hands might be the ruin of us all, by giving an account of our strength and condition." There was a ferocious announcement before the group set out, that anyone who lagged behind "must expect to be shot to death."

Forty-four of the surviving buccaneers resolved to make the bold attempt. They demanded from Captain Sharpe—and received—five captured slaves as part of their booty. The slaves were to carry their marching rations, a quantity of flour ready-sifted for making bread and dumplings en route, and twenty or thirty pounds of chocolate "rubb'd up . . . with sugar to sweeten it." They also selected a large cook pot from the ship's stores, and persuaded an Indian auxiliary to accompany them. This Indian was a native of Darien, as the isthmus was called, and he had joined the buccaneers a year earlier on their way into the Pacific. He proved to be useless as a guide but he could speak Spanish and was invaluable as an interpreter. Better, two of the Miskito Indian strikers decided to go with them. The Miskitos were able to hunt fish and turtles to feed the group as they made their way in small boats for 600 miles along the coast to the Gulf of San Miguel in present-day Panama.

Here they had planned to paddle up the river which emptied into the head of the gulf, and travel inland as far as possible by water. But the Spanish had anticipated their route. A guard ship and garrison were stationed at the river mouth, and the buccaneers hastily diverted before they were observed. They found a small creek a few miles to the north, sank their boats so as to leave no trace of their presence, and made ready for their epic dash across the isthmus. "While we were landing and fixing our Snap-sacks to march," wrote Dampier, "our Miskito Indians struck a plentiful Dish of Fish which we immediately dresst, and therewith satisfied our Hunger." Then the group of adventurers, including Wafer and

"John Hingson, Mariner," later arrested with him by Captain Rowe, turned their backs on the sea.

The buccaneers had heavy loads. An armed buccaneer normally carried an unwieldy musket weighing about sixteen pounds, a pound or two of gunpowder in a flask, and at least a dozen lead bullets in a box or bag weighing another pound. Then there was his cutlass, or "hangar," which served as a machete; perhaps a pistol; and a knapsack with spare clothes, tobacco, and personal possessions. All this added up to a burden probably in excess of thirty pounds. The buccaneers dumped all their surplus possessions when they scuppered the boats at the head of the creek before they set out on their trek across the isthmus. But of course they retained their booty. One buccaneer, "a weakly man," strapped a bag of 400 pieces of eight on his back. Another buccaneer had a bag of 300 pieces of eight. Weighing more than 18 pounds, it was to be the death of him.

"Being landed, May the 1st, we began our march about 3 a Clock in the afternoon," Dampier recorded in his notebook. There were no Indian guides so the column headed across country, "directing our course by our pocket compasses, N.E." That afternoon they covered only two miles before reaching the foot of a small hill. Unwilling to begin the climb and already exhausted, they built "small hutts" and lay down to rest. Until midnight it rained heavily.

The next morning dawned fair, and the column began to ascend the heavily forested hillside, until the vanguard found an Indian trail leading through the trees. At first the buccaneers followed the track, but then the path deflected too much to the east, and they abandoned it. They were beginning to learn that Indian trails that looked promising at the start often proved to be a disappointment. Sometimes the correct path was a track that initially seemed to lead in quite the wrong direction. Later they realized that the local Indians sometimes had no idea what lay over the next ridge. Many Indians never traveled far from their village. They shunned territory that might harbor their enemies or evil spirits.

At a loss to know which way to go, several buccaneers reverted to their role as masthead lookouts: they climbed into the tops of the tallest trees and scanned the green expanse of the forest canopy. On the north slope of the hill, they glimpsed the roofs of an Indian village. The slope was too steep to go there directly, and the column had to follow a round-about track to arrive there.

The buccaneers' reception in the village was friendly. It was still early afternoon and most of the Indian men were away at work, tending their forest plantations or hunting. But their wives were willing to sell food—yams, potatoes, plantains, and the small wild pigs called peccaries—and they offered their visitors bowls of *chicha,* maize beer. A difficulty now arose: no one in the village spoke Spanish, and the buccaneers found it impossible to explain in sign language exactly where they wanted to go. The situation hardly improved in the evening when the menfolk came home. Finally the travelers learned that a day's march away lived an Indian who did speak Spanish well. On payment of a hatchet, one of the villagers, an elderly man, agreed to lead the column there the next day.

Before seven o'clock next morning, the column was trudging out of the village. The travelers already knew the advantage of covering as much ground as possible in the cool of the day. Nevertheless, one of the buccaneers was so exhausted by midmorning that he began to drop back. Fearing that he would be shot as straggler, he slipped away unnoticed.

By noon the travelers had arrived at the house of the Spanish-speaking Indian, and were trying to explain the reason for their visit—to find out the best route to the northern coast. The Indian was dismissive. "He seemed to be very dubious of entertaining any discourse with us, and gave very impertinent answers to the questions that we demanded of him." The Indian said he had no idea of how to get across the cordillera, and his manner was so aggressive that Dampier concluded "he was not our friend." The buccaneers kept their tempers and tried to humor him. They knew how desperately they needed an Indian guide, and that "it was neither time nor place to be angry with the Indians, all our lives lying in their hand."

The buccaneers offered the bad-tempered Indian every inducement they could muster. They displayed "Beads, Money, Hatchets, Macheats [machetes] or long Knives" as payment if he would help them. The Indian was adamant. He would not assist the travelers. Then one of the buccaneers pulled out from his bag a curious item of plunder: a sky-blue petticoat. He draped it on the Indian's wife, and she "was so much pleased with the Present that she immediately began to chatter to her Husband, and soon brought him to a better humour."

The petticoat tipped the balance. Obedient to his delighted wife, the Indian now admitted that he did know a route across the mountains but could not travel himself because he had cut his foot two days earlier and was lame. Instead, he translated to the column's original guide, the old man from the village, where the buccaneers wanted to go and arranged that the old man should continue on for another two days, receiving a second hatchet for his pay.

The Indian "way to the North Side" was not what the buccaneers had expected. The Indians had "no Paths to travel from one part of the Country to another . . . [so] . . . guided themselves by the rivers." To their dismay the guide took the column on a long, wet, slippery scramble from one streambed to the next. Progress was only eleven or twelve miles a day, and the conditions were disheartening. The weather had a predictable pattern: a dry morning, followed by a wet afternoon, and a drenching night. "Tho whether it rained or shined, it was much at one with us," Dampier noted wearily, "for I verily believe we crost the Rivers thirty times this Day." In the evening the travelers cut branches with their cutlasses, made small huts, crawled in, and lay down in their wet clothes and sodden boots to try to get some rest. Two men always had to stay awake, "otherwise our own slaves might have knocked us on the head while we slept." Amid such hardship, the fear of Spanish pursuit quickly began to fade so that "we began to have few other cares than how to get Guides and Food, [and] the Spaniards were seldom in our thoughts."

Dampier was having trouble keeping the pages of his journal dry. He rolled up the sheets of paper and stuffed them into a length of bamboo, sealing the cut ends of the tube with wax. It was a technique similar to the way the buccaneers protected their flintlock muskets. When carrying a musket in a dugout canoe or through a dripping rain forest, a conscientious musketeer covered the lock of his gun with a case and then sealed it with wax to keep out the water.

But the gunpowder as well as the flintlock had to be kept dry, and it was much more difficult to shield the gunpowder from the effects of the prevailing damp. The problem was not so much with the musket cartouches, or cartridges, the prepared loads of gunpowder and shot rolled in paper. These were carried in a cartouche box with a tightly fitting lid. The sensitive material was the priming powder, which had to be placed in the firing pan of the flintlock. A buccaneer carried his loose gunpowder in the standard powder flask made from a cow's horn. The horn had been softened in steam or boiling water, flattened, the open end blocked with a broad plug, and the tip cut off to provide a convenient pouring nozzle which could be closed with a small cork or stopper. But the powder flask was not completely airtight. The rain forest's all-pervading humidity, seldom less than 70 percent, slowly permeated the interior of the flask. The gunpowder absorbed the moisture and grew damp and useless. Damp gunpowder was a much more common cause for a "flash in the pan"—when the shower of sparks from the gunflint failed to ignite the priming powder— than any malfunction of the flint mechanism. It was routine for a musketeer to dry out his personal stock of gunpowder or risk a misfire.

After five days of soggy marching the column had traveled almost forty miles and was about a third of the way through its journey. Ahead lay the crest of the Serrania de Maje, the first of the two main ridges that form the backbone of the isthmus at this transit. In this wilderness—

surprising in such a remote part of the country—they came upon the isolated house of a young Indian who had lived for a time in the home of the bishop of Panama and therefore spoke excellent Spanish. The young man quickly struck up a friendship with the buccaneer's own interpreter, the Spanish-speaking Indian who had accompanied the buccaneers from the day they had left their ship. The young man must have been feeling the isolation of his forest home because he invited the new Indian arrival to stay and help him with the work of clearing plantations and to marry his sister. To the consternation of the buccaneers, their interpreter-companion promptly accepted. This was very awkward. The buccaneers did not want to lose their interpreter, and although he had been with them for over a year, they did not trust him absolutely. They suspected treachery, perhaps that he would inform the Spanish authorities. In the end they agreed to let him go only on condition that he stay with the column for another two or three days' march, by which time the travelers would be clear of any possible pursuit by the Spaniards.

Sorting out this problem took the best part of the day, which was 5 May. Naturally, the men took the chance to light campfires, cook meals, dry their clothes, and relax. One man decided he would take the opportunity to dry out his gunpowder. Removing a silver dish from his plunder bag, he tipped the gunpowder into it, and held the dish close to the heat of the fire. According to Dampier, it was the surgeon Lionel Wafer who was holding the dish in his hand when "a careless fellow passed by with his Pipe lighted and set fire to his powder which blew up." Wafer himself said that he was only "sitting on the ground near one of our men who was drying of gunpowder in a Silver Plate, but not managing it as he should, it blew up."

Whoever was at fault, the blast of the close-range explosion tore open Wafer's leg.

After the initial shock of the detonation the young surgeon examined the extent of his injury. He saw that it had "scorch'd my knee to that degree that the bone was left bare, the flesh being torn away, and my Thigh burnt for a great way above it." The column, he knew, could not stop nor slow down for him. The buccaneers still had to put as much distance as possible between themselves and a potential Spanish pursuit, and his injury was no different from a gunshot wound taken in battle. In great pain, Wafer realized that his best chance was to try to keep up with his companions until they reached the coast, where he could get back aboard ship and recuperate.

His comrades-in-arms were sympathetic and helpful. They wanted to retain their surgeon. His skill might be needed later, and there was "none to look after us but him." So they redistributed the porters' loads and detailed one of the slaves to carry Wafer's baggage, including the remainder of the medical supplies. The surgeon was to hobble unburdened in the rear of the column.

The wet season had now begun. One hundred twenty inches of rain—sometimes more—falls on this part of the Isthmus of Panama each year. Even its "dry season" is a misnomer as there can be heavy downpours on any day throughout the year. But from May onward, the precipitation increases noticeably. Heavy clouds gather over the cordillera and merge into a solid gray cloudcover which brushes the higher ridges and shuts out the sky. The sun disappears completely in the murk, and daylight dims. Thunder shakes the forest canopy, followed by the onrushing sound of torrential rainstorms. When a rainstorm arrives, it can last for a few minutes or for several hours. If the downpour loiters in one place, there is a sense that the roaring cascade of water will never stop. When it does cease, the silence is quickly filled by the manic dripping of thousands upon thousands of runoff trickles spattering down from leaf to leaf, and the gurgle of water draining through tree roots.

The farther east the buccaneers went into the cordillera, the wetter it would become. The rain in the isthmus arrives from the east, originating as moisture carried by the trade winds. Forced upward by the mountain slopes on the Caribbean side of the isthmus, the moisture condenses and falls most heavily on the windward slopes. Lionel Wafer, William Dampier, and the other buccaneers were marching up the rainfall gradient. The rainy season would grow more pronounced with each day that passed, and with each mile they covered.

Their pathway, the rivers, became treacherous. On 6 May, the day after Wafer's accident, the column set out again after hiring new guides. They crossed the first river in a local canoe, shuttling in batches from one bank to the other. But there was no canoe available at the next river, so they had to wade across. A few miles farther on, their guide informed them that they would have to wade again, back to the opposite bank. Twice more they had to ford the river, floundering on the slippery boulders of the riverbed and struggling to keep on their footing as the current plucked at their bodies. On the final crossing the river was so deep that "our tallest men stood in the deepest place, and handed over the sick, weak and short Men." The injured surgeon, Lionel Wafer, only just made it to the opposite bank. The current picked him up off his feet and swept him downstream "for several paces" before an eddy deposited him on a bend in the river, and he scrambled ashore. Two other stragglers, Robert Spratlin and William Bowman, lagged even farther behind than the injured surgeon. They arrived on the riverbank in time to watch Wafer nearly drown. Seeing his narrow escape, they lost their nerve and decided not to make the attempt to get across until the water level dropped. The rest of the men sat on the opposite bank and waited for half an hour. But instead of falling, the river rose even higher. The men in the main column shouted across the water to Spratlin and Bowman and "bid them be of good comfort and stay till the River did fall." Then they marched on.

After another two miles they stopped for the night and made their usual lean-to huts of branches on the riverbank. They had scarcely set up the huts when the river rose even higher, bursting its banks, and the travelers were forced to abandon their huts and retreat to higher ground in the forest. It was too dark to construct more huts and the buccaneers lay down in small groups under the larger trees and tried to get some rest. To add to their discomfort, said Dampier, "The greatest part of the night we had extraordinary hard rain with much Lightening and terrible claps of Thunder."

Sheltering from the downpour, the travelers failed to keep a proper watch. All but one of the slaves and prisoners took their chance to escape in the night. The exception was a drowsy slave "who was hid in some hole and knew nothing of their design, or else fell asleep." When the buccaneers took stock of their losses next morning, they found that the runaways had fled with Wafer's musket and all his money. More wretched from Wafer's point of view was that the slave designated to carry his kit had run away with all the medicines "and thereby left me depriv'd of wherewithal to dress my Sore." The only equipment the surgeon still possessed was a small box of surgical instruments that he had slipped into his pocket and a handful of "medicaments" he had rolled up in a cloth.

Their guide now broke the unwelcome news that the column had to cross the river yet again. The buccaneers assembled on the bank. The water level had fallen considerably in the night, but the current was still running very strongly and though the river was narrow, it looked to be too deep to wade. Not all of the buccaneers knew how to swim, and even those who did wondered how they would get across with their heavy plunder. A council decided that the best plan would be for one of the swimmers to go across on his own, pulling a line behind him. This rope would then be used to haul across the bags and sacks, and afterward the nonswimmers. A man named George Gayny volunteered to go first. He took the free end of the line and, unwisely, fastened it around his neck. Even more stupidly he took his plunder with him, a bag of silver coins. A colleague stood on the bank with the rest of the coil, ready to feed out the rope as needed. Gayny plunged into the river and was halfway across when "the Line in drawing after him chanced to kink or grow entangled." The line handler checked the line, to give himself time to clear the tangle. The sudden tug on the rope plucked Gayny off-balance. He was seen to turn on his back in the current and lose his forward momentum. Rather than strangle Gayny with the taut rope, the line handler threw the rest of the coil into the river, "thinking that he [Gayny] might recover himself."

The flood was too strong. In a moment it swept Gayny, rope and all, out of sight. He was whirled away and "having three hundred dollars at his back, was carried down and never seen more by us." Sometime later the two stragglers, Spratlin and Bowman, who had been left on the far bank, came across Gayny's body. The corpse was lying in a side creek where a side current had driven it ashore. The bag of plunder was still lashed to Gayny's back. The two stragglers did not touch the silver. They "meddled not with any of it, being only in care how to work their way through this wild unknown Country."

The column eventually got across the river by making a bridge. They felled the largest tree they could find, and balanced their way over.

At last it seemed that they had reached easier country. They entered a broad valley where the trees were more widely spaced so they could advance more quickly. Progress had dropped to as little as six miles a day when they were struggling with the rivers, but it now increased to twelve miles. For food they "ransackt" the swiddens, the occasional patches of slash-and-burn agriculture where the natives would cut back the jungle and grow plantains and yams for a year or two, after which they opened up another clearing when the meager soil was exhausted. One guide handed the group over to the next, and on the fourth day since Wafer's accident, 9 May, they reached an Indian village, the first since leaving the coastal plain, to find the entire Indian community assembled and waiting "in a large house to receive us."

Unfortunately they had come in "the hungry time." This was the interval between the abandonment of the exhausted plantations and the fruiting of the new plantings. The influx of forty armed and hungry foreigners overwhelmed the food resources of the village. The Indians "made us welcome to such as they had, which was very mean," Dampier wrote, "for these were new Plantations, the Corn being not eared . . . . Potatoes, Yams and Plantains they had none, but what they brought from their old Plantations." Once again the problem of interpreters arose. The buccaneers had kept their word and allowed their Spanish-speaking Indian guide to return back to the house where he had been promised a wife. Now the travelers had to struggle to make themselves understood. They asked for guides to take them on to the Caribbean coast, and as quickly as possible. They were under the mistaken impression that they were nearer to their destination than they actually were. They were tired of squelching through the rain forest, sleeping in makeshift huts made of branches, swatting at insects, living off unripe plantains, and constantly being soaked by rain and river water.

Their impatience showed. Two Indians who had a smattering of Spanish agreed, on promise of payment, to lead the buccaneers onward. But they cautioned the buccaneers to wait for a day and rest. The buccaneers would have none of it. They wanted to be on their way, and next morning they set out, determined to plunge forward, even without guides. Reluctantly the two guides went with them, though it is not clear whether they were coerced. The buccaneers left a sour atmosphere behind them.

They also left behind three of their own men. Richard Gopson had always been an unlikely buccaneer. He was an "ingenious Man and Good Scholar" who could read classical Greek. Earlier in his life he had been apprenticed to a druggist in London, and he was rather bookish. In his luggage he carried a copy of the New Testament in Greek. This he would read aloud "and translate extempore into English to such of the Company as were dispos'd to hear him." The second relict was John Hingson, "Mariner," who would be arrested with Wafer eight years later by the *Dumbarton*. Both Hingson and Gopson were "so fatigued with the journey that they could go no further," Wafer later wrote in his account of the adventure.

Wafer recalled how "there had been an Order made among us at our first landing, to kill any who should flag in the Journey." But he acknowledged that "this was made only to terrify any from loitering and being taken by the Spaniards, who by Tortures might extort from them a Discovery of our March." The reality was now very different. The Spaniards were too far behind to be a threat, and the three men were genuinely incapable of keeping up with the column. So "this rigourous Order was not executed, but the Company took a very kind leave both of these [men], and of me."

The three were now a fresh batch of maroons, left deep in the jungle by their own wish. It was the same manner of voluntary abandonment that Alexander Selkirk had chosen, and there was another reason for Lionel Wafer's fate to interest Defoe. Selkirk's story provided inspiration for Robinson Crusoe's adventures; Wafer's tale foreshadowed a deeper purpose of Defoe's novel.

Robinson Crusoe and Lionel Wafer were both advocates, one symbolic, the other real, for one of Defoe's favorite themes—the creation of new colonies in the Americas. When Wafer returned to London, the surgeon became involved in a grandiose scheme to set up a colony in Panama where he was marooned. When Robinson Crusoe returns home, he too nurtures a "new Collony" on the island where he was shipwrecked.

Crusoe demonstrates that his island can be made to flourish. He clears the brush, raises flocks of goats, plows, seeds and harvests crops. In short, he is the model of an ideal hard-working, resourceful colonist. When he and Man Friday leave their island, they abandon there three of the mutineers whose ship Crusoe has captured. Sixteen Spanish and Portuguese sailors will soon join them. They have been living as castaways on the nearby mainland coast, and Crusoe sends a canoe to fetch them.

Many years later Crusoe is a widower and approaching retirement, and he is curious to see how the islanders have managed. He goes back to the scene of his adventures aboard a merchant ship. He finds that the Spaniards and the "villains" have settled their differences and that his island is prospering. Women have been brought in, and there are twenty children. Crusoe hands over "supplies of all necessary things, and particularly of Arms, Powder, Shot, Cloaths, Tools" and after staying twenty days sails onward to Brazil, leaving behind "two Workmen which I brought with me, viz. A Carpenter and a Smith." From Brazil he sends yet more colonists to his island, including seven more women to be wives for the settlers, and a small vessel loaded with cows, sheep, and pigs, "which, when I came again, were considerably increas'd." On the very last page of *The Life and Strange Surprizing Adventures*, Robinson Crusoe rejoices in the creation of a flourishing, wealthy, happy colony on his once-desert island and he sails away, promising a sequel of fresh travels and adventures.

The all-too-real colony that was to follow Wafer to Panama was, by contrast, an epic catastrophe. Between 1698 and 1700, some three thousand men, women, and children set out to make their lives on the shores of the isthmus. Only three hundred of them ever returned home. The rest were left in unmarked graves at the edge of the rain forest, drowned, were buried at sea, or were snapped up as cheap labor in other, more successful colonies in the New World. Scotland, the country that sent the victims to their tragic fate, went into shock. At least £200,000—a sizable part of the country's available capital—had been squandered, and the national psyche was deeply scarred. After eighteen months on the coast of Panama all there was to show was an abandoned site, labeled by mapmakers Caledonia and its derelict town, New Edinburgh. Many of the humble dead who lay buried there, the ordinary "planters," had been Gaelic speakers. Had they survived, they might have put to the test Lionel Wafer's claim that the language of the local Indians, though quite different in vocabulary, used the same sounds as Scots Gaelic.

Appropriately, my companion when I went to Caledonia in search of Lionel Wafer's life as a maroon was a Scot from the Outer Hebrides.

Murdo had a Celt's mixture of fair skin, dark eyes, dark hair, and fine features. With his good looks, outgoing energy, and an engaging Scots accent, he was a bachelor who regularly attracted acquisitive feminine glances. Thirty-two years old, he was a teacher of geography at the secondary school on the island of Benbecula, but had previously

worked in radio and television. He was passionate about the story of the
Scots colony in Panama. For four years he had tried to interest television
companies in making a documentary about this pivotal event in
Scotland's history. He had written trailer pieces for radio, drafted television scripts, located Scots sponsors, and helped to organize exhibitions
on the Scots Darien colony, as it came to be known. Always, at the last
moment, the project had slipped from his grasp—for lack of funds, a
change in television schedules, bureaucratic inertia. Murdo had grown
disheartened by the time I met him by chance on a visit to his school. I
mentioned that I was traveling to the Isthmus of Panama and needed a
Spanish speaker to go with me. Murdo instantly volunteered. He had
spent three years teaching at a school in Bogota in Columbia, he told
me. There he had learned to speak what he called "taxi driver Spanish,"
largely from fellow supporters of a Bogota soccer team. "Taxi driver
Spanish" would be the common language of the Indians of the Panama
coast, and Murdo had another aptitude: he had the proverbial Scots
habit of thrift. He always asked for a discount and carefully scrutinized
every bill. Traveling with Murdo would help stretch our budget.

Our final destination was a small island off Panama's Caribbean coast,
close to the Colombian border. The island is still called Kalidonia. Close
by lie Puerto Escoces, Roca Escoces, Punta Escoces, and Canal Escoces.
The cluster of names—Harbor, Reef, Point, and Channel of the Scots—
distracts from the fact that an even smaller island immediately adjacent
to Kalidonia once had an equally significant name—Golden Island, the
rendezvous of the buccaneers and the point of departure for Wafer,
Dampier, and the "Merry Boys" when they set off on their original
march across the isthmus to the Pacific. The buccaneers' overland trail
to the Pacific was an essential ingredient in the Scots' scheme for their
colony. The directors of the enterprise reasoned that if the buccaneer
road could be improved to carry merchandise between the Caribbean
and the Pacific, then their colony would become an international trade
center and "emporium of the world." They hired an ex-buccaneer as the
pilot of their colonizing fleet and gave him orders to steer for Golden

Island. There the leaders of the expedition were to sign a treaty of friendship with the Indians and create "Caledonia."

Golden Island has an Indian name now—Suletupu. All the coast from the Colombian border for 140 miles to the northwest—more than a thousand square miles of mainland and archipelago—belongs to the same Indian people who signed the treaty of friendship with the Scots. They are the Kuna, the people among whom Lionel Wafer was stranded.

At six o'clock in the morning, the sight of Kuna women waiting in a drab airport lounge in Panama City jolts awake the bleariest traveler. The women dress for the journey in their most vivid wardrobe. Every square inch of clothing is patterned with intricate designs and motifs. Carmine, yellow, orange predominate. Each woman is resplendent in bright red and yellow head scarf, patterned blouse with puffed-up shoulders and astonishing embroidered body panels, front and back, and a wraparound skirt below which a bare knee leads to tight leggings made of a myriad of brightly colored beads meticulously wound around the calf as far as the ankle. The feet are bare. Matching bands of colored beads extend from elbow to wrist. Loops of silver coins hang in broad necklaces on the chest, and from the central cartilage of the nose dangles a small, thick golden crescent. Alongside the Kuna women their menfolk look positively drab in a plain white shirt, jeans, and, if they are feeling formal, a small black panama hat.

The Kunas are dwarfed by the average Panamanian—it used to be said that only African pigmies have a smaller average height than the Kunas—but the diminutive Kunas radiate self-confidence. They have good reason to do so. The government of Panama has agreed that the 50,000 Kunas living in the country are a people apart and their land is to be respected as their own. The region is autonomous, officially the Region of San Blas. The Kunas call it simply Kuna Yalah and regard it as inalienable territory. No one can own land there who is not born a Kuna. When you fly from Panama City and arrive on one of the tiny airstrips dotted along the coast, a four-and-a-half-foot-tall Kuna woman dressed in the same flamboyant but more faded clothes approaches every stranger and demands a landing tax. The Kuna people are determined to preserve their race as well as maintain their cultural and territorial identity, and in many ways they are profoundly exclusive. A Kuna man may marry outside his people, and even though the liaison is accepted, his wife and children will not be welcome back in Kuna Yalah. If a Kuna woman marries outside the tribe, that is a scandal.

When Lionel Wafer lived among them, the Kunas were spread right across the isthmus, in the river valleys and on the coast. Then something strange happened. Sometime (the date is unclear but it seems to have been in the mid-nineteenth century), the vast majority of the Kunas abandoned the uplands and moved toward the Caribbean. They paddled offshore in dugout canoes and settled on a chain of tiny islands which are barely more than sand and coral reef tops. The Kunas say they moved to avoid the snakes and insects and illnesses of the jungle.

The move to the islands was an extraordinary decision. Of the fifty distinct Kuna communities, forty of them now live on small islands where almost nothing grows except coconut palms and a few cultivated breadfruit. The soil is too sandy, and the land on the islands they selected is rarely more than a few feet above sea level. To grow food, the Kuna must start out at dawn every day and paddle across to the mainland, walk to their clearings in the rain forest, clean and plant and prune the crops, carry the produce in sacks and on shoulder poles back to their canoes, and then paddle home in the afternoon. It is grinding labor. Even more remarkable is that few of the islands have springs of fresh water. Formerly, hauling and rationing water was a way of life. Every drop of drinking water had to be collected in earthenware jars from the streams on the mainland and paddled across to the villages. Plastic undersea pipes have now been laid from the mainland. Fresh water can be piped in, but dry land is not so easily gained. Some islands are no more than five or six hundred yards across. At spring tides the sea creeps up and inundates the floors of the outer huts.

As the small plane we had caught in Panama City banked and began its descent I looked down on the roofs of our immediate destination, the island of Mulatupu Sasardi, population four thousand, according to the guidebook. Murdo and I had flown there because the community has the longest airstrip close to the island of Kalidonia. All four thousand inhabitants of Mulatupu Sasardi live crammed together on the crown of a single coral and sand outcrop. Seen from the air, the pale thatched roofs cover every square foot of the chosen island, with the exception of a central basketball court and a tracery of footpaths. The houses extend to the beach and beyond, some of them being built out over the water on artificial bases. The place appears as a thatched village floating on the ocean, isolated from reality. I felt I was looking down at an entire people who had chosen to withdraw from the normal world. They had deliberately marooned themselves.

Murdo and I took a ride on the municipal dugout sent to collect passengers from the airstrip on the neighboring, deserted, island. We were the only non-Kunas. The boatman brought us to the wooden jetty on Mulatupu Sasardi and deposited us under a sign that warned visitors to return to their vessels by dusk. The warning was aimed at hucksters who putter up from Colombia in ancient wooden motorboats of *African Queen* style to exchange foodstuffs and cheap clothes for the Kuna crop of coconuts. The warning does not yet apply to foreign tourists, but we were told to report to the village council, state our business, and ask permission to stay. The council office was on the upper floor of a tin-roofed building beside the basketball court–cum–main square. The secretary to the council was a small elderly Kuna with the timeless air of a minor functionary; on his otherwise bare desk were a tin cash box and ledger. He told us that the village council would meet next day and decide how long we could stay.

The guidebook is enthusiastic about Mulatupu Sasardi, stating, "The Kuna here are extremely friendly"—not the case farther north, earlier pages note, as cruise ship tourism has soured relations between the Kunas and outsiders. There is mention of "a very basic hotel" with a bucket in a barrel for taking a shower, the pleasing behavior of Kuna children who run up to the visitor with welcoming cries, and a single eating house serving delicious chicken and run by a Kuna woman "who has a smile that would melt a glacier." On all three counts the guidebook was wildly wrong. Murdo and I found neither hotel nor guesthouse, the children had seen enough tourists to learn to pester them, and the only place to buy a meal was a grubby bakery by the jetty where bread and eggs were served with great reluctance and a surly scowl. We stayed overnight in the hut of an elderly and friendly Kuna who clearly was not planning to pay any attention to whatever the council would decide.

The reason for this melancholy state of affairs was that Mulatupu Sasardi is a double community. Mulatupians and Sasardians had chosen to live on one island, and for some reason the two village councils had quarreled. Each now had its own agenda. When the *sahilas,* the village elders, meet, they bicker over who owns the cultivation rights along the coast and compete to fleece the unwary foreign tourists. Previously, violent crime was virtually unknown; now, petty theft was common, a tourist had been robbed, a Kuna girl had been raped, and the place was in a state of semianarchy. When Murdo and I appeared in front of a committee of elders, the Mulatupian branch, we were asked for a four-hundred-dollar fee if we wanted to pursue our research into the extinct Scots colony. Murdo was outraged. Mulatupu was living up to its name, which translates as "island of the buzzard vultures." Murdo and I hired a dugout canoe and quietly slipped away to Kalidonia. There, when we got to know the Kunas better, our acquaintances wrinkled their noses in distaste when they heard that we had tried to negotiate with the Mulatupu elders.

On Kalidonia we still needed permission if we were to stay. But the sandy footpaths of Kalidonia were wider and cleaner than those in Mulatupu Sasardi, the cane-and-thatch houses were set farther apart and were in better condition, and there was a feeling of wariness rather than distrust as the Kalidonians gazed at us from their doorways when

Murdo and I walked from the jetty to the house of the chief *sahila,* whose support would be crucial.

Leonidas, the *sahila*-in-chief of Kalidonia, was away on the mainland tending to his plantain groves when we arrived at the cane fence of his compound and pushed open the wood-plank gate. His eldest daughter, Leonilla, greeted us and asked us to come in and await his return. Anywhere in the world Leonilla would have been regarded as a beauty. We learned later that she had appeared in an advertisement promoting the sale of the Kunas' modern cash crop, the hand-embroidered panels called *molas* which decorate the women's blouses and are also produced for sale to tourists in Panama City and to foreign collectors. Athletically petite, she had a perfect copper-brown complexion and always looked like a fashion plate, though she had two small children and, with her sister, Rosa, played a major part in running Leonidas's household. When the two sisters were not preparing food, sweeping the bare earth floor, or engaged in all the chores of child rearing, they sat in the day hammocks that swung between the wooden posts holding up the thatch roof of the porch. There, bent over and their needles darting, they stitched *mola* after *mola.*

Leonidas pushed his way in through the gate at four in the afternoon. He had a machete on one shoulder and a bunch of plantains held in one hand. With his slight stoop and wiry frame, he looked like an illustration of the kindly woodcutter returning home in a Victorian book of children's stories.

Leonidas must have been at hard physical work for six hours in the steamy rain forest. Yet he appeared active, as if he were just beginning the day. Sixty-three years old, he looked fifty. Dressed in sweat-stained shirt and dark trousers with broad bare feet, he exuded a gnarled competence. Greeting us with a nod, he disappeared to wash and then came back to hear what we had to say. "Taxi driver Spanish" was the perfect medium as Murdo ask permission for us to stay so that we might compare life on Kalidonia with what the *pirata* Wafer had described three hundred years ago. Leonidas brightened. He had never heard of this English *pirata*, but if he wrote about the Kunas then Leonidas would like to know what he said. Leonidas's first responsibility as *sahila*-in-chief of Kalidonia was to teach his people their own traditions so that they could carry their way of life into the future. He would propose to the council of elders that Murdo and I should be allowed to stay.

That night Leonidas returned from the *onmaked nega*, the meeting house to tell us that the council had agreed to our request. There was a condition attached: we had to live in the *sahila*'s house and we must respect the customs of the village. On certain days we would be confined to Leonidas's compound and could not wander among the houses. "On what days?" asked Murdo. On the day of *chicha fuerte*, Leonidas replied— on the day of strong drink. It was the day, I guessed from Wafer's experience, when every adult male islander was obliged to get hopelessly intoxicated.

Wafer and his two fellow maroons, Gopson and Hingson, were not made welcome in the Kuna village where they had been left behind. The situation grew worse three or four days later when Spratlin and Bowman, the other two stragglers, lurched in. Now they were five extra mouths to feed. The Kunas, wrote Wafer, "look'd on us very scurvily, throwing green plantains to us as we sat cringing and shivering as you would Bones to a Dog." Fortunately the Indian in whose hut they were billeted took pity on them and in the night would slip out of the village, gather ripe plantains, and feed them secretly. With his help Wafer began learning some Kuna words.

Their ill treatment, Wafer felt, was uncharacteristic of the Kunas, who were "generally a kind and free-hearted People." Despite the antipathy of the villagers, their *ina duleds*, "men of medicine," began to doctor Wafer's damaged leg. They prepared curative herbs by chewing them in their mouths to produce a wet paste which they spread on a plantain leaf. Then they laid this compress over the raw wound. Every day they

changed this dressing and applied fresh paste. As a practicing field surgeon, Wafer was greatly impressed by the result. Their treatment was
"so effectual that in about 20 days use of this Poultess, which they applied fresh every day, I was perfectly cured." To Wafer such a rapid recovery from a blast injury—and he must have seen several of them after
buccaneer battles—was little short of miraculous. The only after-effect
was "a Weakness in that Knee, which remain'd long after, a Benum-
medness which I sometimes find in it to this day."

As soon as Wafer was able to walk, the villagers arranged to rid themselves of their unwelcome guests. Guides took the five buccaneers out
from the village and along the track that the main buccaneer column
had followed. After three days, when their traveling supplies—a small ration of dried maize—was consumed, the guides pointed out the track
the white men should take, and turned back, leaving their charges bewil-
dered in the rain forest.

The first part of the trek across the isthmus had been bad enough.
Now the attempt of five unaccompanied buccaneers to grope their way
to the Caribbean coast was a far worse ordeal. The rainy season was in
full force. Flash floods filled the river valleys along which the travelers
tried to find their way. They had no food and only a pocket compass to
guide them. The first day they made no move at all but stayed miserably
on the hillside where their guides had left them. The following morning
they tried following a riverbank that led in the right direction, northward, and were greatly encouraged to come across a tree trunk that had
been felled so it lay across the river as a bridge. On the far side were
"some old raggs hanging on a tree," and the travellers concluded that
they were in the tracks of the main buccaneer column.

They decided to cross the river using the same bridge. But the tree
trunk was now so slippery with rain and decay that they had to inch forward, one at a time, sitting astride the log. Despite their caution,
Bowman, who was the last to try the crossing, lost his grip, slid sideways,
and slipped off. He tumbled straight into the torrent below. His companions thought it was going to be a repetition of George Gayny's drowning

because Bowman, like Gayny, was carrying his booty, four hundred pieces of eight, strapped to his back. They watched as Bowman was swept away in the current and disappeared from their sight. Unable to find a path along the bank to go to help him, they gave him up for lost.

Crossing the river proved to be a mistake. Flash floods had covered the tracks of the main column with a layer of silt and ooze, and the travelers, now reduced to four, decided to go back across the river by the slippery log and continue along the bank. To their surprise they found Bowman sitting on the muddy bank a quarter of a mile downstream. The current had tossed him against the bank and he had been able to grab some branches and haul himself out of the water.

The buccaneers were drooping from lack of food. The last time they had eaten was three days earlier, and now they were fortunate to come upon a "macaw tree." The tree has a evil appearance. Vicious-looking four-inch spikes stick out in rows from the trunk. But the macaw tree is a fruiting palm, and the fruit contains an oily seed which is edible. The travelers collected up a quantity of the ripe fruit, ate the seeds greedily, and carried away the surplus. They imagined that they had crossed the watershed and were on the north-facing slope, where the rivers drain into the Caribbean. Reaching the next river broad enough to navigate, they set about cutting down bamboos and small trees and using lengths of liana to tie them into small, bulky rafts. The scheme was to launch the rafts and use them as body floats, riding downstream to their destination.

It was getting dark by the time the rafts were ready, so the buccaneers fastened the bamboo-and-wood bundles to the riverbank and set up camp, resolving to start on their river trip next morning. Soon after dusk, a tremendous tropical storm rolled in, and "It fell Raining as if Heaven and Earth would meet, which storm was accompanied with Horrid claps of Thunder and such flashes of Lightning." Barrages of lightning bolts crackled all around the travelers, so close that they felt they would be choked by the sulfurous smell. As the storm increased in fury, they heard another sound. It was the roar of the river bursting its banks. Lit by the blaze of the lightning strikes, they saw the flash flood surging toward their campsite. They leapt to their feet and ran for safety. Each man went his own way. There was no high ground for refuge. Wafer, separated from his fellows, hobbled desperately from tree to tree looking for a way to climb out of reach of the flood water. But most of the nearby trees were huge, stately cottonwoods whose trunks extended upward for forty or fifty feet before the first branch. Running "to save my life" he came on a massive old cottonwood that had a hole rotted in one side, about four feet off the ground, and he sprang for it like a fugitive squirrel and wriggled in. The cavity was just big enough to contain his body, and he spent the entire night curled up, "head and heels together" inside the tree, feeling the huge cottonwood shudder as the floodwaters butted loose logs and other flotsam against its trunk. He fell asleep with exhaustion, only to awake and find that he was up to his knees in water. While the lightning flashes continued to hit around his refuge, he spent the next hours praying for salvation and lost all track of time until the tremendous storm moved away and the clouds dispersed. Peeking out from his hole in the tree he could see the morning star and knew "that day was at hand."

With dawn, the flood subsided almost as quickly as it had risen. By the time the sun was fully up, Wafer was able to prize himself from his hiding hole and, stiff and weary, slide down to the ground. The campfire of the previous night had been totally swept away, and there was no sign of his companions. He called and called, and "made shift to ramble to the Place . . . but found no Body there." Weak from hunger—in the previous four days he had eaten only the macaw berries—and in despair, he fainted.

He awoke on the wet ground to the sound of a voice. It was his friend Hingson, who had survived the flood in a small tree and was now returning to camp. Soon afterward the other three buccaneers appeared, all with the same story. They had saved themselves by climbing into trees. After mutual congratulation on their escape, the five men searched for the rafts they had left tied to the trees the previous evening.

They were downcast to find that the bamboo-and-branch bundles were waterlogged. The flood had found hairline cracks in the bamboos and filled their air chambers. The rafts, over which they had labored, were useless.

Only later did they learn that the sinking of the rafts was a stroke of good fortune. Had they boarded them and set off downstream they would have floated into the hands of the Spanish. The buccaneers had overestimated their progress through the rain forest. They were still on the Pacific slope, and the river that they confidently assumed would drain to the Caribbean would have delivered them back to the Spanish blockade.

Unaware of their lucky escape, but totally disheartened, the five men decided to retrace their path on foot. Nothing seemed to go right for them. They came upon a forest deer curled up and fast asleep. Aching with hunger, one of the buccaneers stalked the animal and crept so close that he could bring the muzzle of his musket to point-blank range. But he had failed to wad the musket properly by jamming a small pad of cloth down the barrel to keep the musket ball in place. As he pointed the weapon downward at the sleeping deer, the musket ball rolled gently out of the barrel and dropped to the ground just as the musketeer pulled the trigger. The bang of the explosion woke the deer which leapt to its feet and bounded off. Moments later it plunged into the river, swam across, and was gone.

Driven by their hunger, the travelers decided to follow the track left by a peccary. They knew that the wild pigs looked for food in the abandoned swiddens of the forest Indians, and the buccaneers hoped they might find a few morsels of left-over plantain. Their theory proved correct. Before long they came to an abandoned plantation and, a little beyond it, a new "plantain walk" with every sign that it was being actively cultivated.

At this point, after so much suffering, the five castaways lost their nerve. They did not know whom they would encounter, whether the Indians would be friendly or hostile, whether they would kill the strangers or turn them over to the Spaniards. After debating the matter, it was decided that starvation was the more real threat. Four of the buccaneers hid while one, Wafer, emerged from the forest and limped to the nearest Indian hut. To his chagrin, and to the amazement of the Kunas who lived there, he found that he was back among the very same Indians that they had left eight days earlier. The five buccaneers had blundered in a circle and were back where they had started. Wafer, overcome by the heat inside the hut and the heady smell of a pot of meat boiling over the fire, fell on the ground and passed out.

José Arosemena, *ina duled* of Kalidonia, was ten years younger than Leonidas, and was his close friend. There was no difficulty in arranging for him to drop by the *sahila's* compound to tell Murdo and me about his work. Unfortunately, José arrived walking with a bad limp. A moray eel had bitten him on the foot while he was fishing, and the wound was healing slowly. It made an unconvincing introduction to the village healer. Also, José was unremarkable to look at. Dressed in a pale-blue short-sleeved shirt and frayed flannel trousers, he could have been any worried clerk in a store trying to understand a demanding customer's requirements. He was frowning and nervous as he listened to Murdo's questions. But his answers, delivered in a gravelly voice, were matter-of-fact and cogent. He himself was the son of an *ina duled,* and that was how he had begun in the profession. Anyone could become an *ina duled,* he said. It required only the desire to learn the craft, the patience to do so, and an experienced *ina duled* willing to let you watch him. A trainee *ina duled* learned by watching and assisting. José made the process sound almost humdrum. It was a matter of observing, helping, learning. You came to understand which herbs, bark, leaves, and seeds cured which diseases, how to treat certain illnesses, where to go in the mountains to find the simples you needed, and how to recognize them. Every so often the experienced *ina duled* would "show" a patient to his apprentice and ask him to diagnose the problem, obtain the correct herbs, and carry out the treatment. "Sometimes the student fails the test," José added humbly. José had watched and helped his father for twenty years. After his father died he left the island and went to live with another *ina duled* for five years, then with another for four years. Afterward José traveled to the home of a fourth medicine man and accompanied him for a year until his death. I added up the total "medical training" that José took so lightly. It was thirty years. Only after his fourth and last teacher had died, said José, did he feel confident that he had acquired the proper skills.

Murdo asked José how he would treat a leg wound where the bone was showing. The *ina duled* misunderstood the question and imagined a fractured leg. He would bind it straight and let the break mend. What about the broken flesh? José would cover it with a paste of herbs and have the patient rest. Only in the length of time for healing did José's prognosis differ from the experience that Wafer described for his own wound: six to seven months for a complete mend.

Healing a leg wound was straightforward. The three most challenging conditions for an *ina duled* to treat were snakebite, madness, and preparation for an easy delivery during childbirth. Pregnancy required the preparation of a special potion which the woman had to drink regularly, and a dilute solution of the same preparation in which she should bathe. If she followed the regime properly, the birth would be easy and the baby healthy. Subsequently, when talking to a Panamanian woman doctor working in the public maternity wards, I learned that Kuna women in the labor wards were watched closely. The Kuna mothers insisted on regular draughts of the medicine they brought with them. Often they gave birth so quietly and quickly that the nurses missed the birth completely.

José had a plantation worker's hands—large, well worn, and with prominent knuckles. Being an *ina duled* was not a full-time profession. He went to the jungle like the other villagers to tend his plantain trees, or set off in his dugout canoe to jig for small fish with a hand line. He was very modest. He was only one of three *ina duleds* on Kalidonia, he said. When Murdo asked him if he worked with *nuchu*, carved wooden spirit dolls, José shook his head vehemently. Oh no, he said, he was just a *curandero,* a herbal doctor. Wise and learned men like Leonidas knew how to work with smoke and the *nuchu,* who communicate between the spirit world and an invalid's soul. If there was a serious emergency, José acted on the advice of physicians much more competent than himself.

Two days earlier, a powerfully venomous snake—"a cobra," as Leonidas put it—had bitten a man from Kalidonia. The snakebite victim had been on the mainland, spearfishing in the river at night with a torch when the snake sank its fangs into him. He was nearly dead when found. All of Kalidonia went into a high state of alarm on hearing the news. An *ina duled* hurried into the mountains to collect a fresh supply of herbs. The injured man was brought back from the mainland. He was not carried to his house in Kalidonia but to an uninhabited island close by. There he was placed in a specially built isolation hut, quarantined not from disease, but from the malign spirits that he had aroused. The vital harmony of nature, Leonidas explained to us, was out of kilter. The spirit world was in turmoil. On the mainland the evil spirits, the *boni-gana,* were active. They were ranging the forest and the sierra. He and the village council immediately recalled every Kalidonian from the mainland. They paddled back in their canoes without demur and crept into their houses. That evening Leonidas asked Murdo and me not to leave his compound. We should stay quietly in his house. For the rest of that day, and for the next three evenings, the whole of Kalidonia was hushed. The silence was more for the benefit of the spirit world than the repose of the snakebite victim. The Kalidonians were waiting, almost as if holding their breath, for the spirit world to calm. The forest would be alive with serpents, said Leonidas. When a *boni* in the guise of a cobra bit a man, many other *bonigana* would come to that part of the forest. Everyone was forbidden to travel to the mainland to attend to the plantations.

Meanwhile the victim in his isolation was receiving treatment. An *ina duled* specializing in the treatment of snakebite arrived. He and his assistants examined the patient and prepared special concoctions of bitter herbs. They administered the medicine as a drink and as a body wash. They burned tobacco, peppers and special plants inside the hut to produce clouds of acrid smoke. An *igar wisid*, a chant singer, intoned magic formulae. The purpose was not to counteract the venom but to revive the victim's soul spirit. A cobra *boni* had attacked his inner soul, which now lay close to extinction and death. The smoke fended off the other malign *bonigana* that might have been attracted to the weakened victim. The potions and baths revived and strengthened the spirit soul. The chants called to it as it lay, a weak shadow. José and Leonidas were confident that the treatment was correct. In the previous twelve months three men had died after snakebite because they were too far into the forest to be brought back to the islanders for this treatment. Two other snakebite victims had been retrieved, and both—like the man who was being treated while Murdo and I stayed quietly in Leonidas's compound—survived.

Leonidas had been elected the chief *sahila* of Kalidonia four years earlier. His predecessor, an elderly man, had died in a fishing accident. While he was dropping the stone anchor from his canoe, the anchor line caught around his leg and he was pulled from the canoe and drowned. He was missing for days and no one knew what had happened until a *nele*, a soothsayer-shaman, was called in from a neighboring island. For three days the *nele* stayed in a darkened hut, communing with the spirits and burning tobacco and cacao beans. Then he emerged to tell the people of Kalidonia that they would find the body on the adjacent coast. The next day the body was found where predicted. Once the corpse was recovered, the people of Kalidonia met to elect their new chief *sahila*. Everyone in the community over the age of eighteen, men and women, had a vote. They selected from a panel of the five junior *sahilas*, and Leonidas must have been the obvious choice. He had served in all the ranks of the village hierarchy, starting as a youthful "staff holder," whose task is to walk the lanes of the island every dusk carrying his authority stick. With an echoing cry like a London rag-and-bone man staff holders summon the people to attend the gathering house. During those gatherings the staff holders walk up and down the ranks of villagers seated on low benches, scowl at unruly children, and use their staffs to prod those who had dropped off asleep during the long chanting speeches of the *sahilas*. At intervals they yell "Don't sleep! Listen well!"

From the rank of staff holder Leonidas graduated by vote to junior *sahila,* and then to *agar,* the spokesman whose task is to interpret the opaque language of the chief *sahila* as he recites the foundation stories of the Kunas. Now Leonidas would hold the post of *"sahila numero uno,"* as Murdo put it, for the rest of his life.

Lacenta was the name of the *sahila*-in-chief whom Wafer met. Lacenta was a *sahila* of the highest rank, a *cacique,* and he lived in considerable style touring the country with a retinue of attendants. When he heard about the marooned buccaneers, he had them brought to his village. There, in storybook fashion, Wafer won Lacenta's favor by healing one of the *sahila*'s seven wives.

She was suffering from fever, and the *ina duleds* were treating her with phlebotomy, the practice of bloodletting. Wafer, of course, was thoroughly familiar with phlebotomy. Throughout Europe it was rated as a highly effective medical procedure. In a belief not far removed from the Kuna concept that evil spirits invaded the body and caused sickness, European doctors held that many illnesses resulted from an imbalance or excess of the "humors." The four humors were linked to the elements of earth, fire, air and water, and were represented in the body as blood, phlegm, yellow bile, and black bile. To cure a sick patient, even one with mental illness, the doctors "drew off" the excess or imbalanced humors by cutting into veins with lancets and drawing off quantities of blood; by "cupping," using glass suction cups stuck to the skin; or by "blistering" which involved rubbing the skin with blistering agents such as mustard and a powder made from dried beetles. Surgeons routinely prescribed bloodletting even for healthy patients who they felt would benefit from a flushing out of the bloodstream.

Wafer, however, had never seen anything like the way the Kuna took off blood from Lacenta's wife. The *ina duled* sat the feverish woman on a boulder in the river and then "with a small bow" began firing miniature arrows into her naked body, "shooting them as fast as he can, and not missing any part." Wafer recognized the principle at once because the arrows were "gaged so they penetrate no farther . . . than our lancets." But it seemed to him a very haphazard approach. If "by chance" the *ina duled* "hit a vein which is full of wind, and the blood spurts out a little, they will leap and skip about . . . by way of rejoicing and triumph."

After watching this excruciating target practice, Wafer suggested to Lacenta that he knew a better way to take blood. The *sahila* gave permission for a demonstration, and Wafer produced his little box of lancets. He tightened a strip of bark around the woman's arm as a tourniquet, found a vein, and cut. Unfortunately, in his enthusiasm he cut deep, and the blood gushed out spectacularly. Lacenta was horrified. He seized a spear and for a moment was about to stab the surgeon. But Wafer kept his nerve and asked the *sahila* to be patient. He then drew off twelve ounces of blood, bound up the arm, and advised that the woman should rest until the following day. Luckily for him, the fever had broken by next morning so both Wafer and Lacenta were convinced that phlebotomy had effected the cure.

Naturally Lacenta made a great fuss of his new medicine man. The *sahila* "bow'd and kissed my hand," Wafer claimed, and the young surgeon was carried in a hammock from village to village "administring both Physick and Phlebotomy to those that wanted." Lacenta then insisted that Wafer accompany him at all times. No foreigner would be granted such a privileged insight into Kuna life for another 250 years.

Wafer enjoyed his time with the Kunas. He attended a Kuna wedding which culminated in all the male guests rushing out of the festivities, shouting and cheering, with axes in their hands. In a group they ran to a tract of virgin forest where they began "cutting down the woods and clearing the ground as fast as they can." For seven days they worked "with the greatest vigour imaginable" while the women and children followed behind planting "maize or whatever is agreeable." Only when the wedding guests had built a hut for the young couple to live in as well as providing the plantation that would feed them was it time for "the Company [to] make merry." Then the Kunas got down to serious drinking.

Their alcohol was *chicha*, made from fermented maize, and "tis very intoxicating . . . and makes them belch very much." Before the party began, the bridegroom took the precaution of collecting up all his guests' weapons and hanging them out of reach on the ridge pole of his house because the Kunas "were very quarrelsome in the drink." Once the visitors were disarmed, the party drank day and night until every drop of the wedding stock of *chicha* had been consumed. During these marathon sessions, "Some are always drinking, while others are drunk and sleeping." After three or four days, "when all the drink is out, and they have recovered their Senses, "the Kuna men returned to their own homes. There each man was helped into his hammock by two or three women who, as "he lies snoring, . . . sprinkle water on his body to cool him, washing his hands, feet and face; stroking off that water with their hands as it grows warm, and throwing on fresh." Ten or twelve Kuna drunkards sprawling helpless in a row of hammocks was a sight Wafer never forgot.

The women would wait until the men had finished their drinking sessions before starting their own "dancings and merriments." Then they, too, "drink by themselves till they are fuddled."

The music of the Kuna panpipes was too "whining" for Wafer's taste, but he was entertained when thirty or forty men linked arms to form a ring and then shuffled gently to the music "with a wriggling antick gestures" in their traditional dances. From time to time an individual dancer sprang from the circle to perform feats of tumbling and juggling. When the group was exhausted, they all jumped into the river to wash off the sweat. A dance session generally began with a short drinking bout and could last all day, but, Wafer noted, "They don't dance after they have drunk very hard."

Wafer was expanding his Kuna vocabulary and always asking questions. He was particularly mystified by the "milk-white" Indians. They were unlike anything he had seen or heard of in any other part of the world, In fact they were so abnormal that he feared that readers of his book might not believe that such humans existed. Their skin color was "much like that of a white horse" and covered in a fine white down. Even their hair and eyebrows were white, and the shape of their eyes was unusual. Their eyelids "bend and open in an oblong figure, pointing downward at the corners, and forming an Arch or Figure of a Crescent." The Kunas called them "Moon-ey'd," and Wafer said that on "Moon-shiny nights" they were "all Life and Activity, running . . . into the Woods, skipping about like Wild Bucks, and running as fast by Moon-light even in the Gloom and Shade of the Woods as the other Indians by Day." Wafer rejected the obvious explanation that these strangely pale Indians were the result of intermarriage between white-skinned Europeans and Kunas. He had seen a pure-white "moon-ey'd" child less than a year old whose mother and father were "copper coloured" like most Kunas. Besides, so few Europeans passed that way that it seemed highly unlikely they could have created so many white offspring. Wafer estimated that for every two or three hundred normal Kuna one was "Milk-white."

He asked Lacenta for an explanation. The *sahila* told him that "moon eyes" were born as the result of their mothers' "looking on the Moon at the time of Conception." But this explanation did not satisfy Wafer either. He noted that the "moon ey'd" tended to be weaker and more sickly than the average Kunas and that they died young. He suspected a physiological cause for the "white Indians" and felt sorry for them because they were uncomfortable in bright sunshine, which made their eyes water profusely. The Kunas treated them with disdain.

There were three albinos on Kalidonia Leonidas told us—a woman, a young man, and a boy. Three albinos in an island population of a little more than a thousand was much the same ratio that Wafer had guessed, though calculations in the early twentieth century for the whole of Kuna

Yalah put the ratio rather higher, with albinos forming as much as 2 or 3 percent of the total population. Until recently, the treatment of the albinos was as degrading as in Lacenta's time. Marriages between albinos were taboo; male albinos were forbidden to marry at all; and so severe was the stigma of an albino birth that the infant might be smothered. A generation ago on Mulatupu Sasardi it was still the custom for the albinos to go on the roofs of the houses and shoot arrows at the full moon. Now, by contrast, there was an albino member of the Mulatupu council.

The three albinos on Kalidonia were fully integrated into the community, thanks, I suspected, to Leonidas. When I told him of Lacenta's explanation of how an albino was created by the mother gazing at the full moon, Leonidas disagreed quietly and firmly. "No." he said, "The albinos are a special people. They are our older brothers and sisters." Leonidas was the keeper and teacher of Kuna lore for his community, like all *sahilas*-in-chief. He instructed his people that albinos were the offspring of the first children born to the creator-father, Mago, and his wife, Ologwandule. Leonidas tried to explain to Murdo and me how the Great Father and Great Mother had brought into existence the ancestors of the human race and taught them how to fish and hunt and many things, including how to make *chicha*. But whenever he described the foundation legends of his people, Leonidas got very muddled. He would have been difficult to follow even if he had not been struggling to translate his ideas into "taxi driver Spanish" for Murdo's benefit. The moment he began to talk of Kuna lore, Leonidas slipped into a mode of recitation. He repeated phrases and names learned by rote. They were fragments of the enormously long recitations by the most learned *sahilas*, which they declaimed while lying in a hammock—the posture of dignity—in the congress house. But Leonidas was not a scholarly nor a learned *sahila*. He had been elected to be *"numero uno"* in Kalidonia because he was sincere and genuine, and his people trusted him. Now, seeing that Murdo and I were looking baffled, Leonidas summarized: "The moon children are actually better than us."

Four days after the incident of the snakebite Leonidas judged that the forest was quiet again and the evil spirits had settled down. He invited Murdo and me to accompany him on a trip to the village plantations on the mainland. With us came twenty-three-year-old Vitello, an albino. He was also a village hero. Six months earlier he was working in the forest, clearing the undergrowth for plantains, when a "cobra" appeared on the path ahead of him. All the other Kunas working alongside Vitello fled in panic. But Vitello chopped the viper with his machete, cutting it in half so that the blood and venom sprayed his chest. "The snake was so close to me, I could do nothing else," Vitello said modestly. "That was how it happened."

It was difficult to judge whether it was shyness about his strange appearance—his skin was morbid white and his hair and eyebrows a coarse yellow—or the bright light that made Vitello glance away most of the time as if embarrassed. His eyelids fluttered constantly or they were half closed to protect his eyes with their strange cloudy greenish-brown irises. He suffered terribly from sunburn. His lips were permanently cracked and raw, and his face was covered in red blisters and sores. His hands were even worse. The skin was puffed and swollen, and every cut and scratch made an angry red weal. But he was not weakly like the albinos Wafer had observed. Vitello was big and strapping, and as soon as we got into the shady jungle and out of the sunshine, Vitello kept pace with the indefatigable Leonidas. The two of them swung machetes, hacking back the undergrowth, slicing away surplus leaves from the productive plants, and chopping down the fruiting trees to get at the heavy bunches of green plantains.

Our first trip was thwarted, like Wafer's cross-country travels, by the rivers. We left Kalidonia in one of the dugout canoes which was usually pulled up on the beach behind Leonidas's house. Leonidas's son by his first marriage, Rocky, owned an outboard engine, so we set out later than the rest of the villagers, who had departed from their homes well before dawn. No one had been able to tend their plantations for three days, so now the mile-wide strait that divides Kalidonia from the mainland was already speckled with the black silhouettes of some twenty dugout canoes being paddled sturdily. The hulls of the canoes were so low in the water that they could barely be seen. Instead, the heads, torsos, and rhythmically moving arms of the paddlers crept across the slow undulations of a low swell advancing in the blue-gray light toward the fringe of white mist that hid the far shore.

At the landing beach we put palm tree trunks as rollers under the canoes and dragged them out of reach of the tide. Then the different canoe crews walked off, machetes in hand, and disappeared into the maze of footpaths leading to their plantations. They would scatter through the secondary forest, each man to his own plantation, and return at the agreed time—usually at noon—to rejoin their canoes and return home. The vegetation was so dense that it was impossible to see more than a few yards into the greenery. So the workers left little markers, usually a twig stuck in the soft ground, at junctions along the footpaths to show which way they had gone. On their return journey they would collect up the markers so that their companions, as they were returning to the canoes, would know who had already gone back to the landing beach and, if someone failed to return, where to look for him in the jungle. It was little wonder that Wafer and his companions had gotten lost in the forest.

Murdo and I followed Leonidas trotting along with his machete on his shoulder and looking more than ever like a woodcutter from a fairy story. The path jinked this way and that; sometimes it was covered six inches deep in fallen leaves, elsewhere it was a muddy groove leading into shallow streams laced with tangles of tree roots. Near the seaside the sandy soil was riddled with the burrow holes of crabs. Occasionally Leonidas stopped to point out a fruiting tree or a plant that was useful. It soon became clear that the Kunas had tended the area for generations. The tallest trees were called *kupu* and grew straight for about 60 feet. The first branches were at least 30 feet above the ground, and the clean trunks provided ideal timber for dugout canoes. The hard shells of the fig-shaped fruit were turned into toys and games for children. The fruit of the rough-barked *chi chi* tree, shaped like a peach, produced a sticky sap that the Kuna women mixed with charcoal to make the black stripes they painted on their noses. *Chi chi* leaves were burned under the hammocks of sick people to ward off evil spirits. We passed clumps of a cane with a long, green, rodlike stalk which rang like metal when tapped with the blade of machete. The cane was used in plaiting baskets—a male occupation among the Kunas—and for making fences. Occasionally a plant with a purple flower like a clematis provided groundcover, and there was a single scarlet hibiscus. But in general the color of the forest was a range of dark succulent greens, the color of constant humid growth. According to Leonidas, the jungle plants would completely smother a plantation within five months if the encroaching vegetation was not cut back. Against the dark-green foliage fluttered orange butterflies speckled with bronze. "All butterflies are lucky," Leonidas said to me. "An hour before you and Murdo I arrived, one of my daughters saw a butterfly in my house and announced that something very lucky would take place." He gave a significant look.

Our luck ran out, however, when we reached the river Acla. It crossed our path and emptied into the sea about a mile from the place where we had left the canoes. The footpath crossed the estuary by a ford which ran along the crest of the bar at the river mouth. We found three Kunas already standing on the riverbank and looking doubtful. The sea was heaping waves across the sand bar, then sucking back in a brisk undertow. The breaking surf on the ford looked too deep to be passed in safety. Nevertheless one of the Kunas decided to try. He removed his clothes and placed them in a bundle on his head, and then, dressed only in his underpants, stepped gingerly into the water. In this situation the Kunas' small stature was a disadvantage. The scout timed his advance, hoping to scuttle across between the waves. But when a surging wave submerged him to his shoulders, then nearly pulled him out to sea, he gave up the attempt and scampered back to safety. I had wandered fifty yards up the riverbank, wondering whether it would be possible to swim across where the river current was less rapid. Trying to judge the speed of the current, I watched a log drifting slowly down toward the man on the river bar. When the log was about twenty yards short of the Kunas I realized I was watching not a log, but the snout of a cayman cruising gently downstream. I beckoned to Leonidas and pointed. There was great excitement. It seemed that a very large cayman had taken a Kuna—the uncle of Vitello, the albino—at this spot a year previously. The project of crossing the river that day was abandoned.

The following day, when the waves and tide were lower, we success-fully crossed the ford and reached Leonidas's plantation. While Leonidas and Vitello were cutting back the undergrowth, a band of howler mon-keys came swinging and shouting into the *kupu* trees close by. The mon-keys stayed there for an hour. They ran back and forth on the branches fifty yards away, swung by their tails, and kept up a territorial hooting and yelling. They were so bold that I wondered whether they would do what Wafer had claimed—"skipping from Bough to Bough, with the young ones hanging on the old ones backs, making faces at us, chatter-ing, and if they had the opportunity, pissing down purposely on our heads." I remarked to Leonidas that the howler monkeys seemed almost tame, and he told me that it was very common to hear the hooting calls of the howlers but that never in his entire life had he known the mon-keys to come so close or stay for so long. Once again he looked thought-ful, and I wondered, knowing how the Kunas find a close link between all life on earth, whether plant or animal or human, what sort of reputa-tion Murdo and I were acquiring.

Murdo had established himself as a favorite of Leonidas's family. He was so friendly and enthusiastic that the two daughters, Leonilla and Rosie, began to smile the moment Murdo embarked on a lively, gesticu-lating conversation in his Spanish. It helped that Murdo was a school-master by profession, because Leonilla's husband, Eladio, was the village schoolmaster on Kalidonia, and the two teachers could compare experi-ences. When Kunas marry, the man moves into the wife's family com-pound, so Leonidas's household was substantial. With sons, daughters, sons-in-law, and grandchildren, there were more than a dozen people living in the cluster of thatched huts within the compound's cane fence. Murdo's theory was that Leonidas's calm and equable nature came from having to coexist with so many exuberant children in such close quarters. Murdo himself coped effortlessly with the urchins who peeked in through the gate and the privileged few invited by Leonidas's grandchildren, who watched, open-mouthed, as Murdo put his contact lenses in his eyes.

Every evening Leonidas donned a clean shirt with the sleeves rolled down, dark trousers, and his formal hat, and set off to the congress hall. Sometimes he carried one of his authority sticks. His favorite was a small staff about a yard long, carved into a spiral. It was brightly varnished and decorated with a human figure carved on the head, a seated figure with crossed arms and tall wings like an archangel. Leonidas made the staffs himself as emblems of his office, and there was one whose knob, painted green and blue, was clearly a self-portrait—a short, standing figure in jacket, trousers, and a neat little hat. The congress hall was situated near the island jetty. It was an oversize version of the traditional Kuna house, a massive barnlike structure with a high thatched roof and low sidewalls of cane. There Leonidas joined his fellow *sahilas* reclining in a row of hammocks suspended in the gloomy, unlit interior of the building. All the villagers were supposed to assemble on the ranks of wooden benches and listen while the *sahilas* discussed the concerns of the community and sang the chants that enshrined Kuna lore. But the sessions could last three or four hours, and sometimes the audience was sparse. Yet Leonidas never shirked his office. Often it was ten or eleven at night before he returned home.

The day of strong drink, of *chicha fuerte*, was under discussion. The event was to celebrate the end of clearing the plantations before planting began, and was to be held in a special building, the *inna nega*, or *chicha* hall. This was another huge, thatched shed next to the congress hall. *Chicha fuerte* was made from sugar cane—the weaker *chicha* was made from maize—and gallons of cane juice were already fermenting in several large wooden troughs. The actual day of *chicha fuerte* depended on when the alcohol was ready to drink. *Chicha* tasters, "the chemists," Leonidas called them, came each day to sample the brew, determine the degree of fermentation, and predict the best time for the party. Shortly before the *chicha fuerte* was ready, a reserve supply of beer was ordered from Mulatupu.

At six-fifteen on the appointed morning there was a great shout of "Eladio!" from outside the compound's cane fence, and the village schoolmaster went out to join his drinking buddies. His wife, the beautiful Leonilla, stayed behind, looking disapproving. Women were expected to join in the *chicha fuerte* ceremony but both Leonilla and Rosie preferred to stay behind with the children. Their father, Leonidas, left the compound at 7 A.M. dressed in his formal outfit and looking purposeful. Two young constables passed the gate soon after, crying out to remind the community to assemble at the *inna nega*.

Then, for five hours, the whole of Kalidonia went silent. Confined to Leonidas's house as had been agreed earlier as a condition of our visit, Murdo and I listened for signs of merriment. There was nothing. The *chicha* hall was six hundred yards away, hidden in the cluster of thatched huts. We could hear only the occasional scuffles of a child and in the background the rumble of the surf breaking on the reefs that protect Kalidonia from the trade winds. Shortly before noon Eladio appeared, looking flustered. The *chicha fuerte* had all been drunk, and the reserve supply of beer in cans had not arrived as promised. He went off in a canoe with the outboard engine to hurry up the delivery boat. The long, quiet day dragged on until Murdo and I could no longer contain our curiosity. We sallied out cautiously. The sandy lanes were deserted. Our route took us past the huge thatched hangar of the *inna nega* and we averted our eyes decorously. But there was nothing to see except for a couple of huge empty *chicha* tubs on the sand outside the door. Then we heard it. The *inna nega* was humming. The sound was low and unwavering in pitch. The enormous thatched *chicha* house resembled a huge hive. The noise was the sound made by a swarm of angry bees muttering and buzzing. We slunk back to Leonidas's compound.

We deliberately left the compound gate ajar, and in the late afternoon Leonidas came in view. The *sahila*-in-chief of Kalidonia was walking home very unsteadily between two of the junior *sahilas*. All three men were holding one another up with a grave solemnity as they headed for Leonidas's gate. Our host crossed his threshold, and his two companions accepted two cans of beer from Leonilla and went fumbling toward their own homes while Leonidas disappeared into his hut. Murdo and I—judging that the *chicha* ceremony was now over and we were free to explore—went for a stroll. All the adult Kunas we saw on the street—men and women—were completely intoxicated. They were weaving and stumbling, owl-eyed with concentration. Murdo and I prudently edged around them or turned aside down alleyways. But we were ignored. We came to the jetty by the little harbor. Standing in the shallows was a Kuna youth, aged about sixteen. He was fully dressed and up to his waist in the sea. In one hand he held up a clear glass bottle. It contained rum. He brought the bottle to his lips with a wide ceremonious sweep of his arm, took a swig, and toppled backward in slow motion. . . He disappeared completely underwater except for his hand and the bottle, which remained above the surface like the hand holding Excalibur. He struggled back to his feet, spluttered and shook himself, took another pull at the bottle, and fell slowly backward once more. Again and again, he rose and drank and sedately fell. Finally the bottle was empty, and another young Kuna of about the same age waded purposefully into the sea, took his swaying friend gently by the arm, and pulled him to dry land. There the drinker's mother was waiting—a short, stocky woman in full traditional dress of colored head scarf, embroidered blouse, beaded leggings, and golden nose ring. She took hold of her son on one side, his friend held him up on the other, and the trio walked away sedately. The scene was the classic picture of the drunkard homeward bound. But on Kalidonia there was no disapproval, rather the reverse. On *chicha fuerte* day the young drunk had done his duty.

Wafer proposed Golden Island as the site for a new colony of the sort that Defoe conjures up from Robinson Crusoe's former home. Wafer knew the island well. He had "been ashore at this Golden Island and was lying in the harbour near it for about a fortnight." It had, he said, many natural advantages. Though small in area, the island was "rocky and steep all round to the Sea (and thereby naturally fortified)." The landing place "was a small sandy bay on the south side," from where the hillside rose gently upward in a pleasant slope that was "moderately high and cover'd with small trees and shrubs." The harbor itself was first class. The approach for a sailing vessel was by "a fair deep Channel between it and the Main." Ships could enter or leave the anchorage from either side of the island, and this was one reason why Golden Island had been so popular with buccaneers and pirates. A harbor with two exits offers a chance to escape and is difficult to blockade.

Golden Island now belongs to the Kalidonians. They call it Suletepe because its profile seen from Kalidonia is the shape of a crouching *sule,* or painted rabbit, a shy nocturnal animal like an oversize guinea pig that inhabits the high forests of the cordillera. Suletepe lies so close to Kalidonia that it took Leonidas less than ten minutes to ferry Murdo and me there in his canoe.

The harbor was surprising small. No more than four or five ships could anchor there; it was utterly deserted now. Yet the vessels would be in perfect calm, in 28 feet of water and sheltered from the prevailing northeast winds by Golden Island itself. The wind was blowing at close to thirty knots when Leonidas brought us there, but the water in the anchorage barely ruffled. Our entry was between protecting reefs and islets of dead coral, and the buccaneer ships were able to drop anchor in good holding ground less than fifty yards from the beach. Best of all, any vessels in the anchorage were hidden. No one could see them from the sea, and from the landward side their masts were lost from view against the green mass of Golden Island, and their hulls were cloaked by the surrounding fringe of mangrove swamp. The Kuna name of this secret refuge, said Leonidas, was "the place where the caymans come to bask."

Leonidas made the canoe fast to a convenient coconut palm at the landing place and led us through a pleasant grove of mature coconuts. There is no gold on Golden Island—the name is a glamorous fiction— but it was easy to understand Wafer's enthusiasm for its potential as a spot for a settlement. On the rich soil near the beach the Kalidonians were cultivating mango, gourds, and breadfruit. They had set young banana plants in the shade of the coconut palms. Higher, on the shoulder of the hill overlooking the harbor, was a broad field of cassava plants. Leonidas led us along a footpath that circled the island. From flowering vines and ferns came the sound of bird songs and marching lines of leaf-cutter ants struggled across our path with their burdens. To our left the terrain rose steeply to the 470-foot-high central peak and was covered with secondary forest. Here were small balsa trees, and a half dozen "cedar pines" of Golden Island towering starkly against the sky with massive pale gray trunks and contorted branches, leafless at that time of year. Where a great tree trunk had recently fallen across the path, the fleshy tendrils of a cactuslike jungle plant were already climbing over the host, making thin green veins on the pale bark. Surprisingly—for Wafer had not mentioned it specifically—there was fresh water on the island. Two small springs trickle down each side of the central hill, cutting deep grooves into the slope, and empty into the sea among boulders on the beach. This is where the visiting crews must have filled their water barrels. On the northeastern shore was a sweep of sandy beach where the sea turtles once came to lay their eggs.

Five minutes' walk brought us to the south-facing side of Golden Island. From there we looked across to the mainland, three miles away. Directly opposite was the mouth of the deep bay which is Puerto

Escoces. Here perished the hapless Gaelic-speaking "planters" whose failed endeavor gripped Murdo's imagination. Now that I had seen the advantages of Golden Island, I wondered whether the outcome might have been different had the Scots established their colony on the island as Wafer the maroon had recommended. Then Defoe's fiction of an island colony that flourished in the wake of Robinson Crusoe's sojourn might have become a fact.

Bursts of surf springing from the rocks of Punta Escoces were the warning. They were waves smashing into the headland, driven ashore by the prevailing northeast wind. A little to the right, another spouting fountain of whitewater marked Roca Escoces, a dangerous reef. The headland and the rock define the entrance to Scots Bay. With extraordinary lack of foresight, the leaders of the colony chose a harbor that was downwind of the prevailing wind, and was a nautical trap. As the first fleet from Scotland entered the harbor, in November 1698, the *Unicorn*, packed with colonists, collided with Roca Escoces. The ship bounced off and survived, though leaky, but it was an ill-omen. Once the fleet was inside the bay, it was difficult to emerge again. Only a well-handled and agile ship could beat to windward out of the bay. The clumsy Scots transport vessels were marooned for weeks on end until the wind changed. A visiting French vessel tried to sail out on Christmas Eve 1699 with her crew either hung over or drunk. The waves rolling into the mouth of the harbor picked her up and tossed her on the lee shore. She sank in full view of the colonists.

The Scots colony lasted less than eighteen months. With heart-breaking mistiming, a second fleet of colonists arrived soon after the first group of planters had sailed away leaving four hundred graves in pitiful rows. Disease and dissension destroyed the second installation, and a Spanish military expedition landed and accepted the surrender of the survivors. If the Scots had settled on Golden Island, they would have done better. They could have fortified the slopes, as Wafer suggested, and fended off any Spanish attack. Their supply ships would have come and gone as they wished. Above all, they would have been spared the diseases and fevers of the mainland. Like the Kunas they would have found the islands a much healthier location.

Today you have to search closely to find the least sign of the Scots colony. The jungle has smothered nearly every trace. There are some tumbled dry stone walls, a shallow ditch dug as a defensive moat, and nothing more unless you scratch the soil and, if you are fortunate, turn up fragments of clay tobacco pipes. Divers found the wreck of an ill-fated supply ship, the *Olive Branch,* close offshore under eight feet of silt. She was carelessly set alight at her mooring by the ship's cooper who was using a lighted candle to search for brandy below decks. She burned and sank with all her stores on board.

Looking across at the graveyard of Scots hopes, I wondered whether anything in this tropical landscape would have reminded the settlers of their homeland. I could imagine only the gray granite rocks that lay on the foreshore, and the swirling mist that the steady wind whips up from the sea and carries far inland. The Kunas think of Puerto Escoces as a place inhabited by evil ghosts. A man of Kalidonia, said Leonidas, sold the site of New Edinburgh to a man from Mulatupu for the value of two machetes. Coconuts grow there but no one likes to stay for long in such a place. There is only a temporary camp for the workers, and the new owners periodically hold mass exorcisms to cleanse the site of ghosts.

After four months with the *cacique,* Lacenta, Wafer persuaded him to let his five foreign guests go on their way. Wafer and his companions were escorted to the Caribbean coast to La Sounds Key, a harbor known to be popular with visiting buccaneers. But there were no ships waiting. Wafer consulted with the local conjurers, for he had come to believe that the Kuna shamans were able to foretell the future. The shamans would seclude themselves in a house and "make most hideous Yellings and Shrieks, imitating the voices of all kind of Beasts and Birds." They clattered stones, blew conch shells, drummed on hollow bamboos, and made "a jarring Noise . . . with strings fastened to the large bones of beasts." Any foreign objects interfered with their magic and were banned. The conjurers found a bag of seamen's clothes and threw them out of the house "with great disdain," then they fell to work again "all in a Muck-sweat." They prophesied that two ships would arrive in ten days time, that a gun would be lost, and that a man would die.

It all turned out as they foretold. The two pirate ships appeared on schedule; Gopson, the scholarly, Greek-reading buccaneer, lost his musket when the canoe carrying the buccaneers to the ships overturned in the surf; and poor Gopson himself was dragged half-dead from the water. He died three days later aboard ship.

Wafer never mentioned what is today the most celebrated feature of Kuna culture—their stitching of the intricate and beautiful *molas*. It seems that in his time the Kuna women did not practice the craft, nor did they wear the distinctive bands of beads on their arms and legs. Instead they draped rope upon rope of beads around their necks and mixed natural pigments with oils to make paints and decorate the bodies of their men. Their brushes were sticks chewed soft, and they used them to "make figures of birds, beasts, men, trees or the like, up and down and in every part of the body more especially the Face." These pictures were creative and "of differing dimensions as their fancies lead them," and their favorite colors were "Red, Yellow and Blue, very bright and lovely." Wafer was so enchanted by the body painting that he gave up wearing his seaman's smock and breeches when he was with the Kunas. Instead he wore a breech cloth and had his body painted all over. To complete the Kuna look, he took to wearing a gold ring in his nose. He was dressed in this way and covered in body paint when he went aboard the buccaneer ship at La Sounds Cay with his companions. His former shipmates greeted his four companions while Wafer, who had a sense of humor, stayed squatting down on deck among the Kunas. It was some time before one of the buccaneers looked among the Kunas, and suddenly exclaimed, "Here's our doctor!"

Back in practice as a buccaneer surgeon for the next seven years, Wafer went on to join the *Batchelor's Delight,* help rescue Will the Moskito, and fall afoul of Captain Rowe and HMS *Dumbarton* on antipirate patrol. He and his disreputable friends, Hingson and Davis, had to spend two years in a Jamestown gaol before a clever lawyer got them acquitted. They succeeded not only in escaping the charge of piracy, but—on getting back to London—successfully sued to recover their booty, which Captain Rowe had seized. In 1698, when the colony of New Caledonia was being planned, the Scots promoters of the enterprise considered sending Wafer back to the Kuna country as an adviser. But after interviewing him—and extracting most of his information gratis—the Scots dropped the scheme when Wafer asked for a salary of £750. Instead they paid Wafer twenty guineas to delay publication of his memoirs of life among the Kunas. The Scots did not want commercial competitors to learn too soon that a lucrative colony could be created in the place where the surgeon had been marooned. It was only after the first batch of doomed colonists had been set ashore that Wafer's book was published—the same book that was to appear in the "lost list" of the auctioneer Payne when he sold off the contents of Defoe's library.

B efore Murdo and I left Kalidonia, Leonidas made mementos for us. Using a borrowed pencil, he drew two pictures on a scrap of cardboard: for Murdo a three-masted ship flying the cross of St. Andrew and the rising sun, which was the emblem of the Scots Darien company; for me a profile of "painted-rabbit island" and a hat-wearing Kuna paddling a canoe. His daughters, Leonilla and Rosie, took the sketches and stitched the pictures as *molas* for us. They also, with many giggles, split the fruit of a *chi chi* tree to extract the sticky juice, pounded charcoal from the hearth, and made a batch of their cosmetic ink. Using a thin stick they drew a black line down Murdo's nose.

Leonidas, as our mentor, also asked a favor. When we came to our homes, he would like us to send him videotapes of all the conversations when he had told us about life on Kalidonia and Kuna lore. One day, he said, there would be electricity on Kalidonia, and television and a machine to play the videotapes. Perhaps he would be dead by then, but if his people could watch the tapes, he would still be their teacher.

As for Murdo the teacher, I wondered how his pupils in the Outer Hebrides would react if he came back from Kalidonia with a black Kuna paint stripe still running down his nose.

While walking on the shore, Crusoe finds a turtle,
which he takes for food.

Chapter V
SALT TORTUGA

"Wayed ankor . . . from the lagoon at St. Georges . . . beutifal sailing day."

The sentence, with its pleasingly idiosyncratic spelling, could have come from the era of Robinson Crusoe. The penmanship was suitably antique. The letters were rounded and erratic. They rambled this way, then that, and paid little attention to the ruled lines on the page. They looked as if they had been scratched with a quill pen on a rumpled sheet of parchment. I found myself thinking that this was how maroons and castaways of the late seventeenth century could have begun their journals. Yet the words were fresh on the page. They were the first entry in the logbook of the vessel carrying me on the final phase of my quest for Robinson Crusoe. The skipper had written them. Far from being a seventeenth-century mariner, he had just celebrated his twenty-third birthday.

Ashley—known, of course, as Ash—was the proud owner of the only boat I could find to satisfy the requirements I set: I wanted to sail to three small Caribbean islands marked on the map that apparently led Defoe to locate Crusoe's island off the mouth of the Orinoco River. This map, it will be remembered, is printed in *A New Voyage Round the World*, the book by William Dampier, the buccaneer captain, published in 1697. His descriptions of the Caribbean were a source for many of Defoe's ideas about the geography of the place where Robinson Crusoe is cast away. Now I intended to check out these three islands to see whether one of them might fit the description of Crusoe's island better than the nonexistent island off the Orinoco. The three genuine islands—all clearly located by Herman Moll, the well-known chartmaker—had each witnessed a dramatic shipwreck or a marooning, which Defoe could have known about when he came to write his novel. Visiting these islands I hoped to discover what conditions these castaways and maroons really had to face, and whether their adventures matched Crusoe's experiences. It was also my chance to sample the sailing conditions faced by mariners in the days of Robinson Crusoe. I planned to make the 1,400-mile journey in a old small wooden sailboat without an engine. I would arrive on the islands like the men whose stories I was investigating, with the help of only the wind and current.

The vessel for the voyage was lying in St. George's Harbour in the West Indian island of Grenada. She was ninety-nine years old, had never been fitted with an engine, and was built to an English fishing boat design that dated back at least to the mid–1800s. She had her original sail plan—including the heavy gaff rig—and no electric power, and there was very little in the way of modern gear. She was called *Ziska* after a Bohemian folk hero, a warlord in the days of religious strife in Central Europe.

The fact that her owner wrote in a late-seventeenth-century hand and with a complete disregard for modern rules of spelling and grammar had nothing to do with nostalgia for the past. It was because Ash was so dyslexic that he virtually gave up formal schooling when he was fourteen years old. At that same time he discovered a passion—and a talent—for the restoration of wooden boats. His family lived near the coast in southeast England, and Ash hung about boatyards and scrimped and saved until he could salvage and restore *Ziska*. Then he sailed away to sea, across the Atlantic to the sunlit lure of the Caribbean. Three centuries earlier, I imagined, he would have gone wandering like young Lionel Wafer and perhaps finished up as a buccaneer. He would have been made welcome because Ash was a meticulous shipwright. Coltishly thin, blond, and with bright blue eyes made all the more startling by his deep tan, Ash looked even younger than he was. *Ziska* was his home, his joy, and his obsession. Around his upper left biceps was tattooed a blue band which depicted dolphins, waves, and a gaff-rigged sailboat.

It was convenient that *Ziska* was lying in St. George's Harbor. The first maroon on my list of those to investigate started his adventure close by on the island of Barbados. Henry Pitman was a surgeon, like Wafer, and an unlucky one. He had arrived in Barbados as a felon. In 1685 he had taken part in the unsuccessful rebellion of the Duke of Monmouth against King James II. Arrested while fleeing from the defeat at the battle of Sedgemoor, Pitman claimed that he had been a noncombatant. He told his captors that he had merely served in his capacity as a doctor, and tended the injuries of soldiers whether they were rebels or loyal to the Crown. His excuses were rejected. The arresting officers stripped him of his clothes, rifled his pockets, and threw him in gaol pending trial on a charge of treason. After a preliminary interrogation, he appeared at the assizes in the town of Wells. There he faced a panel of judges headed by the soon-to-be notorious lord chief justice of England, "Hanging Jeffreys."

This was the era when Judge George Jeffreys was gaining his odious nickname. He and his fellows on the panel of judges devised a method of dealing rapidly with the hundreds of suspected rebels. The court offered the prisoners a choice: either they could plead guilty and throw themselves on the mercy of the court, or they could claim that they were innocent and be subjected to a full cross-examination. But in the latter case, if they were found guilty, the sentence was automatic—execution. To make his point, Judge Jeffreys deliberately selected for his first batch of cases some twenty-eight prisoners against whom there was strong evidence. When they pleaded "not guilty," he heard their cases and cross-examined them, pronounced them guilty, and the same afternoon signed warrants for their execution. Not surprisingly, the vast majority of the remaining prisoners preferred to enter a guilty plea and await a lesser sentence. Some were even expecting pardons. To their dismay Judge Jeffreys ordered the execution of 230 prisoners—the bitter catchphrase now became "Confess and be hanged!"—and shipped most of the rest off to the "Caribbee Islands" as convicts. There they were to serve ten years forced labor.

The mass transportation swept away Pitman and his brother, also implicated in the rebellion, while their family tried to reduce the impact of the sentence. They paid a bribe to the businessman who had been given charge of the convicts' transportation. In return, he promised that the two brothers would not be sold on arrival in Barbados like the other prisoners. Instead they would be handed over to a sympathetic master who would pay them wages and treat them fairly.

It was hardly surprising that in the unscrupulous world of "the Caribbees" this promise was promptly broken. In Barbados Henry Pitman and his brother found themselves sold off like cattle. They read with outrage the lieutenant governor's proclamation, which detailed the conditions of their employment. As punishment for their "late wicked inhuman and damnable Rebellion" they were to serve the full ten years with no possibility whatsoever of remission. They were obliged to carry out "all such labour or services as they shall be commanded to perform and do by their Owners, Masters or Mistresses, or their Overseers." The secretary to the governor was to keep an up-to-date list of all the felons on the island, and no one would be allowed to leave Barbados without a "Ticket," or passport, which could only be issued after the list had been checked. If any "convict rebel" was caught trying to escape secretly from the island, he would be given "thirty nine lashes on his bare body," set in the pillory, and branded on the forehead with a hot iron with the letters "F.T.," for "fugitive traitor."

The proclamation also attempted to close down any practical means of escape. It ordered every owner or keeper of "any small vessel, sloop, shallop, wherry, fishing boat or any other sort of boat belonging to the island" to register his boat with the local magistrates and lodge a bond of two hundred pounds. He would forfeit this bond if any "servant" used his vessel to get away from Barbados, with or without the owner's knowledge. When a shipwright made a new boat, he too had to add it to the boat register or risk confiscation. Of course, no "servant" would be allowed to keep a boat.

Even a shrewd marriage would not help a "convict rebel" shorten his punishment. Should he try to obtain remission by marrying a local woman and changing his status from rebel to citizen, his ownership would be shifted to a new master forthwith. The woman who had married him would be fined two hundred pounds and "suffer Six Month's imprisonment for such her intermarrying with any of the said rebels convict." A similar penalty would be inflicted on anyone so rash as to "suffer or consent to the marriage of their daughters or other near relations."

In short, Pitman and hundreds of condemned rebels like him were confined to Barbados for ten full years in conditions of legalized slavery.

It was fifteen months before Henry Pitman came to the conclusion that he had to escape. He had been abominably treated. His master, a planter, refused to give him decent clothing and fed him so poorly on an unvarying diet of "salt Irish beef," salt fish, and maize dumplings that Pitman suffered from frequent bouts of diarrhea. At the same time the planter expected Pitman to continue his work as a surgeon, and pocketed any fees that he earned from his clients. When Pitman complained about his food and the quality of his lodgings, he was brusquely warned that they could be made even worse. Stubbornly Pitman asked to be transferred to do manual work alongside the slaves in the field. His planter-master thrashed him with a cane and put him in the stocks. Only the pity of the planter's wife obtained Pitman's release after twelve hours in the blazing sunshine. Pitman's sole satisfaction was that his owner eventually slid into such heavy debt that he could not keep up his payments on the original purchase of his "servant." He was obliged to return Pitman and his brother to the businessman who had imported him from the assizes in England. At this stage Pitman's brother died, and Pitman was left with the bitter feeling that he himself was reduced to nothing more than the status of "unsold goods."

He started to lay plans to acquire a boat.

He began by contacting John Nuthall, an impoverished woodcarver working on Barbados. Nuthall was not a "convict rebel," so he was allowed to own a small boat on condition that he registered it with the island secretariat. However, Pitman knew that Nuthall wanted to get off Barbados: he was an undischarged debtor, meaning that he still owed money. If Nuthall absconded from Barbados and disappeared he would leave his creditors behind. In a series of secret meetings Pitman offered to organize and pay all the expenses of an escape. Nuthall quickly fell in with the scheme, and Pitman handed him twelve pounds to buy a ship's boat. The money came from the sale of goods that his family had smuggled out to him. Nuthall acquired a ship's tender from a merchant ship, a slaver arrived from West Africa, though the boat was very small. A "skiff" is how Pitman describes it.

The local magistrates were suspicious when Nuthall went to register the little boat, as the proclamation required. They demanded to know how Nuthall, a bankrupt, had obtained the money to buy the boat. Nervously Nuthall reported back to Pitman. He advised that the best way to lull suspicions was to sink the boat deliberately. Once the skiff was under water, officialdom would lose interest. The policy of "out of sight, out of mind" seemed to work, and Pitman began putting together, in secret, the necessary supplies for their departure.

Pitman and Nuthall decided their best course was to try to reach the Dutch-owned island of Curaçao. There they would be beyond the reach of English law. From Barbados to Curaçao is a distance of six hundred miles. For food the surgeon calculated that the fugitives would be able to manage with a hundredweight of bread, a cask of fresh water, and a few bottles of Madeira wine and beer and a quantity of cheese. Pitman also laid in a stock of boat-building material in case they had to make repairs at sea, describing how he obtained nails, some spare planks, and a large tarpaulin. Included on his list of necessities were a hatchet, a saw, and a hammer. Pitman also obtained a stock of ready-made candles for his trip. But in the hurlyburly of the departure they became "bruised into one mass of tallow."

Buying all these items meant that Pitman was running short on cash, so he drew in two more accomplices. Thomas Austin and John Whicker were both "convict rebels" and keen to escape. Between them they were able to find the extra money for the supplies and to help Nuthall fend off his most immediate creditors. The plotters knew they would be foolish to stop at any islands en route where they might be recognized and arrested. So Pitman got his hands on a basic set of navigational equipment—compass, quadrant, chart, a half-hour glass, half-minute glass, and a log and line for measuring speed and calculating distance. He was the only member of the crew who knew how to use them.

Locating and hiding all these items widened the circle of Pitman's accomplices even further. More and more partners were added to the plot until there were nine in total. This was too many for the little boat to carry safely or comfortably. But Pitman pressed ahead. He concealed the food and other stores in the house of a friend who lived near the harbor, and for security reasons kept most of the members of the team ignorant as to when or how the escape would take place. John Whicker was his go-between. Fortunately, Whicker had a job at a little-used warehouse near the wharf which Pitman planned to use as the embarkation point. Whicker informed the conspirators that when Pitman gave the word, they should assemble at this warehouse, bringing side arms with them if possible.

Pitman saw his chance when the governor of the neighboring island of Nevis paid a visit to Barbados. Naturally the governor of Barbados announced that he would honor his distinguished guest with a ceremony of welcome. The Barbados militia received orders to dress up in their uniforms and make a parade. Pitman anticipated that after the parade, the tired, hot, and sweaty soldiers would go off to the taverns to carouse and get drunk, and their guard would be slack. He sent word to Nuthall to have the little boat raised from her watery hiding place, to bail her out, and bring her to the wharf. Meanwhile Pitman arranged for the stores to be carried down to the harbor from his friend's house, and told Whicker to inform the conspirators that they were to assemble at the warehouse after dark.

At one hour before midnight on 9 May 1687, the escapees quietly made their way to the rendezvous. They stationed one man at the foot of the pier to give warning if the militia approached, then began loading the stores into their tiny boat. To their alarm they had not finished the task when the lookout alerted them that a militia patrol was heading toward the wharf. The conspirators scattered and ran away in the dark. Pitman scuttled off to his friend's house and hid. He was convinced that the plot had been discovered and he risked, as he put it, "a burnt forehead and sore back." He was wondering whether or not he should make a run for the mountains when there was a low call at the window. Pitman recognized the voice of one of his accomplices. Apparently the arrival of the militia had been a false alarm. The soldiers had come only to look for one of their comrades and ask him to join their revels. Not finding him, they had wandered away from the wharf without paying any attention to the escape boat tied up against the quay. Pitman was now so close to losing his nerve that he was only persuaded to go back to the wharf after his colleagues pointed out that he was the only navigator among them. Thomas Austin, one of the original conspirators, took a different view. The prospect of setting out in such a small, open boat overwhelmed him at the last moment. He "was so possessed with fear of being cast away, that he would not go with us."

In the warm darkness of a Caribbean night, eight frightened and desperate men climbed down from the wharf into their little boat and cast off. Besides John Nuthall, the woodcarver, there was another debtor, Thomas Walker. All the rest were "rebel convicts," former supporters of the Duke of Monmouth, and Pitman lists their names: John Whicker, Peter Bagwell, William Woodcock, John Cooke, and a man called Jeremiah Atkins.

The runaways first had to sneak past the fort guarding the entrance to the harbor. It was less than a pistol shot away, so close that they dared not bail water from the leaky boat for fear that the splashes would alert the guard. They rowed softly past the sentries, then eased their way past an English man-of-war anchored in the roadstead. Only when they were out of earshot could they begin to scoop out the water from their half-sinking cockleshell. By then the skiff was so waterlogged that their matches and tinder were soaked and useless. They were unable to burn a light to see their compass. For the rest of the voyage, whenever it was dark, they steered by the stars and, when it was cloudy, by the wind.

The wind pattern of the Caribbean dictated their course. They had no choice in such an overloaded and unhandy boat but to go downwind, southwest with the northeast trade wind at their backs. So they set up a small mast, rigged a sail, and with Pitman as their navigator set their course "as near as I could judge, intending to make the Great Grenada."

They quickly discovered that the little skiff Nuthall had purchased for twelve pounds was a bad buy. The vessel leaked alarmingly. "She was so thin," Pitman wrote, "so feeble, so heavily ladened and wrought [twisted and flexed] so exceedingly by reason of the great motion of the sea that we could not possibly make her tight." As they moved farther offshore, the crew tried every means to stop the leaks. They ripped up their shirts, wiped the rags in tallow, then stuffed the strips of cloth into the gaps between the planks. But it did little good. The water continued to pour in, and the men "were forced to keep one person almost continually, day and night, to throw out the water, during our whole voyage."

They had only a large wooden bowl and a tub to bail with, and quite soon they lost the bowl. One of the crew carelessly let the bowl slip from his wet fingers as he was flinging water overboard, a classic mistake. They were traveling with a strong breeze behind them and there was no way of turning round to pick up the bailer. The bowl went bobbing away in their wake. Now, wrote Pitman, "We had nothing left to throw out the water with but our tub; which obliged them to be more careful of it, for our lives were concerned therein."

By then several members of the crew no longer cared whether they lived or died. They were suffering from seasickness as the tiny boat lurched and swayed in the waves. Several wanted to turn back to Barbados. But Pitman pointed out that was now impossible. There was no way back against the headwind.

The light of dawn showed Barbados as a distant shadow on the horizon behind them, and looking back the fugitives were relieved to see there was no sign of pursuit. There was no sail of a guard ship or man-of-war coming in chase. They were alone on the sea.

Their sense of relief changed to anxiety at nightfall. A "brisk gale of wind" arose; the waves smashed the skiff's rudder, and she could no longer be steered on the increasingly turbulent sea. There was a very real risk of broaching and capsizing. The frightened crew had to take down the sail. Now Pitman's forethought was rewarded. The spare lengths of plank, the hammer, and the nails were retrieved from the bilges. One of the fugitives was a joiner by trade, and he nailed together a splint round the broken rudder, a crude but effective repair. "That done," says Pitman, "we went cheerily on again."

The next day, 11 May, they had "indifferent good weather." The crew were sufficiently recovered from their bout of seasickness to do some work to try to improve the little boat. To increase her seaworthiness, they raised the sides nine inches by adding weather-cloths, strips of tarpaulin nailed to the oars, which they rigged around the gunwhale. With the remainder of the tarpaulin they constructed a "tilt," an awning, to shade the stern of the boat and give some protection from sunburn.

On 12 May, the third day of their escape, the Grenadilloes—the islands now called the Grenadines—came in sight, and Pitman realized that they were off course. His intention had been to stand well clear of the islands, but now the current had carried them off their intended track. If he did not veer away, the refugees risked coming ashore on the main island of Grenada and falling into the hands of the English garrison there.

He steered his little vessel on a more southerly course, and the overloaded skiff slipped round the south side of Grenada and out into the broad passage that separates the arc of the Windward Islands from the mainland coast of South America. A hundred miles to the south lay Trinidad. Beyond Trinidad was Boca Grande, the mouth of the Orinoco and site of Defoe's fantasy, "Crusoe's island."

Pitman was learning that his main position-finding instrument, the quadrant, was of little use in such a difficult environment. He had brought along the device so he could measure the angle of the sun at noon and establish a daily latitude. But the small boat was proving too unstable a platform for him to take an accurate reading, and the sun was so high at the zenith that any reading was very vague. Reluctantly he decided that he could not rely on celestial navigation. Instead he would have to find his way by line of sight. He would set his course according to the islands marked on the chart, and sail from one island to the next as each came up over the horizon. It meant that he had to abandon the shorter, direct, course to Curaçao and take a longer route, island-hopping in a curve that followed the South American coast.

Next to come into view, on 14 May, were Los Testigos, "The Witnesses." This cluster of small islands was to the south-southwest, confirming that the skiff had kept to the right course since Grenada, their last landfall. The same day, far ahead, they caught a glimpse of the larger island of Margarita. Exhausted after steering the boat almost continuously for four nights and days, Pitman decided to get some rest. He handed the helm over to a companion, told him to steer for the distant loom of Margarita, and lay down to snatch a few hours of sleep.

He awoke with a start. The sail had been lowered. Looking over the gunwhale Pitman saw that the skiff was very close to the shore of Margarita and that his companions were getting ready to land. They had decided, without consulting Pitman, to find somewhere to refill their water cask because their drinking water "stank so extremely." Pitman hastily quashed the scheme. He could see a fire burning on the beach not far from their landing place. The fire, so he believed, had been lit by natives who were waiting to capture the runaways and eat them. "I caused the sail again to be hoisted up, and hasted away with all expedition," he wrote, "and . . . soon got out of fear or danger of those savage cannibals."

It was a bizarre misapprehension that there were cannibals on Margarita. The island had been a Spanish possession for three centuries. By the time Pitman sailed past in his little skiff, Margarita had been pacified, colonized, and christianized for so long that the cathedral in its capital, La Asuncion, was already two hundred years old. With an area of just 355 square miles and an open terrain, there was no corner where a cannibal band could hide out. Nor had its native people, the Guaiqueri, eaten human flesh. Yet Pitman sheered away from Margarita convinced that he was saving himself and his companions from becoming the victims of a cannibal feast on the beach. It was a whimsical concept and, notably, it is mirrored in Defoe's fantasy that cannibal Indians cut up and cooked their human victims on the beach of "Crusoe's island."

Pitman must have been convinced about the cannibals because next day, 15 May, he again refers to the man-eaters on Margarita. The skiff was halfway along the north coast, and for a second time the crew demanded to go ashore to find fresh water. On this occasion, seeing that the beach was clear of humans, Pitman agreed. He turned the little boat toward what seemed to be a good landing place, an attractive open bay with smooth water. It was a miscalculation. As the boat drew near the shore, "to our great surprise we found the ground near the shore extreamly foul." The sea "heaved us in so fast that we could not possibly have avoided being split on the rocks, had I not leaped into the sea to fend her off."

With Pitman in the water and pushing with his feet against the rocks, and his companions heaving frantically at the two oars, the runaways succeed in clawing off the shore. Pitman, wet and exhausted, scrambled aboard. It was, he said, a miraculous escape and "our hearts were filled with joy, and our mouths with praises to the LORD, who had so wonderfully preserved us from being cast away on this island." His words and tone are echoed by the speech and thoughts of Robinson Crusoe when he too is preserved from harm, and—as in Defoe's tale—the cannibals once again come back in focus. Had their boat been wrecked, Pitman writes, "we must either have been starved ourselves, or have become food for those inhuman man-eaters."

Avoiding the "cannibals," the next stepping stone on their precarious island-hopping route lay fifty miles farther west. It was a low, inconspicuous island the Spanish called Tortuga, for the abundance of turtles which nested on the beaches. To the English, Dutch, and French it was more usually known as the Saltadudos, the Salt Islands or Salt Tortuga, from the pans of sea salt found there. At high tides the sea floods a low-lying area on the southwest corner of the island and leaves standing water about a foot deep. The sun constantly evaporates the water, creating a thin rime of salt. The Spanish laid claim to the island as it lay only 45 miles off the mainland coast, but it was—and still is—uninhabited. At the end of the evaporation season, in November or December, foreign vessels often called at Salt Tortuga to shovel up the salt and take it away for sale. Occasionally Spanish patrol ships pounced on the interlopers and seized the foreign ships as poachers. But for most of the year Salt Tortuga was left abandoned, a small, squat, insignificant island sweltering in the heat.

Pitman and his crew headed out toward Salt Tortuga on May 15. It was now the sixth day of their voyage, and they had completed about two thirds of their journey to Curaçao. After a few hours the wind picked up, and Pitman began to be nervous. His anxiety was increased at dusk by the appearance of a white ring around the moon, a traditional omen of heavy weather. "I thought [it] presaged ill weather," he wrote, "and to our great sorrow, [this] proved too true." At about nine o'clock that night, "a dreadful storm" arose. The sea, which had been smooth, "began to foam." Their heavily loaded skiff "was tossed and tumbled from one side to the other and so violently driven and hurried away by the fury of the wind and sea, that I was afraid we should be driven by the island [Salt Tortuga] in the nighttime."

To slow down their hectic progress, the crew brought their little boat's bow into wind and tried to hold her up against the waves, maintaining station. But soon, for their own safety and before the skiff was overturned, they were obliged to put about and run downwind, still bailing and now praying for salvation. It was at this time of greatest anxiety that Pitman and his crew believed they heard a voice calling to them. It was "an unexpected voice which (to our thinking) seemed to hallow [hallo] to us at a great distance." Pitman uses the same devout tones as Robinson when he too is completely downcast. The mysterious voice, the surgeon wrote, was "a sign that the Omnipotent (who is never unmindful of the cries of his people in distress) heard our prayers." Within hours the brief gale had abated and the sea state eased, as "GOD, of his infinite mercy and unspeakable Goodness, commanded the violence of the winds to cease, and allayed the fury of the raging waves."

"Eternal praises to his Name for evermore!" concluded Pitman piously.

The first glimmer of dawn showed that the gale had blown the little skiff almost on top of Salt Tortuga. The low outline of the island lay just ahead, and Pitman steered for a landing. The crew were now in poor shape. The gale had knocked the last of their energy out of them. They had endured nearly a week crammed together in a small boat, living on short rations, drinking foul water, wet with spray or exposed to the tropical sun beating down on them and reflecting off the sea, and always bailing. Below them the thin hull of their vessel was increasingly shaky. Battered and twisted by the storm waves, the makeshift caulking—the tallow-soaked rags stuffed between the planks—had spewed out from the gaps. The boat was in urgent need of fresh caulking if she was to complete the final 230 miles to Curaçao. This time Pitman did not hesitate. The runaways had to get ashore to rest, find fresh water if possible, and repair their boat. He steered along the north side of Salt Tortuga, and the crew scanned the beach, looking for a suitable place to land.

They identified a likely spot where a small coral islet gave a measure of protection to the beach, and made for it. To their surprise they saw a canoe put out from shore and come toward them. Fearful images of cannibals and savage natives sprang to mind, and the runaways grabbed for their weapons. They had brought "muskets and blunderbusses" with them but now discovered that in their hasty midnight departure they had left the only bag of bullets on the quayside in Barbados. They loaded their guns with bits of broken glass from the bottles, poured gunpowder into the flashpans, and stood by, determined to fight off any attack.

Their alarm increased when they noted that the crew of the approaching canoe were using paddles "like Indians," not rowing with oars. Convinced that they had stumbled on a marauding group of natives, Pitman turned the skiff around, the crew hoisted sail and they tried to flee.

Then someone looked more closely and noted that the crew of the "Indian canoe" were shouting and waving hats. Indians did not wear hats.

Pitman and his crew slowed their panicky flight and allowed the strange canoe to come closer. Now they could see that the occupants were white men. The refugees from Barbados called out "What were they?"

The reply came back that they were "Englishmen in distress, etc," waiting "for an opportunity to go off the island."

Pitman suspected nothing. He did not question why a canoe loaded with distressed mariners was seeking help from a skiff full to the brim with refugees. He had no way of knowing the consequences as he turned the little boat and meekly followed the canoe to land. The little skiff lacked an anchor so she had to be beached. The runaways' newfound friends helped them pull their little boat up on the sand and welcomed them to Salt Tortuga.

The introductions were guarded on both sides. Pitman and the other "convict rebels" were reluctant to reveal their status as runaway prisoners. The self-styled "Englishmen in distress" on Salt Tortuga were hiding the fact that they were really pirates.

Real identities began to surface when Nuthall and Walker, the two debtors, betrayed their companions. Seeking to ingratiate themselves with the mysterious strangers, they explained that they were runaway debtors, but all the others from the skiff were former supporters of the Duke of Monmouth and therefore, by implication, dyed-in-the-wool malefactors. The response was the opposite of what they anticipated. Their hosts on Tortuga applauded the "rebel convicts" and said that had they been given the chance, they too would have fought on Monmouth's side.

They were, they said, a roving detachment from a forty-eight-gun ship—ostensibly a privateer—under the command of "Captain Yanche," a Dutch captain. He had sent them to raid the mainland coast for supplies. Captain Yanche was planning a major assault on the Spanish town of St. Augustine in Florida and needed stocks of food as well as several *piraguas,* large native canoes, to use as landing craft in an amphibious assault. Unfortunately the detachment, some thirty men, had run into trouble. While "turning turtle" on the beach, they had been attacked by Indians, lost two men killed, and been driven off. Later, they succeeded in capturing several canoes and also an Indian prisoner. He had taken them to his plantations on condition that they would set him free once they had gathered their food. The raiders must have been sadly inexperienced because two of them, including their quartermaster, had eaten poison cassava without squeezing out the toxic juice first. The two men had died. The survivors of the raiding party then withdrew, taking the captive Indian with them, and headed for their agreed rendezvous with Captain Yanche. There was no sign of the forty-eight-gun pirate ship at the meeting place nor did they know where Yanche might have gone. So they paddled their *piraguas* to Salt Tortuga and were waiting, hoping to be picked up by one of the salt-collecting ships or intercept and seize a passing merchant ship.

Captain Yanche's name should have warned Pitman and his colleagues to danger. Captain Yanche, or "Yanky Duch," as he was sometimes known, was infamous. He claimed to be a privateer but acted like a pirate. His base of operations was the small island of Petit Guaves off the island of Hispaniola. The French governor there was willing to sell "commissions" and letters of marque left blank and undated so the captain could fill in his own details. Yanche rarely had difficulty in finding crew because he had a lucky streak. He had taken part in the lucrative raid on Vera Cruz in May 1683, when even the lowliest member of his crew received 800 pesos from the division of the plunder. The following year Yanche and another Dutch captain captured three rich Spanish vessels off Cartagena. And just eight months before Pitman met up with his detachment of ruffians, Yanche had boarded and seized a Spanish ship worth fifty thousand dollars.

At the outset Yanche's men were generous to the eight escapees from Barbados. They showed them a well for fresh water they had dug near their own huts and gave them food. Pitman and his companions rigged up a sail as an awning, lay down on the sand in the shade, and fell asleep, utterly worn out.

When they had rested, the runaways turned their attention to repairing the sea-worn skiff. They wanted to be on their way to Curaçao as soon as they had plugged the worst of the leaks in hull. They also resolved to build a light deck over the forward part of the skiff. This deck would give some protection from the waves slopping in over the gunwhale and from the rain. If they were unlucky enough to be caught by another storm, a deck might save the little boat from swamping. Lengths of tree bark were the only materials they could find to make the decking, and they had started work when Yanche's men began to meddle.

The "privateers," as Pitman politely called them, repeatedly asked the newcomers to change their plan. They pointed out "the insufficiency of our boat and the dangers we were so lately exposed to." Yanche's men suggested that the runaways should abandon their journey to Curaçao and, instead, throw in their lot with their new friends. It was better to "go with them a privateering . . . than to hazard our lives by a second attempt."

Why Yanche's men were so insistent can be guessed at—they did not want news leaking out that there was a pirate force camped on Salt Tortuga. The pirates depended on surprise. Yanche's men were operating in small vulnerable *piraguas,* and to be successful they had to take their victims unawares, ambushing them as they sailed past. If Pitman and his colleagues reached Curaçao, it would not be long before the Dutch authorities heard about the pirates. The Dutch themselves would probably take no direct action, but all merchant shipping would delay sailing or avoid the danger zone.

The "privateers" succeeded in putting their argument so enticingly that several of the runaways from Barbados were willing to join them. Then Pitman, as he self-righteously put it, "persuaded them to the contrary." At that juncture Yanche's men dropped any pretense of friendliness and revealed their truly piratical nature. To stop the runaways from attempting to sail to Curaçao, the pirates removed the sail from the skiff for their own use, then set fire to the runaways' boat, and burned it to cinders.

There was nothing that Pitman and his seven colleagues could do to prevent them. They were heavily outnumbered by Yanche's men, twenty-eight to eight. They watched helplessly as the pirates then picked out the nails from the ashes of the conflagration and used them to fasten extra side planks to their *piraguas*. At that stage it was obvious that the pirates themselves were getting ready to leave the island.

Pitman, to his credit, kept his wits about him. He offered to buy the Indian whom the pirates had captured earlier on the mainland and never set free. He paid "30 pieces of eight" for the man, who, he expected, "would be serviceable unto us in catching fish etc."

On 25 May 1687 all but four of the pirates pushed off to sea in their *piraguas* to resume their raiding. The four who stayed behind had elected to take their chances on Salt Tortuga with Pitman and his colleagues, including Jeremiah Atkins and the newly bought Indian. The maroons were left with the rough huts the pirates had formerly occupied, a few swords and muskets, and the hulk of a small Spanish boat Yanche's men had rejected as it lacked either a sail or a rudder. The next salt-collecting ships were not due to visit Salt Tortuga for another eight or nine months. Until then the maroons would have to learn to survive, or "GOD, by a particular Providence should direct some vessel or other to touch here."

Ziska caught the eye. Ash had recently painted her hull a jaunty sky blue, and scraped and oiled the mast and bowsprit to a healthy glow. Swinging on her anchor in the lagoon at St. George's among modern fiber-glass yachts and chromium-trimmed motor cruisers, she looked picturesque, shipshape, and rather small. She was only thirty-eight feet long but was surprisingly broad in the beam. She seemed to squat down into the water with her nose in the air. *Ziska*'s sister ships had been designed to trawl for shrimp on the shallow fishing banks off the northwest coast of England, and the low stern had made it easier to hoist nets and trawls out of the sea. Technically known as cutter-rigged fishing smacks, they sailed from port at dawn and, if possible, returned the same evening. They had been built for speed, to be nimble in narrow muddy channels when the tide was out, and easily handled by a small crew, often no more than a man and a boy. Sometimes the fishing smacks stayed out overnight or they might cross the Irish Sea, so they could survive moderately heavy weather. But her builder could never have imagined, ninety-nine years earlier when he built *Ziska* for a private owner who wanted the fishing-boat design used as a private yacht, that she would be sailing the Caribbean. He would probably have been amazed that she was still afloat.

Ash looked after his treasure fastidiously and on very slender means. Every rope seemed to have had a former life on another vessel; the sails had been acquired at second or third hand, as had the anchor, the anchor chain, the winch, any item of gear one cared to mention. The compass was so venerable that the marks on the compass card were faded to the point of obscurity, and the card itself floated beneath a large bubble trapped under scratched glass. Below deck it was even more obvious that external elegance had an internal price to pay. The entire stern section of the vessel was given over to a ragtag store of bits and pieces of salvaged and battered gear that might one day prove useful. There were half-used cans of paint, rags, shackles, lengths of wire, scraps of timber. Here Ash had his work bench. It was fitted with a rack of secondhand but carefully honed tools and dominated by a massive iron bench vice bolted in the center. The workbench was, I discovered, designated as my bunk. I had eighteen inches of head room, and if I wished to lie flat I had to open the jaws of the vice to full width.

Ziska's stark fishing boat ancestry was equally apparent in the main cabin. You could not stand upright except in one small area just below the hatch leading down into the cabin. The accommodation was spartan, cluttered, and—in Grenada's heat—exceedingly stuffy. The absence of any engine was caused by lack of space as much as by Ash's limited budget. There was hardly any place to put a motor. No engine meant no electric power, no radio, no electronic navigation aids. Lighting, above and below deck, was accomplished with paraffin lamps. They too were past their prime. Cleaning soot from the lamp glasses, trimming the wicks, refilling the little brass tanks, was a smelly, messy, and ultimately futile chore: the red and green navigation lamps on deck usually sputtered and died, or were so dim that you had to peer closely to see whether they were lit. Apart from an equally fickle stern light hanging near the helmsman, *Ziska* crept along at night as a dark shadow. Remembering Pitman and his troubles with the "bruised mass of tallow" for his candles, I purchased a hand torch so we could at least flash an occasional light on the faded compass card.

Lamp cleaning duties fell to Tristan, whom Ash had enlisted the previous week as a volunteer deck hand. A year or so older than Ash, Tristan was a member of that nomadic band of young men and women with an aura of perpetual bronzed good health who migrate with the boats of the wealthy yacht-racing and yacht-chartering community. They provide the deck hands, boatmen, cooks, and working crew. He had joined Ash now that the sailing season in the West Indies was drawing to a close and the expensive boats were leaving the area before the hurricane season. Tristan bore an astonishing resemblance to Henry VIII in Holbein's portrait of the king standing bulkily, hands on hips, sturdy legs apart, glaring at the artist. Tristan even had the same ruddy complexion. On *Ziska* he was to have a difficult role. It was clear that Ash really preferred to sail on *Ziska* single-handed. He had a close relationship with his beloved boat, and though Ash was prepared to tolerate my presence in my quest for Robinson Crusoe, Tristan risked being seen as an intruder.

If Ash had any such doubts about the fourth member of our team, they soon vanished. Trondur Patursson looks, acts, and is the supreme sailor of traditional boats. Raised on the Faeroe Islands in the North Atlantic, he had first gone to sea in his early teens, working on the ferry to Denmark. "Four hours every day cleaning brass in the ship" was how he remembered it. He subsequently worked as a deck hand on fishing boats off Greenland and Newfoundland, and long-lined for shark in the Gulf of Mexico, and he owned his own small wooden sailboat almost as venerable as *Ziska*. Now one of Scandinavia's leading maritime artists, he had accompanied me on transoceanic voyages aboard replica vessels as varied as a medieval skin boat and a bamboo raft. With his shaggy hair and beard shot with gray, he obviously impressed a slightly worried-looking Ash. As Trondur came aboard *Ziska* he had a cardboard tube under his arm. It contained an item he had forged at my request just before he left his northern workshop—the head for a light harpoon. I had a notion that if anyone could show me how castaways had managed to survive, it would be Trondur.

We sailed *Ziska* from the lagoon at St. George's on the morning of May 4. The timing was apt. We left the anchorage in the same month, almost the same week, that Pitman and his seven companions slunk past Grenada to avoid detection as they headed for Curaçao in their little boat. *Ziska* was more seaworthy than their open skiff, but I wanted to sample the sailing conditions the refugees encountered. The benign reputation of West Indian weather is of constant gentle zephyrs, bright sunshine, and blue skies. The reality is different. . . . The previous week had seen a brisk gale that bottled up the charter boats in harbor, several downpours, and a near calm. All that could be said was that none of these weather conditions had lasted for long. Sooner or later the northeast trade winds return.

When *Ziska* cleared St. George's, bound for Margarita, the weather was what Pitman had described as "indifferent good"—a few clouds, spells of warm sunshine, and a moderate breeze. Ash used a long stern oar to spin his yacht deftly through 180 degrees in the crowded anchorage. Trondur and Tristan set the jib, and a breath of wind gave enough steerage way as we threaded a path out from the mass of boats and into the channel. For the first few miles we were in Grenada's lee and in smooth water. The mainsail rose. After the near silence of the engineless departure the outbreak of clattering and groaning and slatting was an assault on the ears. I recalled how Pitman and his colleagues had rowed softly away from the wharf in Barbados, not daring to bail the water for fear the sentries would hear the splashes. Only later, when well clear of the harbor, had they hoisted sail. Aboard *Ziska* the din of setting the heavy gaff sail would have been heard half a mile away on a quiet night. There was the piercing high-pitched squeak of the wooden jaws of the gaff, the spar at the top of the sail sliding ponderously up the wooden mast, the erratic flap and clatter of the heavy canvas following it, the grumbling run of heavy rope through the blocks, and, above all, the sound of *Ziska*'s hull adapting noisily to the strain. When the sheets were hauled in and the mainsail exerted pressure, *Ziska* groaned with effort, then groaned again. Ten minutes later, as we cleared the wind shadow and the full strength of the breeze filled the sails, the backstay, a rope supporting the mast, gave several sharp cracking sounds as it tensed rigid, and the boat talked once more, a deep moan running right down through her frames to her keel. Within moments she was heeling to the wind, and the first of the wave tops skipped from the sea, broke on to the deck and came swirling down to wet the helmsman's feet. *Ziska*'s class of fishing smacks, I had read, were notoriously wet on deck. Luckily the water was warm as *Ziska* ran purposefully to intercept the wake of the surgeon Pitman and seven desperate runaways.

Pitman did not write of a magnificent sunset, the brilliance of the starry night sky, or the splendid sleek, black vision and plosive breath as a minke whale surfaced within fifty yards—all of which we witnessed in the next twenty-four hours. The men in Pitman's boat were scared of bad weather, of being carried off course by the currents, of the skiff filling through her leaky seams and sinking. Had a whale surfaced alongside, they would have feared a capsize.

The next entry in the log—"Trondur landed 2 baracooda just befor dinner one with fresh gashes in side from a shark . . . we ate the 2 for dinner and were apsolutely stuft"—confirmed Trondur's role as the onboard hunter-gatherer. He had trailed a line overboard as soon as we cleared the land, and the two barracuda were in the frying pan before dark. Trondur made much of his living from the sea as he had done when a young man. But now it was by drawing, painting, sculpting, or creating evocative stained-glass images of the ocean and its creatures, whether fish or whales or birds. Yet he never ceased to regard the ocean as a primary resource for food if you had the skill to harvest it.

That evening the wind died away, and *Ziska* lolled, nearly motionless, through the night and most of the following day. Ash spent the long hours prettifying his little dinghy, its hull upturned on the cabin roof. Lost to the world, his nose pressed almost to the work, he scraped away minor imperfections with the edge of a chisel and smoothed the slightest scratch with fine sandpaper. Trondur fished, the line weighted with a link of anchor chain to sink it down into the still water. Tristan read the stock of yachting magazines that formed Ash's library. I watched the sea birds to identify the species that had kept mariners and castaways alive.

I saw boobies and noddies and tropicbirds. They flew past in small groups, seldom more than three or four together. Dampier described the brown booby (*Sula leucogaster*), as "a very simple creature." A member of the gannet family, it would "hardly go out of a man's way." The booby received its mocking name, so it was said, from the English sailors who thought it so stupid that they could stand on the deck and extend their arms as perches and the boobies would alight. The sailors wrung their necks. "Their flesh," said Dampier, "is black and eats fishy, but are often eaten by the privateers." The brown noddy (*Anous stolidus*), was more of a disappointment in size and taste. A dingy grayish-brown seabird, it was only "about the bigness of an English black bird, and indifferent good meat." The best catch, according to Dampier, was the red-billed tropicbird (*Phaeton aethereus*). The sailors cared less for its deft aerobatics or the elegance of the trailing tail feathers than for its flavor. It was "as big as a pigeon, but round and plump like a partridge. . . . They are very good food."

Astern, small patrols of pelicans flapped sedately past in line. They tucked their heads back against their bodies as they flew only a few yards above the calm sea. Their slow wing beats and sense of heavy purpose made them look like flying stomachs or aldermen on their way to a civic banquet. One solitary pelican, a large brown specimen, landed ponderously on the sea fifty yards away and, bobbing there, regarded our motionless vessel with a beady eye, a white feathered cheek above the massive beak. Pelicans, too, provided food for seventeenth-century mariners, though the bird's flesh is so tough that they recommended first burying the carcass in hot sand for a couple of days to tenderize the meat. The sack, the membrane below the bill, made a handy tobacco pouch when stretched with a musket ball.

Everything that swam in the sea or flew above it was potential food for hungry sailors. Dolphins and porpoises were sought after. Porpoise meat, or "sea pig," was said to taste like pork. Others, more accurately, compared the taste of dolphin steak to the finest beef. A single medium-size dolphin provides forty pounds of rich dark-red meat. There were still plenty of dolphins in the Caribbean. In midafternoon a patch of the calm sea suddenly broke into a profusion of wavelets as if a rip tide were running. The wavelets proved to be the sleek shiny backs and dorsal fins of one to two hundred dolphins coming to the surface, then rising and falling rapidly. They were hunting as a group, lunging at the small fish they had herded into a tightly packed shoal. Above them the seabirds clustered excitedly to hover and dive, then snatch at the sprats.

Later, at two in the morning, when I was on watch, there was a sudden plunge close by, a puffing exhalation of breath, and a dolphin, a much larger one, made its presence known. Within minutes the animal had returned with its companions to use *Ziska* as the focal point for some complicated underwater maneuvers. Between eight and ten dolphins rushed back and forth just below keel depth for half an hour, leaving fizzing bubble trails as they thrust along, the side-to-side undulations of their bodies clearly visible. They ran under the boat in pairs, raced off to one side, then turned and raced back, then vanished until I thought they had gone away, only to come suddenly barreling in from another angle. They formed into teams of four and two, divided again into pairs, changed partners, surfaced in unison so their snorts were almost simultaneous. The white curves and streaming trails they left in the dark sea were like the sinuous white banners waved by bamboo-wielding Chinese acrobats. At the end of the display there was nothing for perhaps five minutes, and I was sure the dolphins had moved elsewhere. Under *Ziska* the sea was a dark indigo barely illuminated by a sliver of moon and the stars. Abruptly and silently—and I had no idea how the dolphins achieved the effect—a great mass of small white bubbles silently arose from directly beneath the boat. The white incandescent glow spread upward and outward, radiating out from the hull until for a moment the boat was floating on a foaming orb of luminescence.

For twenty-four hours *Ziska* made little progress through the water. Yet we had not been motionless. The current had been silently taking us along. The dominant current in the straits between the Windward Islands and South America flows west, with the trade winds. Pitman had found himself swept too far toward the Grenadines. Now, unknown to us, *Ziska* was also being carried forward at between one and two knots. Like Pitman we were relying on line-of-sight navigation, and in the wake of his little skiff we kept a lookout for "the Witnesses," the islands of Los Testigos, which had been his signpost. We saw them at eight in the morning, peaks of land fine off the port bow. When a light breeze came up, we altered course toward them. Six hours later the peaks had reared higher from the sea, and through the haze more high ground appeared on either hand. It was much too substantial to be the Testigos. I checked the chart. We were twenty miles off course. The Testigos were north, not south, of us, and we were heading directly for the mainland coast of Venezuela. We adjusted the helm, and *Ziska* veered toward Margarita.

Without modern navigation aids, we had been as much at the mercy of the currents as Pitman's little skiff, and almost as vague about where we were. When we arrived at Margarita in the early hours of the following morning, it had taken thirty-six hours to travel from Grenada, the same length of time that Pitman and his little overloaded skiff took to reach the "cannibal" island.

In Margarita the advice was to stock up with food and water if we planned to continue on to Salt Tortuga. An occasional weekend yachtsmen visits Salt Tortuga, and commercial fishermen have built a couple of camps there. But it has no permanent population. The fishermen go home to their families on Margarita every few weeks and pick up supplies, or light aircraft bring out fresh food. Ominously, we were told that it was easy to identify the best anchorage on the island: we had to look for two prominent wrecks lying on the shoreline, a rusty fishing boat hull and a beached and broken yacht.

The yacht, it turned out, was easy to spot. It lay cast up on the shore, tilted over on its side and was carmine red. We could see the wreck almost from the moment we began to distinguish the low, blue-gray profile of Salt Tortuga at midmorning on May 10. We had hove to the previous night during the passage from Margarita so that we would approach with the sun high enough to reveal the coral reef outliers. Fortunately the water was as transparent as the most blatant travel poster, and it was easy to skirt the dark arm of reef that protects the anchorage. The spectacular aquamarine of the shallows and the strip of dazzling white sand were the only concessions to the image of a lush tropical island. Tortuga was low and flat. Behind the beach dune we could see only a thin edge of sage green. Apart from the corrugated metal roofs of the fishermen's sheds shimmering in the heat, nothing broke the horizon. There was no hill, nothing to relieve the flat landscape, not a single tree. Salt Tortuga was a flat, bleak, hot prospect.

Trondur caught a booby as we arrived. He baited a hook with a chunk of left-over barracuda, floated the lure behind the boat on light line, and waited. Soon the booby earned its reputation as "a very simple creature." The size of a small and undernourished goose, the bird fluttered closer to take a look, then landed awkwardly, spreading out its ungainly webbed feet as it flopped down on to the sea. Paddling over to the bait, the booby opened its large yellow beak and gobbled down the morsel. Trondur tugged. The startled booby was hauled aboard, flapping futilely. Its neck was quickly wrung; and Trondur had provided our supper.

We ate the booby on the beach later that same afternoon. *Ziska* lay before us, safely anchored in water of such clarity that she seemed to float on glass. A single fishing boat had looked into the bay and gone. There was no one else. We made a fire of driftwood and sat on sand of extraordinary fineness. It was as soft and yielding as finely milled white flour. Trondur skinned and disjointed the booby, and the morsels were skewered on twigs and propped over the embers. The pieces of booby took a very long time to cook, and the dark flesh did, as Dampier promised, "eat fishy." Nor was there much substance to chew on. If boobies were "often eaten by the privateers," they must have needed at least one bird per man or gone hungry. When we tired of gnawing on the charred flesh, we tossed the remnants to the dog the fishermen had left behind to guard their shacks. Initially the dog had done its duty and come to bark ferociously. Then, losing heart, it had crept closer and begged for scraps. When we left the beach and rowed back to *Ziska* in Ash's tiny dinghy, the dog sat down on the crest of the dune and looked bereft. Then it lifted its muzzle and began to howl and howl. His wailing made Salt Tortuga seemed an even more abandoned place.

Pitman published a little book about his escape from Barbados and his adventure as a maroon on Salt Tortuga thirty years *before* Daniel Defoe wrote *The Life and Strange Surprizing Adventures of Robinson Crusoe*. Pitman's lively account has a notably similar title: *A Relation of the great suffering and strange adventures of Henry Pitman, Chirurgeon*. It went on public sale on 13 June 1689 "at the sign of the Ship in St. Paul's Churchyard." This was the premises of John Taylor, a London bookseller. Pitman's booklet runs to just thirty-six pages in modern typeface. A further nine pages describe the remarkable way in which his comrade-in-adventure, John Whicker, succeeded in escaping from Salt Tortuga. This compares to over two hundred pages to tell Robinson Crusoe's story. Defoe had much more room to expand and embroider his tale of a castaway, and he introduced all sorts of additional themes and episodes not found in Pitman's terse account. Yet so many details from Pitman's story surface in one form or another in the tale of Robinson Crusoe that it is hard to avoid the conclusion that Daniel Defoe must have got his hands on Pitman's *Relation*.

Both narrators, the one real, the other fictional, begin their adventures by enduring a form of slavery and then fleeing in a small boat. Pitman suffers as a "convict felon" before fleeing in his skiff from Barbados; Crusoe starts his adventure by being made a slave by Barbary corsairs. He is aboard a merchant ship captured by the brigands and is brought to the coast of North Africa, where he lives the life of a slave until, after two years, he too begins to think how he can obtain his freedom.

His master has taken a tender from the merchant ship and is using it for day fishing trips. Crusoe now plots to take this tender; he stocks it with a store of food and other supplies, including "a large basket of Rusk or bisket," three jars of water, several bottles of liquor, "a great lump of Bees-Wax which weighed above half a hundred weight, with a Parcel of Twine or Thread, a Hatchet, a Saw and a Hammer, all [of] which were of great use to us afterwards." These tools and supplies that Crusoe prepares bear a strong resemblance to Pitman's real stores list as he gets ready to escape Barbados, and there is an uncanny resonance between Crusoe's "great lump of Bees-Wax," which he uses "to make Candles," and Pitman's stock of ready-made candles, which become "bruised into one mass of tallow."

But it is when Pitman begins to describe his island life on Salt Tortuga that the foretaste of Robinson Crusoe becomes increasingly striking. "Before I proceed to give account of our manner of life in this place,"

Pitman begins, "I think it necessary to give a short description of the island itself." He calculates Salt Tortuga—accurately enough—as being twelve miles in length and two or three broad. The east and west end of the island were sandy "for the most part." The middle consisted of "hard and craggy rocks that are very porous and resemble honeycombs," so the maroons gave them a nickname, Honeycomb Rocks. There were plenty of bushes growing out of the sand, and shrubs between the rocks. But there were no trees. On the southeast corner were found the *salinas,* the salt pans for which the English named the island, though the Spaniards knew the place only as Tortuga, "from the plenty of turtles that resort thither."

These turtles formed "the chiefest of our diet," Pitman remembered. The first priority of the four pirates who had stayed behind was to show the new arrivals how to "turn turtle." Every night the maroons walked quietly along the beach looking for the fresh tracks of the hen turtles. It was important for the castaways to patrol stealthily because a turtle about to emerge from the sea will turn and retreat if startled. Typically a hen turtle goes ashore to lay eggs a few weeks after mating. She hauls herself up the beach on her fore flippers, scrapes out a body pit and deposits in the hole between 50 and 200 glistening white eggs the size and shape of Ping-Pong balls. The female then covers the nest with sand, turns around, and begins to crawl ponderously back to the sea. The whole process takes two to three hours, and leaves a distinctive groove in the sand, with a series of hollows on each side where the front flippers have served as levers to propel the animal forward. Once she is a few yards up the beach, the turtle is helpless. She is even more vulnerable when the laying process has begun and she lies there quietly dropping the egg stream. The hunter has only to turn the turtle on its back—not always an easy task with an animal weighing between 100 and 250 pounds—and the animal is immobilized. This technique works for green turtles but not for hawksbill turtles which are more agile. If overturned, the hawksbills can lever themselves back over again with their flippers and return to the sea.

Pitman and his companions would "turn" their turtle at night and leave the animals where they lay. The next morning they walked back to the spot, either to butcher the animal or, more usually, to build a sun screen over the catch. Properly shaded from the sun, the turtle is able to survive for four or five days, a great advantage to the maroons, who could keep a supply of fresh food ready on demand.

They had difficulty in opening the turtle shells at first, snapping their knife blades as they tried to prize the upper carapace from the plastron, the lower shell. They did better when they replaced the broken knives with heavier, stronger tools they fabricated from the swords they had brought with them. They broke the sword blades "into suitable lengths and softened them in the fire, and then rubbed them on a stone to a fit shape and thinness; and after we had hardened them again, we fixed them in hafts and made them more serviceable than our former [knives]."

Once they had opened the shells, they roasted strips of turtle flesh "by the fire on wooden spits." They found that the meat was "very delightsome and pleasant to the taste, much resembling the veal." For a special treat the maroons took the opened and half-scraped shells and propped them up on forked sticks thrust into the sand, facing the embers. This grilled the edible shell lining, the succulent calapash and calipee. As this was the height of the egg-laying season, April to June, there was an ample supply of turtle. But the maroons were aware that their turtle harvest would soon dwindle and, expecting a long stay, they took the precaution of slicing the surplus turtle meat into fine strips, rubbing them with salt, and then draping the fillets on wooden racks to dry in the sunshine and turn them into biltong or jerky.

Turtles also crawl up on Robinson Crusoe's island as Defoe imagines it. Crusoe explores his island and arrives at a beach some distance from the point where he was wrecked ashore. There he finds that "the shore was covered with innumerable Turtles." Defoe then makes it clear that if Crusoe had come across the turtles sooner, his early days on the island would have been easier. Catching turtles was simpler than hunting wild goats. It is only after Crusoe tames his flock of goats and starts growing crops that he has a more reliable food source. Even then he still needs turtle eggs when he is sick. A fever-stricken Crusoe manages to choke down some goat's meat but gets ready three turtle's eggs by his bed so that when the fever comes back, he can eat the eggs "roasted in the ashes" and washed down with diluted rum.

Sea turtle eggs, Pitman explains to his reader, are "fully as large as hen's eggs, but with this difference that these are round and covered only with a thick strong membrane or skin." He and his colleagues collected the eggs and beat the yolks together in calabashes with some salt. Then they poured the mixture onto a shard of broken pottery they had found lying on the beach and had greased with turtle fat. Using this makeshift skillet they cooked the eggs over the campfire "like pancakes," which they then ate as a substitute for bread.

Their need for a better cook pot—and the difficulty of making it—leads Pitman to one of his most Crusoe-esque details. He explains how he and his companions grew weary of eating their turtle flesh always roasted. They wanted—as did Crusoe in Defoe's story—the choice of being able to cook the flesh as a stew. But they did not have a suitable stew pot. They possessed only "two or three earthen jars left by the privateers, some few calabashes, and shells of fish that we found by the seaside." So the maroons carried out a number of experiments with making their own crockery. They searched for suitable clay or earth but not finding any, they tried mixing "the finest sand with the yolks of turtles' eggs" into a thick paste. To give the paste enough substance for them to mold the pots into shape, they then added goats' hair to the mix (this is the only time Pitman mentions goats on Salt Tortuga, though Dampier said there were goats on the island, "but not many"). Finally they put their clumsy pots out to dry, though whether to bake in the sun or near the fire Pitman does not say. Not surprisingly Pitman admits glumly that "we could not possibly make them endure the drying." The pots collapsed and the maroons had to revert "to eat[ing] our turtle roasted by the fire on wooden spits."

Defoe has Robinson Crusoe follow a similar routine: Crusoe decides he should try making pots, first as storage jars and later to use as a casserole to cook up goat stew. He finds some clay and begins trying to make the shapes. But, he allows, "It would make the Reader pity me, or rather laugh at me, to tell how many awkward ways I took to raise this Paste, what odd misshapen ugly things I made, how many fell in, and how many fell out, the Clay not being stiff enough to bear its own weight." After many trials and bungled attempts recalling Pitman's experience, Crusoe finally succeeds in making "two large earthen ugly things, I cannot call them Jarrs" by baking them in the sun. By chance a shard of this earthenware is hardened into a glaze in the embers of his fire, and he then goes on to make a fire-resistant pot to cook his stew.

Crusoe echoes Pitman's tale again when he uses his new pottery skills to make a clay tobacco pipe. Crusoe had "been used to smoke." He finds wild tobacco growing on his island and regrets that he has not salvaged any tobacco pipes from the wreck of his ship. He turns his hand to making a crude pipe. It was "a very ugly clumsy thing when it was done . . . yet it was hard and firm and would draw the Smoke, [and] I was exceedingly comforted with it." Thirty years earlier Pitman had reported how he and his companions discovered on Salt Tortuga a substitute for tobacco. "There is" he wrote, "a pleasant fragrant herb [which] grows out of the sand among the rocks which we call Wild Sage whose leaves we smoked instead of tobacco." Lacking the clay and skill to make Crusoe's rough clay pipe, Pitman satisfied his craving by gathering wild sage and then "for want of a pipe I smoked it in a crab's claw."

Crusoe-style turtles, tool and pot making, and wild tobacco are joined on Salt Tortuga by a Man Friday figure. He is the Indian whom Pitman had ransomed from the pirates. Yanche's men had brought the captive to Salt Tortuga from the adjacent mainland, and Pitman purchased him, thinking the Indian would have useful survival skills. Now, Pitman records, "I went abroad with my Indian a-fishing, at which he was so dextrous that with his bow and arrow he would shoot a small fish at a great distance." When Pitman is not fishing or exploring the island on foot, he and his colleagues spend "most of our time" in their huts "sometimes reading or writing"; Crusoe did likewise. They also walked inland to gather wild fruit; so did Robinson Crusoe. On Salt Tortuga the fruit came in the form of small red berries "about the bigness of a small nut, in taste resembling a strawberry," which they found embedded in the body of a low cactus they called Turk's heads.

Ziska's voyage had already demonstrated that Pitman's account of how he had arrived on Salt Tortuga was credible. The course he and his colleagues had taken in the little skiff when they fled from Barbados was correct. The passage time to Margarita and on to Salt Tortuga matched the prevailing winds and currents. The main features he gave for the island—its size, location, and so forth—were all reasonably accurate. But these were details Pitman could have taken from a sea chart or gleaned secondhand, and then added to his yarn to make it seem more authentic. If I was to consider seriously the possibility that Pitman's astonishing tale was a major source for the adventures of Robinson Crusoe, then I had to be sure that Pitman's story was itself genuine. The events themselves—the midnight escape in the open boat, the cruel marooning at the hands of Yanche's men, the climactic reversal of fortune when the second set of pirates arrives—were so dramatic that they were worthy of Robinson Crusoe, but also they were so far-fetched that they could be fiction. Was Pitman's yarn a pure fabrication like Defoe's? Had someone invented this resourceful surgeon who escapes from slavery and lives on a desert island? If the details in Pitman's story were pinpoint accurate, then his story was likely to be true. If, however, the reality of Tortuga did not match Pitman's description, then the surgeon's adventures could be considered no more real than the *Strange Surprizing Adventures of Robinson Crusoe*, written "by himself." Defoe, writing in haste, famously trips up on several key details—at one stage he misplaces "Crusoe's island" by ten degrees of latitude and has to correct the error in a later edition of his book, and at another point he switches latitude with longitude and confuses the equator with the International Date Line.

On the morning after our arrival on Salt Tortuga, Trondur, Tristan, and I set out to explore the island. Ash, true to form, preferred to stay behind on his beloved *Ziska* and work on the upkeep of his yacht.

We began our trek at the carmine-red wreck of the yacht. The broken hull lay five minutes' walk along the floury white sand to the west of us, where the rocks began. The vessel had once been someone's dream. "*–IBERTY* Austria" was written across her stern. Now the vessel was a ruin. The waves had tossed it up on the ironbound shore. At high tide the water sluiced in and out noisily through a great hole punched in the port side. The mast had long since been plundered. Every single item of deck gear, even down to the hatch covers, had been stripped off her. She lay a bare, battered hull whose fiber-glass skin was starting to flake in the sun. I was reminded of the hulk the pirates left Pitman and his colleagues after they had stolen all the gear and sails. If fiber-glass burned more easily, I imagined, *IBERTY* would have been set on fire by her scavengers.

We had been warned in Margarita that to go exploring on Tortuga, we needed three things: a compass, a supply of drinking water, and stout footwear. Walking inland from the wrecked yacht with our bottle of water, the reasons for the advice became clear. The landscape stretched out bleak and flat before us. A few low knolls were too far away and insignificant to be much use as landmarks. The vegetation was uniform—low scrub, a few bushes, no trees. It was exactly as Pitman had described. Overhead the sky was a washed-out blue with dragged-out wisps of high cirrus, and a heat haze was beginning to develop. There was a feeling of utter emptiness, as if a portion of the Australian outback had been dropped down on the rim of the Caribbean.

Only the wind gave a general sense of direction. It came steadily from our left—the east—not strong but rustling across the scrub and providing a strangely hollow sensation with its insistent presence. Sharper sounds—the rattle of a stone under foot, the distant twitter of an unseen bird—seemed to vanish upward into the empty sky. There was no moisture. Every plant was adapted to surviving drought. Some cut evaporation to a minimum. Their few leaves were small or shriveled into spines. Others stored fluid in their fleshy bodies. Most hugged the ground defensively. The dominant colors were drab, the bleached grays and browns of an arid land.

We walked gingerly. The surface of the ground was rough plates of rock, the split and shattered remnants of ancient coral. The plates were loose. They shifted and tilted beneath our weight. Every time a rock slipped and struck against its neighbor, there was a flat clattering sound as if metal struck metal. The surfaces of the rocks were pockmarked and rough, their edges sawtoothed. None of us owned the heavy walking boots we had been advised to procure, and we were wearing sandals. Within half an hour the leading edges of the heavy sandals I wore were shredded. I wondered at the fortitude of Pitman and his colleagues. They had walked clear across the island to reach the *salinas* and fetch salt for preserving the dried turtle. They carried their water in a cask and "those uneven rocks . . . soon wore out our shoes and compelled us to make use of our soft and tender feet." It was "very irksome" Pitman recalled rather lightly. Then, as the weeks passed, "the bottoms of our feet were hardened into such a callous substance that there were scarcely any rocks so hard but we could boldly trample them."

He made no mention of the loose spines from the Turk's heads (*Melocactus caesius*). They lay strewn across the ground like caltrops, the spikes scattered on the ground to lame cavalry horses. Each spine was as long and thin and piercing as a hypodermic needle. Every few paces, one of us came to a sudden halt, usually with a grunt of pain, and stooped down to remove a spine that had driven clean through half an inch of a sandal's hardened rubber sole and into the foot, drawing blood. The sources of these barbs were everywhere. The Turk's heads sat on the ground like bloated pineapples, topped with a fuzzy crown like a turban.

The bulbous main body of the plant bristled with spikes. When it grew old and collapsed, yet more spikes could be seen, pointing inward into the rotted heart. Some of the healthy ones, however, were in fruit. Buried deep within the pale mauve turban was a pinpoint of red, the gleam of the berry. With the blade of a penknife we prized out the fruits, the size of a small hawthorn hip, and ate them. The taste was blackberry crossed with strawberry. Once again, Pitman's description was correct.

We came across another species of cactus, *Agave cocui,* a plant Pitman said he had used for medicine. He described it as having "an oval body or stump . . . [and] out this grew long thick leaves whose edges were prickly and its juice so exceeding sharp and pungent that it was not easily suffered on the bare skin." Pitman boiled up the leaves with turtle fat, added beeswax to the mix, and used the mush as a "most excellent balsom [poultice] for wounds." The maroons showed great ingenuity. Fibers from the leaves provided thread for stitching, the astringent juice became a soap for washing their clothes, and by burying the body of the cactus in hot sand for five or six days they managed to get the juice to ferment, so it could be used as alcohol. It tasted "like the syrup of baked pears," and they ate "the innermost part of the body or stump. . . like bread." The maroons had displayed an adaptability worthy of Robinson Crusoe, though when we tasted the cactus flesh, it was like munching tough cotton wool. Perhaps we should have cooked it first.

We found no other food in the wasteland except for some bright-scarlet pods on a low bush. They hung in spirals and when the pods split open revealed a row of black seeds surrounded by a soft sweet white pith that tasted like lichee. We nibbled on the seeds while the small birds, resembling larks and finches, who had been feeding on the seeds sat in the shrubs and scolded us.

It took two hours to walk across the island and reach the salt pans, in a small valley crusted with a gray, cracked soft sand, where you had to tread carefully to avoid breaking through the soft surface. This was not the season for salt gathering, and the *salinas* were mixed with mud and roots of mangroves. Here the southern half of the island had risen to a slight elevation, never more than 120 feet, so there were gullies and an occasional rock slope, but it was still a very bare terrain. Salt Tortuga has been racked by earthquakes and battered by hurricanes in the last century, so the present topography is not identical to its contours in the days when foreign ships came to load salt from this corner of the island. But the long and shallow inlet adjacent to the *salinas* and now called Laguna el Carenero—Careenage Lagoon—was the obvious shelter for the visitors.

We did not linger among the *salinas*. The soggy ground with its mangrove swamp was mosquito territory, and we wanted to be well clear before the insects emerged at dusk. Our return route took us in a loop along the eastern rim of the island. Here a spectacular reef guarded the shore, white surf spilling over into a shallow lagoon. It was noticeable that the wildlife of the island preferred the coastal zone. Small flocks of green parakeets burst shrieking from the scanty bushes. Pelicans wheeled and crash-dived just beyond the reef and then returned to rest on land. Terns spiraled delicately off the ground ahead of us as we approached, using the steady wind to gain altitude, hovering delicately over our heads, then settling down on the rocks behind us after we had passed, rearranging their wing feathers with little flicks of irritation. They were in no hurry. Clearly they did not encounter humans often enough to be made wary of them.

By the time we regained *Ziska's* anchorage, we were hot, tired, and thirsty.

We had been walking for four hours in the hot sun, and had drunk the last of our water when the needle of *Ziska's* mast came in view. There was no mistaking it in that flat and featureless landscape. "Faced with this place," Tristan commented as we crossed one particularly bleak patch, "I think I would have joined the pirates rather than be left marooned here. It is a hopeless place."

The maroons had been on Salt Tortuga for three months when a heavily armed ship and an attendant small sloop were seen approaching. The four pirates who had stayed behind from Yanche's raiding party recognized the newcomers as fellow pirates; they identified the vessels and stood on the beach and signaled. The larger vessel, it turned out, had come to pick them up after meeting the rest of their group. The captain of the pirate ship asked Pitman to come on board. As a surgeon, he would be a valuable addition to the crew, and the captain offered him a berth. Naturally Pitman requested that the captain also take along his seven fellow refugees from Barbados. But this could only be decided by a vote of the entire pirate crew. They "were called together, and after some debates they voted they would take me with them, but none of my companions." The reason for this flint-hearted decision was that the pirates had recently taken part in the capture of a large, well-laden Portuguese ship, and any additional crew members would share in the final division of the booty. Pitman's seven luckless companions were therefore left on the beach, though the pirates "were so kind that they sent them a cask of wine, some bread and cheese, a gammon of bacon," and also "some linen cloth, thread and needles to make them shirts etc." The maroons had been reduced to repairing their clothing with thread made from cactus fiber and needles made of fishbones. The pirate ship then "set sail," wrote Pitman, "leaving my companions on the island, not a little grieved at my departure."

If this colorful episode caught Defoe's attention by appealing to his love for tales of pirate skulduggery, the letter Pitman received some time later would have made an even more powerful impression. The letter reached Pitman when he was back in London and compiling the narrative of his adventures. He had tried to find out what happened to his former colleagues left behind on the island, and received an answer from Whicker. "Dear Doctor," the note began, "In answer to your request, I have given you the following account."

The story that Whicker narrated was so remarkable that Pitman reprinted it in full.

"About a fortnight after you left us," Whicker wrote, "two of our companions, John Nuthall and Thomas Walker left us." These two were the undischarged debtors, and they had never managed to get along with the "convict rebels." The two of them "made sails of the cloth that the privateers left us." They also refurbished the hulk of the Spanish boat that had been lying on the beach ever since they first arrived, made it seaworthy, and set sail from the beach, "designing for Curaçao." They were never heard from again. Whicker suspected that "the boat was so large and unruly and they so unskilful in navigation that I fear they either perished at sea or were driven ashore on the Main."

Now just five of the original maroons remained on the island: Whicker, Bagwell, Woodcock, Cooke, and Jeremiah Atkins.

The very next day, unknown to them, a small vessel dropped anchor in a bay seven miles to the east of their camp. On board were eight white men and a negro—yet more pirates—who had been heading for Tobago, missed their course, and finished up on Salt Tortuga. Now, short of food and water, they came ashore to recuperate. On the beach some days later, they came across a cache of salted turtle meat. It had been left by Whicker and the other maroons from Barbados to keep dry under a turtle shell. The new arrivals thought nothing more about it at the time. The cache of food could have been left by a crew who had already left the island, and there was no one in sight.

Three of the newly arrived pirates were "very unprincipled and loose kind of fellows." They hatched a plot to rob their shipmates of their plunder, steal the boat, and make off, leaving their colleagues marooned. The plotters were in a minority, so they waited until three of their colleagues were away for the day, exploring inland. Then the three conspirators quietly went out to their vessel, collected up all the weapons, and returning ashore came "to the hut where the other two were, and presented a pistol to each of their breasts and swore, "If they would not carry everything aboard, they were dead men!"

The two men, "being surprised" as well as unarmed, "were forced to comply and carry all aboard."

The three men who had gone off to explore had been suspicious enough to take the precaution of hiding their plunder by burying it in the sand. The plotters waited for their return so they could find out where their loot was hidden. The plotters held all the firearms, so they expected little trouble. They warned the two men they had already robbed that "they would make them examples" if they did not inform them when the three missing crew members returned. Then they went back aboard their ship, taking all the food and water containers with them.

In the evening the three men who had been exploring the island came back to their hut. They had failed to find anything to eat or drink during their walk, and were hungry and very thirsty. They found their hut had been ransacked and stripped bare. Their two distraught colleagues told them that they had been betrayed.

Desperate for something to drink, one of the men went down to the beach and called out to the plotters on the boat, begging for some water. His companions hid.

The plotters called back that they would bring some water and came ashore, but then they seized the man, tied his hands with a length of line, and went looking for the other two.

While they were searching, their prisoner managed to extricate a knife from his pocket, cut the cord binding his wrists, and ran off.

It was at this stage that he remembered the cache of dried turtle. In the faint hope that this might indicate there were other men somewhere on Salt Tortuga, the runaway set out to look for them. "Having travelled about the island until almost ready to faint," Whicker wrote, "he came near our huts." There he saw the five maroons from Barbados. They were busy preparing turtle meat, each man with "nothing on but a pair of drawers." For a moment the runaway came to a halt and stood there fearfully. He thought the maroons were Indians because after three months in the sunshine "we were tanned with the sun almost as yellow."

"At length, he advanced," continues Whicker, "and enquired if we were Englishmen, [which] We told him We were. Then he begged for a little water, which we gave him and some of our turtle."

The runaway now explained his plight and pleaded for help. Whicker and the others readily agreed to assist. They gathered up their muskets and blunderbusses, and walked through the night to the place where the pirate vessel was anchored. There they spread out and hid among the bushes and waited for dawn.

The runaway had told them that early each morning the plotters came ashore to fetch water, presumably from a well or soak they had dug above the high-tide mark. "Morning being come," wrote Whicker, he and his companions saw two of the pirates get ready to leave the ship. They were carrying guns and were accompanied by the negro with the water container.

Whicker and the others waited in ambush until the watering party were ashore, then they showed themselves "with our arms ready cocked." The pirates were taken completely off-guard and were captured without a fight.

Whicker and his colleagues then marched their two prisoners down to the water's edge and showed them to the third of the plotters, who had been left aboard with twelve muskets ready loaded. They called out to him not to fire, but to "jump overboard and swim ashore to us, which he immediately did."

Whicker ends his story briskly. "So taking them all three prisoners, we put them ashore, leaving them some of our provisions. The rest we put aboard in order to prosecute our voyage for New England. So victualling and watering our small frigate in the best manner we could, we left them upon the island, and on the 24th of August [1687] we took our departure from Saltatudos."

Whicker's adventurous escape from Salt Tortuga and Pitman's life as a maroon on a desert island vanished into obscurity for the next two centuries. Then in the 1870s a literary sleuth trawled up Pitman's little book. Edward Arber, a devoted bibliophile, cast his net widely. He abandoned a career as a civil servant at the Admiralty so as to devote his time promoting the merits of English literature of the seventeenth century. He took a job as a university lecturer and began to track down and reissue "at as cheap a price as can be, exact texts, sometimes of books already famous, sometimes of those quite forgotten." When he came across Pitman's slim volume and read how Whicker managed to leave the island, Arber was immediately reminded of Defoe's account of Robinson Crusoe's escape from his island.

In Defoe's tale, Crusoe gets his chance to leave his island when a merchant ship drops anchor near the shore. A small boat heads for the beach. From hiding, Robinson sees that there are eleven men in the boat, and three of them are prisoners. The landing party walks inland, leaving their captives unguarded, and Robinson approaches the three prisoners. He learns that they are the captain of the ship, the mate, and a passenger. The rest of the crew, led by the bosun, have mutinied and seized the ship and are about to maroon their prisoners. Crusoe frees the captain and his men, defeats the landing party with Friday's help, and by series of ruses deals with rest of the mutineers when they come ashore looking for their missing companions. The episode ends with the captain restored to command of his ship, and Crusoe and Friday taking passage for England with their souvenirs, including a goatskin umbrella and a parrot. They leave the bamboozled mutineers marooned on the beach, led by the chief ruffian, Will Atkins.

Arber reprinted the text of *A Relation of the great suffering and strange adventures of Henry Pitman, Chirurgeon*, and inserted a personal note into the text. In it he drew attention to the striking similarity between Crusoe's fictional escape from his island and Whicker's real departure from Salt Tortuga. He also noted the coincidence that the leading villain among Crusoe's mutineers was named Will Atkins, and there was a Jeremiah Atkins among the maroons on Salt Tortuga. At the point in the text of Pitman's book where Whicker and his fellow maroons turn the tables on the pirates and then sail away from Tortuga leaving them ashore with some provisions, Arber—by then Professor Arber—placed a question in brackets:

[? Did DEFOE get his idea of WILL. ATKINS etc from this]

For me the walk across Salt Tortuga succeeded in defining and vali-
dating Pitman's geography. I now knew exactly where Whicker and his
colleagues ambushed the pirates and seized their ship. It was at the
same anchorage where *Ziska* now awaited us, the spot on the beach,
Playa Caldera, where we had eaten Trondur's roast booby. Playa
Caldera was where Whicker and his four colleagues hid behind the
dunes until the pirates came ashore, then took them by surprise. It was
the first anchorage on Salt Tortuga when one approached from the
east, and this fitted with Whicker's assertion in his letter that the pirate
ship had been bound for Tobago but missed its course. More important, Playa Caldera was correctly placed in relation to the place where
Pitman and his colleagues must have first come ashore, lured by
Yanche's men.

Pitman's original camp was seven miles farther east. He described
how his little skiff arrived close off Salt Tortuga in the dawn, and then
"we steered down the north side of it," looking for a place to land until
"we came to the leeward of a small island hard by the other." Here the
exhausted crew "stood in directly for the shore, thinking it a convenient
place to land," only to find the spot already occupied by a camp of
Yanche's men.

The modern chart confirms Pitman's description so exactly that I
guessed he had been keeping a logbook of his journey.

Halfway along the north shore of Tortuga is "the small island." The
Palanquinos Reef shows above water as two or three small islets, Los
Palanquinos, that create a protected anchorage in their lee. Directly opposite Los Palanquinos, on Salt Tortuga itself, is a wide sand promon-
tory, a low dune ridge, and an ideal campsite. From here Whicker and
his comrades marched through the night carrying their blunderbusses
and muskets to lay their ambush at Playa Caldera.

Late that afternoon *Ziska* sailed to Los Palanquinos, directly in the
wake of Pitman's leaky skiff. With a following wind we glided along the

coast of Salt Tortuga until we came into the shelter of the islets, and there dropped anchor. As if we had been expected, someone—passing fishermen, probably—had lashed together a temporary hut on the sand spit. It was a simple shelter of bamboo poles in the classic cone shape of a tepee. The cloth covering had long since gone, and the structure stood there like modern icon for "campsite."

That evening we clambered on the rocks of Los Palanquinos. With Trondur's guidance it was easy to understand how maroons and castaways could survive in that location, even though there are no turtles now on Salt Tortuga's magnificent sweep of beach. Pitman wrote of catching crawfish and described how "for change of diet we sometimes ate a small sort of shellfish that live on the rocks, and are like snails, but much larger, called Wilks"—whelks. We caught no crawfish but many crabs. Trondur dropped a rag over them as they scuttled clear of their hiding places, and he and Ash collected half a bucket of crabs in half an hour. For variety they then gathered a selection of the "wilks," some of them three inches across, and sea urchins. Trondur, shaggy as a musk ox and up to his shins in the seawater, stooping to turn over rocks, then pouncing on his prey, made the perfect Crusoe image.

Tristan and I spent the next day ashore, investigating the natural campsite. Just behind the dune ridge we found the skeleton of a slightly more substantial hut, a couple of vertical wooden posts bleached gray by the sun, and a couple of slumped rails. Rooting around in the scrub and rubbish, Tristan came across the desiccated leg of a small goat, the hair still on it. Clearly this spot was still used by whoever came to use the island, though it was deserted now. We could find no trace of a well, so either the visitor brought water for the goats or, more likely, dug a shallow well which was now dry. A modern castaway no longer need trudge across the island to find salt. On the edge of the sea and fifty yards away from the abandoned hut, Tristan found a bowl-shaped hollow in the rocks which the storm spray had filled with seawater. Now it contained a soft layer of pure salt, white above and pink below.

After the scenes of other shipwrecks and maroonings in Nicaragua, Honduras and Juan Fernandez I could see why Pitman and his companions had chosen to remain at Los Palanquinos. Here was a ready supply of food on the shoreline, a well dug by Yanche's pirates, and a broad expanse of turtle nesting beach to the east. Less obvious was the source of firewood and building materials on an island devoid of large trees. The patterns of tides and currents had not changed, and the sea still deposited all manner of offerings—lengths of timber, old ropes and scraps of fishing nets, and the battered plastic detritus of a modern age. The sand spit at Los Palanquinos was littered with flotsam. To the maroons it was the vital bounty of the sea.

Our search of the natural campsite done, Tristan and I sat on the slope of the beach dune, facing out toward *Ziska* anchored in the lee of the reef. In the foreground, stark on the white expanse of the sand spit, was the bamboo tepee. A line of pelicans stood gravely at the water's edge, making a brown frieze against the blue-green of the Caribbean. It was a stage setting for a castaway story, even if the spot had not matched Pitman's detailed description so exactly. I brought out my camera and held it to my eye. As I looked through the lens, a blurred shadow passed across the image. Thinking it was the camera strap being blown by the wind, I brushed my hand across the lens. There was a light tickling sensation. Puzzled, I held the camera to one side and turned my hand. Clinging to it, and staring at me with bright eyes, was a small emerald-green and gray lizard. I put my hand to the ground and the little creature scuttled off. We had seen these little lizards on our walk across the island, but they had always flickered off as we approached, darting away and hiding in the rock crevices. At Los Palanquinos the lizards reacted very differently. As Tristan and I sat there, more and more lizards appeared, creeping and darting and dodging among the matted stalks and fleshy rice-grain leaves of the pink and yellow sea samphire which covered the dune face. What attracted the lizards I could not tell. Normally so shy, here these creatures were friendly and curious. Soon they were hopping up onto our feet, running up our legs, scuttling along our arms, climbing into our hair.

"Another little insect is worthy to be mentioned, called Lizards," Pitman wrote. "They were so familiar and friendly that they would come boldly among us and do us no harm." Their bodies were "adorned with divers delightsome colours" and they pleased the maroons by feeding on flies and "for that reason they were serviceable to us." The lizards were "so very tame that, when we were eating, they would come on our meat and hands to catch flies."

With lizards climbing through my hair and resting on my shirt collar, it was easy to sense the maroons' pleasure in the society of these tiny, iridescent companions. For me it was the final clinching detail: unless Henry Pitman, maroon and surgeon to the Duke of Monmouth, had himself lived on that beach, there was no way he could have known about the friendly lizards of Salt Tortuga.

My visit to Salt Tortuga had established the veracity of Henry Pitman's claim that he had lived as a true marooner on Salt Tortuga. Now, I still had two more islands to investigate.

Aves, "the Island of Birds," was directly on Henry Pitman's intended route to refuge in Dutch-held Curaçao. Lying 160 miles northwest of Salt Tortuga, the island is correctly shown on the map in Dampier's *New Voyage Round the World*, from which Defoe seems to have quarried much of his Caribbean geography. Dampier also provides a graphic account of the greatest maritime disaster of the age, a catastrophe that made Aves the temporary home to more than fifteen hundred castaways.

About midnight of 11 May 1678, a French invasion fleet crashed headlong into a six-mile-long reef that reaches out in a great hook to the north and then west of Aves. Vice Admiral the Comte d'Estrées had been steering for an attack on Dutch-held Curaçao. Close behind his imposing flagship, *Le Terrible,* came the most powerful naval force in the West Indies, comprising thirty-five vessels, including the royal warships *Le Tormant, Le Belliqueux, Le Bourbon, Le Prince,* and *Le Hercule.* They were on a night passage, and with a "soldier's wind"—a following wind—from the east they should have had no difficulty in bringing the troop transports to their target. Accounts differ as to why eighteen of the ships piled up so tragically on the coral, but the most common explanation is that a privateer ship acting as scout led *Le Terrible* to her destruction. About half the French fleet were mercenaries—ships hired for the campaign or privateers who had joined up in hopes of plunder. The identity of the fatal bellwether is unknown but she came up on the reef, struck, and was rapidly followed by *Le Terrible*. According to Dampier, the vice admiral fired guns to warn the rest of the fleet of the danger and to tell them to stand clear. But the ships following mistook the sound of the guns to mean that their leader had engaged the enemy. Instead they "hoisted up their Topsails, and crouded all sails they could make, and ran full sail ashore after him."

Le Terrible had a light burning at the masthead as she lay shattered on the Aves reef, and her consorts mistook the light as a beacon. In rapid succession they crunched into the coral "all within half a mile of each other." Some accounts say three hundred and others five hundred died in the havoc. Slower and less disciplined vessels bringing up the rear had enough sea room to change course and save themselves. Many of the hired ships made little effort to help the castaways and left the scene of the disaster.

There was so much wreckage on Aves that for years afterward, pirate vessels came to the reef for their refit. They anchored nearby and sent men on to the coral to salvage "masts, yards, timbers." Dampier's own captain, Peter Wright, helped himself to two cannons from the wrecks.

For the castaways, the weather was calm enough for the impaled vessels to stay intact for most of the following day. Sailors and soldiers swam or waded ashore. Some were collected by ships that had lingered safely in deeper water, but many of the other castaways had to wait up to three weeks to be rescued. The landsmen and navy personnel were not "accustomed to such hardships" wrote Dampier, and they "died like rotten sheep." By contrast, the privateers who had been shipwrecked thrived. Dampier talked with some of them and they told him they "could not have enjoyed themselves more." Being wrecked on the reef was better than going to Jamaica "with 30 pounds a man in their pockets." These privateers watched the doomed ships break up and spill their cargo, and they calculated where the flotsam would wash ashore. Then they moved in a "Gang" and stationed themselves so that they were at just the right place, like vultures. "Though much was staved against the Rocks," Dampier reported, "yet abundance of Wine and Brandy floated over the reef, where the Privateers waited to take it up." In the three weeks before the privateers were evacuated, "they were never without 2 or 3 hogsheads of Wine and Brandy in their tents, and barrels of Beef and Pork." Forty Frenchmen stayed on one of the wrecked ships, broke into the liquor store, and got completely drunk, though whether in celebration or to drown their fears it was not clear. They were so intoxicated that they did not stir when the wreck began to break apart. The section of the ship on which they were carousing floated over the reef and out to sea "with all the Men drinking and singing, who being in drink did not mind the danger, but were never heard of afterwards."

In 1998 a diving team found traces of nine vessels from the lost d'Estrées's fleet in less than thirty feet of water. Now more birdwatchers than wreck hunters visit Aves. The island has regained its more auspicious reputation as a roost for vast numbers of seabirds.

Ziska took only twenty-four hours to sail from Salt Tortuga to Aves, more properly called Aves de Barlovento, or Windward Aves, to distinguish it from its smaller neighbor, Aves de Sotavento or Leeward Aves. With her own "soldier's wind" the little yacht covered the distance so briskly that we had to reduce sail and slow her down to reduce the risk of repeating d'Estrées's misadventure and colliding with "the back of the Riff" in the dark. The dawn showed a low green island that was clearly a place for good fishing, both for birds and for men. Two small Venezuelan motor fishing vessels lay at anchor in the lee of the island, and as I clambered high into *Ziska*'s rigging to peer down at the coral patches and wave directions to Ash at the helm, a succession of shrieking gulls darted round my head, irritated by our intrusion.

With the yacht neatly anchored on a patch of sand between the coral ledges, we took the little dinghy to investigate whether the Island of Birds could have provided a home for Crusoe in Defoe's imagined Caribbean world.

It was an eerie place. The island is very small, barely two miles long and two hundred yards wide. The western end is, as Dampier said, "plain even savannah land without any trees." Here the privateersmen dug two or three wells to supply them while they careened ships in an anchorage on the northern side. The remainder of the island is now covered with dense thickets of mangrove, some of it growing thirty or forty feet high, above which rise the tops of a few larger trees. Small, shallow backwaters penetrate the forest of mangrove. The water was the color of pale whiskey and the bottom a sickly yellow that at first sight looked like fine sand. But step on it and the foot sank in slickly up to the knee. It was a slime of bird dung.

Guano blotched the mangrove foliage. In places it was only a few droplets, elsewhere broad splatters and splashes streaked wide swaths of leaves. Sitting in the bushes were the seabirds. They were roosting in their hundreds upon hundreds until it seemed that the mangroves were some bizarre kind of mythical tree that grows avian fruit. The vast majority of the birds were red-footed boobies, and we found them in every stage of growth. There were fat chicks covered in pure white fluffy down, larger than a rugby ball but with the slumped profile of a badly filled bean bag. They squatted on untidy piles of feces-whitened sticks and waited to be fed. Mistaking the movement of our dinghy as the return of their parents, the black eyes would register our presence, a head swiveled, and the beak, black against white, gaped expectantly. Mixed among the chicks were molting fledglings showing two black diagonals of their future wing feathers. They were even bigger and plumper than their siblings. Then came the juvenile birds. They were slim and glossy, with ash-gray beaks and bright shoe-button eyes. They seemed athletic and debonair, until they attempted to fly. Launching themselves from a branch, their svelte elegance turned to desperation as they flapped urgently to gain speed and avoid striking the tepid water. Like novice ice skaters pushing off from the side of the rink and taking unsteady strides before gliding away, the young birds beat their wings in panic, often tipping the water before gaining a few feet of altitude and heading out to sea to learn to fish for themselves. All of the creatures, whether babies, fledglings, or adults, scarcely stirred on their branches as we gently glided among the mangroves. Most striking of all were the boobies' feet. They were broad and webbed and, at first sight, not designed for gripping a roosting branch. Yet they curled around their roosts, and the array of prehensile booby feet looked remarkably like a line of coral pink rubber kitchen gloves.

Trondur had harpooned a medium-sized shark on our passage from Salt Tortuga, so we had plenty of food aboard and no need of "castaway's supplies." But as we passed row upon row of fat and succulent booby chicks, each butterball waiting in arm's reach, Trondur must have felt he was in nature's supermarket checking out the shelves. No castaway could have gone hungry with such a ready source of sea-bird flesh and eggs, but it would have been a fetid and eerie existence. The air had the smell of guano, a slightly metallic tang, and there was a creepy lack of sound. Apart from the occasional raucous bird call, some chattering and clacking, the vast assembly of seabirds just sat and stared.

There were even more boobies roosting on the island before the French fleet was wrecked. D'Estrées's men ate so many of them that "their numbers have been much lessened." Yet it is calculated that more than a thousand of the castaways died of exposure, starvation, and injuries sustained while clawing their way across the coral heads. Aves, I concluded, was as Dampier had described—a place where an abysmal maritime catastrophe had created a freak situation. The Island of Birds was not a location to inspire the idea of Robinson Crusoe the survivor.

The third island on my list provided its surprise. I had imagined a low, whale-backed sand bank barely rising above water level, littered with shells, waterless and grim in the vast expanse of sea. Instead I found a pocket Shangri-la.

The Serrana Bank, a formation of shoals and low cays 250 miles out in the western Caribbean off the northeast coast of Nicaragua, is named after its own castaway. Pedro Serrano was shipwrecked there in the first half of the sixteenth century—the date is uncertain—and his survival story is so extreme as to beggar belief. He maintained that he lived for seven years on an island *that had no fresh water*. It was "a historic feat worthy of the greatest admiration" observed the historian who recorded the story, Garcilaso de la Vega. De la Vega, an often-reliable chronicler of early Spanish America, had heard the castaway's tale from a colleague who had met Pedro Serrano in person and said it was true. Garcilaso checked the map of the Caribbean, located the island, and saw no reason to doubt the castaway's claim.

Serrano recounted that he survived for the first few days by drinking the blood of turtles. Sole survivor of a shipwreck, he swam ashore to find that the island was totally barren. It had neither water nor wood for fuel nor "even grass he could graze upon." It was entirely "covered with bare sand." He circled the island, which he said was about "two leagues" (about five miles) in circumference, and came across enough crabs and shellfish to provide him with food. That evening the sea turtles crawled up to lay their eggs. He caught one "and drawing a knife he used to wear in his belt, and which saved his life, he drank its blood instead of water." He then caught and killed as many turtles as possible, opened their shells for the meat, and laid the turtle shells out on the ground, facing the sky to collect any rain. Some of the turtles were so huge that he could not turn them over. When he tried jumping on their backs they simply carried him into the sea. He managed to capture others whose shells could hold as much as eight gallons of collected rainwater.

Pedro Serrano then turned his attention to making fire. He had his knife blade to use as a steel, so searched around for a stone to make a flint. But there were no stones on his sandy refuge and he had to swim around the fringe of his island, diving down to the sea floor and collecting up all the pebbles he could find. These he brought ashore and tested until he found one that struck sparks. Ripping up his shirt to provide tinder, he succeeded in making a fire, which he carefully sheltered from the frequent rains by building over it a structure of turtle shells. For fuel he collected everything that washed up—"weeds called sea pods, timber from ships lost at sea, shells, fish bones, and other material to feed his fire." When he could no longer endure the scorching sun on an island that offered no shade, Pedro Serrano waded into the sea and submerged himself. Within two months the castaway "was as naked as he was born, for the great rain, the heat, and the humidity of the region rotted the few clothes he had." From time to time he saw passing ships and lit a signal fire, but they either ignored the plume of smoke or failed to see it, and the vessels passed on. Slowly the naked castaway changed into a wild man. Serrano's body adapted to the constant exposure by growing extra hair. His beard and hair grew immensely longer, and his body hair sprouted until it covered him in a thick pelt.

After three years of this strange existence, Serrano had a unsettling shock. "One afternoon when he was not expecting anything, he saw a man on the island," wrote Garcilaso. The stranger ran away in terror, he was so aghast at Serrano's shaggy appearance. Serrano, thinking that the stranger was the Devil come to tempt him, also ran off, shouting "Jesus! Jesus! Oh Lord, deliver me from the demon!" When the stranger heard this, he turned back and shouted out the Credo to prove that he too was a Christian. The two men approached one another, and Serrano learned that the stranger was another castaway. He had been wrecked the previous night and saved himself by floating on a plank. When he saw the smoke from Serrano's fire, he paddled ashore.

Serrano gave food and water to the newcomer, and they agreed to take it in turns to do the tasks of collecting flotsam, gathering shellfish, and guarding the precious fire. "They lived in this way for some days," Garcilaso continues, "but it was not long before they quarrelled and so violently that they lived apart and nearly came to blows." The reason for the altercation was that each accused the other of not doing his chores properly. In the end, however, the two castaways made up their differences and shared their small domain amicably for another four years. Finally a passing vessel did spot their signal smoke, and sent a small boat to collect them. By then both the castaways had grown their extraordinary body fur, and Serrano's beard had reached a spectacular length. Remembering the alarm that his appearance had already caused, Serrano and his companion stood on the beach calling out the Credo and shouting out Christ's name as their rescuers approached.

The tactic worked and they were brought aboard, but Serrano's unnamed companion did not live to enjoy his rescue. He died at sea while returning to Spain, leaving Serrano to make his way to court to be presented to the emperor. The fame of the shaggy castaway went before him. Nobles paid his traveling expenses and Serrano made extra money by exhibiting his hairy body to villagers along his route. He so impressed the emperor—presumably Charles V—that Serrano received a pension of four thousand pesos, to be collected in Peru. But Serrano never got to collect his pension. On his way back to South America he died in Panama. By then, said Garcilaso, he had grown so irked by the length of his beard that he had cut it short, just above his waist. Otherwise, the immense beard spread over his bed and disturbed his sleep.

In many ways Pedro Serrano sounds like a fraud. His progress as a human freak show collecting money from credulous onlookers is particularly suspicious. On the other hand, there is no reason to think that, with weather luck, he could not have survived on rainwater collected in turtle shells. The fishermen who set up temporary camps on Salt Tortuga used to catch and store rainwater in large, upturned conch shells. A single large turtle shell holds enough collected fresh water to last ten days, and the rainfall on the Serrana Bank is sufficiently well distributed throughout the seasons to refill the shells if the rain showers fall in the right place.

Having given Pedro Serrano the benefit of the doubt, we sailed 800 miles slightly north of west to reach his island. It was a direct passage from Aves de Barlovento, quick, uncomfortable, and largely uneventful. At times *Ziska* traveled at speeds of ten knots. As usual she was ill at ease with the wind behind her, and rolled so heavily from side to side that it was difficult to hoist up the boom and mainsail far enough to stop them from dipping into the sea and straining the rig. The waves climbed over her low stern deck and squirted random invasions of seawater through various cracks and crevices. The cabin floor was often soggy. Nothing much happened apart from a near collision in the dark with a small freighter, and the sudden whistling sound of engines and the black silhouette of a surveillance aircraft overflying us in the night. On two occasions a plane circled above us, noting our position and course. It was a reminder that once again we were on the routes of the narco-traffickers.

The Serrana Bank and its sister, Serranilla, or Little Serrana Bank, qualify as two of the more remote specks of land in the entire Caribbean. They belong to Colombia, yet the nearest mainland is Nicaragua. They are Colombian by the same accident of history that threw Pedro Serrano ashore: they lie across the direct route of the galleons that traveled from the Spanish Main to Havana. For four hundred years their lurking coral shoals and reefs have been a serious hazard. Both the Serranas and Serranillas are surrounded by the wrecks of many vessels.

South-West Cay is the only candidate on the Serrana Bank where Pedro Serrano could have struggled ashore. Though smaller than Pedro Serrano's "two leagues" of circumference, South-West Cay is the largest above-water patch of land in twenty square miles of reefs and coral shelf. Even with its warning light on an iron frame tower the place is insignificant. We were within six miles before we sighted the cay from aloft in *Ziska*'s shrouds. The island was no more than a gray-green scratch on the horizon, no larger than a fingernail. The sighting produced a sense of excitement and caution for we were steering in toward a coral platform without benefit of charts or written directions, and without an engine to get us out of trouble. There is no demand for a large-scale chart of Serrana. Officially it is off-bounds. A visit requires official permission from the Colombian authorities, a permission we did not have. We did not even know whether the place was inhabited.

Ash was nervous. He was finding it claustrophobic to share his boat with three other crew, and the notion of bringing *Ziska* so close into an unknown and exposed anchorage was unsettling for him. Once again he was at the helm and asked me to climb the ratlines and search out the best passage through the coral. It was early afternoon and the sun was almost directly overhead, so it was easy to see through the water. The previous day had been bleak and forbidding, with heavy cloud cover and an opaque slate-gray sea. But now the weather was magnificent, with puffs of cloud and a brilliant sun. As I hung on the shrouds and *Ziska* curved round to come into the lee of the island, I looked down and could see the boat's black shadow sharp on the sea floor thirty feet below the surface of the sea.

The island slowly revealed itself. First an expanse of white rock foreshore beneath the light tower, then a low point covered with some sort of dark-green vegetation, and then as we made our final approach an astonishing sight: straight ahead was a gentle curve of white sand beach and behind it a clump of lush palm trees. Farther to the left appeared the orange-brown roof and wooden sides of a large double-fronted cabin on stilts. It had a verandah, some wooden chairs, and a rustic archway at the end of a sandy path leading down to the beach. Some distance away, on the northwest end of the island, stood a flagpole on which hung the yellow, blue, and red flag of Colombia. The place looked like a large and well-kept holiday ranch.

Several small, lightly built sea birds were circling round me as I clung to the rigging, reminding me of our approach to "the Island of Birds." I identified them as some sort of terns, but I had never seen anything like them before. Instead of the usual white underbellies, their stomachs were the most beautiful fluorescent sapphire blue. They gave thin, piercing cries as they dipped and banked, and I gazed at them in wonder, thinking they were some strange and glamorous tropical variant. Then I realized that they were in fact perfectly ordinary sea birds. Their extraordinary color was nothing more than the upward reflection of light from the vivid sea, a light so pure and intense that it brushed everything with a gentle luminescence. The combination of lush dark-green palm trees and a neat cabin on the island where I had expected only desolation and sand made the fluorescent seabirds seem like the final flourish of an artistic impression of a tropical paradise, drawn in poster colors.

Apprehensive, I went ashore with Ash in the little dinghy. I had deduced from the crisply painted wooden pillars lining the path to the cabin, as well as the prominent Colombian flag, that this was a military garrison. The Colombian army had established an outpost to protect its distant territorial claim and deny drug smugglers the use of the island as a forward base. The garrison was there to stop unauthorized access.

I need not have worried. The half dozen young men who emerged from the shelter of the palm trees had short haircuts and were obviously soldiers. But they were not dressed in leopard camouflage, nor were they even carrying weapons. They wore T-shirts and shorts and looked more like vacationers. They were all barefoot. The average age seemed to be eighteen. They cheerfully hauled the dinghy up the sand and escorted Ash and me up the neat approach path and under the rustic wooden archway. BIENVENIDOS A SERRANA was carved into a large wooden board, the letters picked out in red and green. Completing the impression of a holiday resort were a wooden picnic table off to one side, a wooden sunshade, and several wooden chairs. From the sunshade hung another hand-painted sign: MIRADOR—the Lookout.

Our youthful guides climbed the wooden steps leading to the verandah, stamping their bare feet to dislodge the sand. On the open verandah, their leader stopped and called out, "Ola!" casually. After a brief moment one of the doors leading on to the verandah opened and there emerged a somewhat older, heavy-set man. He was dressed only in shorts. He was much darker-skinned than the others, was perhaps in his late thirties, and had the air of a regular army n.c.o. Regarding us with the noncommittal gaze of a long-serving soldier, he gestured for Ash and me to sit down at the wooden table. I passed across passports and ship's papers. The young soldiers clustered around behind the sergeant's back to gaze over his shoulder and stare at the documents with open curiosity. In fractured Spanish I explained we had come to the island to investigate the story of Pedro Serrano. The sergeant looked utterly blank. It was clear that he had never heard of Pedro Serrano. I produced a bottle of whiskey and slid it across the table. The young soldiers looked intrigued, the sergeant looked embarrassed. I guessed that alcohol was forbidden on the post. I left the bottle on the table where it was. The sergeant reached into his pocket, produced a key, and handed it to one of the soldiers, with instructions to fetch some coffee. The soldier unlocked another door and I had a brief glimpse into the base storeroom. It was lined with wooden shelves. There were a few bags of flour, rice, beans, and sugar, some dry biscuits, and some coffee. The rest of the shelves were bare. The soldier returned with the coffee and handed the key back to the sergeant, who carefully replaced it in his pocket. South-West Cay looked like a holiday camp, but the diet was spartan.

Waiting for the coffee to be brewed, the sergeant explained that he and his men were posted to the island for thirty to thirty-five days at a time, or maybe longer. They never knew quite how long they would stay. It depended on the boat that brought them from the island of San Andrés, 160 miles away to the southwest. Sometimes the boat was late. They never knew when they would be collected and the next garrison would be left ashore. In the interval, during their time as guardians of South-West Cay, almost nothing happened. The only people he had known to visit the reef were fishermen from San Andrés or Honduras. Very occasionally they would arrive to dive for lobsters on the reef. But they never stayed for long. Otherwise there were no strangers. He had

never seen a private yacht before. I asked about fresh water on the island. There were two wells, he said. Would it be all right if *Ziska*'s crew
walked about the island? Of course, he answered as if I had not needed
to ask the question.

Ash and I returned to the dinghy on the beach, and the same cluster of
young soldiers accompanied us. By then their colleagues had lost interest and were playing dominoes at one of the wooden tables. Out of
earshot of the sergeant, the boldest of the young men shyly asked if we
had any cigarettes aboard. They looked resigned when we told them
that none of *Ziska*'s crew smoked. Then they asked whether we would
like to send someone ashore that evening to join their soccer match.

Later that afternoon Trondur, Tristan, and I circled the island on foot.
Once again, Ash stayed on board. He worried that his yacht was in a dangerously exposed anchorage. It took only forty-five minutes to walk
right around Pedro Serrano's island, if that is what it was. The young
soldiers had told us that a few turtles did still come up the beach at night,
but we saw no sign of tracks. To the east, the coral platform stretched
out for at least a hundred yards and was exposed at low water, so the animals would have had difficulty in coming ashore except at high tide.
Away to the north a truly vast barrier reef extended, mile after mile of
rock and surf, as far as the eye could see. Only on this northern exposure
of the island was there any sense of the barrens that greeted Serrano.
The prevailing northeast wind and waves had heaped up a gray dune,
and along its face were scraps of flotsam. Here the garrison had planted
small immature palm trees to stabilize the sand. The remainder of the island they had turned into a cross between a bird sanctuary and a maze.

A dense thicket grew ten feet high. It was brushwood juniper, dark-
leaved, close-branched and impenetrable. It lay like a living mantle
across the southern half of the island. The thicket had been carefully
tended. Here and there were paths, laid out and trimmed as if in a formal labyrinth. Where the paths intersected, the soldiers had placed little
signs or planted a palm tree and carved an arrow on the trunk. The floor
of the paths was hard-packed sand riddled with the burrow holes of red

crabs. If you walked quietly and turned a corner it seemed that the floor of the path ahead was alive, covered with the crabs walking on tiptoe. Among the crabs, hopping on the ground, were dozens of immature birds, sooty black in color. They quarreled shrilly and fought. To add to the surreal effect was the flickering strip of sky overhead. Across the narrow space flashed a constant fly-past of adult birds traveling at high speed just above hedge level, and maintaining a constant demonic cackle. The air seethed with birds wheeling and calling ceaselessly. A single bird would suddenly swoop and perch unafraid on a branch almost within touching distance. Sitting in the tangle of twigs it looked like a steel-cut Victorian engraving of a bird-in-a-bush.

They were noddies, a sea bird smaller and swifter than the boobies on Aves. Their greatest concentration was on the southwest corner. Walking there, around the edge of the great thicket, it seemed as if a fire hose were spraying sea birds horizontally. The natural response was to flinch as the birds came racing over the edge of the thicket, almost at head level. Adult birds that were not whizzing through the air were perched, black and white, on upper branches, gripping their perches, which swayed in the wind. Below them at a safer level were their juveniles, bickering among themselves with shrill chirps. Here was a small patch of open ground, overgrown with tall dune grass. Walking across it was like walking across a meadow full of grasshoppers—only the creatures leaping up and falling back among the tall stalks were not grasshoppers, but young noddies learning to fly. They leapt up, flopped, and struggled.

The entire surface of South-West Cay was sand, and the air was as oven hot as Pedro Serrano had implied when he told of wading into the sea to seek relief. But, if his story was really true and he had lived for seven years catching rainwater in turtle shells, he did not know that there was fresh water on the island. Had he dug down in the sand, he could have made the wells that had changed life on the island so utterly. The Serrana Bank named in his memory no longer offers a desert island of the forlorn castaway. It is now an island of the lotus eaters. His successors, the squad of conscripts sent here, must scarcely believe their luck when they are selected to man the garrison post. That evening from *Ziska*'s deck we watched the young soldiers emerge from their pleasant barracks and saunter down to the edge of the beach. They had been joined by their sergeant, and in the golden light of a flawless tropical sunset some kicked around a soccer ball on the white sand, while others splashed and cavorted in the sparkling water. I thought of the little notice that I had found inscribed at the end of one of the alleyways carved through the great thicket. The soldiers had built a token gun position at the point where the pathway emerged on the beach. It was no more than a low breastwork of salvaged tree trunks, not even as forbidding as the palisade that Robinson Crusoe built to protect his island home. On a low flat boulder beside the breastwork, a member of the building squad had painted a list of six names in red letters, presumably the names of his patrol. Beneath the column of names he had added: ♥ Serrana.

"Fines are levied in such cases," the sour-faced customs officer announced aggressively. We had reached the Cayman Islands and returned to the world of petty officialdom. Our misdemeanor was our failure to report *Ziska*'s arrival in port twenty-four hours in advance, over the radio.

"We couldn't let you know," I said apologetically, "because we don't have a radio."

"You should make sure your radio is working. That is no excuse."

"We don't have a radio because we don't have any electricity on board."

The customs man threw us a malevolent glance. He was thin and blond and had close-set eyes. As far as he was concerned, everybody had a radio. He had one, two, even three. There was a radio beside the desk and a walkie-talkie stuck in a charger on his desk, and another marine radio set was making background noises through a loudspeaker. He was on his own side of the glass window, crisply dressed in a clean white shirt and neatly pressed trousers, and in a well-appointed and air conditioned office, surrounded by new furniture. We, the entire crew of *Ziska,* were on the other side of the window cooped up in a tiny, shabby anteroom furnished with cheap linoleum and no furniture. We had been standing there for ten minutes, waiting, and I was speaking through the gap of a small sliding glass panel that would have been more appropriate for a booth selling bus tickets in a Third World country. The customs man was supercilious and contemptuous. We were making a very poor impression. All four of us were dirty, scruffy, and dressed in ragbag clothing. None of us had shaved in weeks. We had just completed our four-teen-hundred-mile voyage and had come directly from the yacht to the harbor office to present ship's papers and passports and obtain inward clearance. The customs officer lacked the imagination to deduce that if we were true suspects, we would never have come to his office to present our papers. He judged by appearances. He picked up his handset and called the Black Gang—the narcotics enforcement team.

We had brought *Ziska* that dawn into the harbor of Georgetown, Grand Cayman Island, about 350 miles north of Serrana Bank. The place was awash with cash. Three giant cruise liners the size and shape of apartment blocks loomed over the anchorage and dispatched shuttle boats to bring tourists to the shops and beaches. Late models of the smartest cars crawled along the crowded roads. The place was a worthy heir to the rapacious traditions of Jamaica's Port Royal when Lionel Wafer set up his medical practice there. Now Cayman took money from tourists, not drunken buccaneers, and nearly every corner of the downtown area was home to one of the hundreds of banks that have given the Cayman Islands their questionable reputation as an offshore financial haven.

The Black Gang had obviously benefited from the government's largesse. When they showed up, they were lavishly equipped. A huge brand-new four-wheel-drive vehicle appeared, so big that it had difficulty finding space to park outside the harbor office. The crew—led by a dog handler who must have stood six foot two and weighed well over two hundred pounds—was dressed in black jump boots and impressive black coveralls with huge baggy pockets and DTF, for Drugs Task Force, emblazoned across the back. They were hung with a remarkable array of equipment. Around their waists were thick webbing belts from which dangled, in a typical case, a pair of handcuffs, a heavy torch, a massive ring of at least twenty keys, two phone pagers, and a walkie-talkie. They jangled and clinked as they walked or, rather, swaggered. Professional training apart, their demeanor was apparently acquired from watching slick American cops-and-gangsters television programs. Their youthful "plainclothes" officer was trying to look the part in his tight T-shirt and high-fashion jeans and he too had the telltale beeper in his waistband. He lounged stylishly in the passenger seat of the giant vehicle, eating the trademark fast food of the television character. Everyone wore suitably cool sun glasses.

The rapid response unit had taken two hours to arrive at their own office. Traffic had been difficult. Then a problem arose about rummaging, the procedure of searching the suspect boat from top to bottom. I had expected the Black Gang to swoop down on the little yacht as she lay at anchor. But there was no patrol boat to ferry the Black Gang from shore to ship, and Ash's little dinghy would have sunk beneath the weight of the burly dog handler and his colleague. So Trondur and Tristan were detained, and Ash and I were ordered to bring the yacht to the inspection dock. We explained that this would be difficult as *Ziska* had no engine and there was no wind. There was another long pause. Perhaps a tow could be arranged, I suggested. After a further hour's delay the patrol boat arrived on the back of a trailer. The shiny new speedboat would have done credit to a para-gliding operation for tourists, except for the row of crossed marijuana leaves painted on the superstructure. Each green leaf recorded a successful drug interception. There weren't many of them.

By now the Black Gang had swelled to eight operatives, and there was another long wait to get the patrol boat down a suitable ramp into the water. The ramp was already occupied by a tourist dive boat that was repairing its engine. As the hours slipped past, the Black Gang's menacing posture began to wilt in the hot sun of the dockside. The youthful plain-clothes officer was on his second paper cup of fried potatoes and there were several crumpled greasy napkins on the floor of the Land Cruiser. Only the dog handler, who was in charge, kept up the gruff pose. When *Ziska* was finally towed alongside the wharf, he was waiting on the quay-side with his sniffer dog on a leash. The dog peered down from the height of the dock to the little boat, took fright, and began to whimper. After several futile tugs on the leash, the dog handler took the creature in his arms and jumped down on deck. He put the animal on deck and it ran to investigate a piece of raw sharkskin. The last time Trondur had harpooned a shark, Ash had wanted to wrap a piece of its skin around the tiller as decoration. Trondur obligingly skinned the animal and Ash had stretched and nailed the skin to dry in the sun. That had been three days earlier, and the skin was now distinctly ripe. The sniffer dog took a deep breath, and lost interest in any further rummaging. Meanwhile her massive master was having trouble squeezing down into Ziska's cramped accommodation. His belt tools kept catching on various pro-jections. He had difficulty in turning round, and the cabin was unbear-ably hot and stuffy. When he finally emerged from the hatchway, his black overalls were crumpled. He was drenched with sweat. He had of course found no drugs of any sort. Maintaining the final shred of his au-thoritarian approach, he lifted his whining dog ashore, and clambered back on the wharf. His junior, the plainclothes operative, followed him. As he jumped across the gap between boat and quay, there was a distinct plop. His telephone pager had flipped from his waistband and fallen into the harbor. Disconsolately he stood on the edge of the quay and peered down. Twenty feet blow, in Georgetown's admirably clean harbor water, the little silhouette of the pager winked back up. "Can any of you fel-lows dive down and get it?" he asked us plaintively. We shook our heads.

The dog handler, Malachy, was not really as fierce as he had pre-tended. After he had mopped his brow, he inquired what we had been doing prowling about the Caribbean in such an antique vessel. I ex-plained our quest for Robinson Crusoe and that we had come to Grand

Cayman, now that our task was done. The crew would go their separate ways. Trondur and Tristan would go by air to Europe, Ash would take *Ziska* single-handed to Florida and away from the hurricane season, and I would stay in Georgetown a few days to visit the libraries and public archives to see if there were any records of castaways. "Oh, you don't have to go to the library for that," Malachy observed. "Go to talk with Andrew Powery. He was cast away on Serrana. He has quite a story to tell."

Finding Andrew Powery was easy. He was a living legend. Persuading his family to arrange a time when I could meet him was rather more difficult. The family was very protective as Andrew Powery was old and very frail. In view of what he had gone through, it was a miracle that he was alive at all.

On 26 October 1932 Andrew Powery sailed from Grand Cayman as a deck hand aboard a local fishing boat, the *Managuan*. She was a small wooden boat, a workaday yawl-rigged vessel of 22 tons. She had no engine and was considered to be rather a slow sailer. What made the *Managuan* slightly unusual was that she had a "fish well," an open box built into the center of the hull and linked to the sea, where fish could be kept alive and sold fresh in port. Andrew Powery, a big strapping twenty-year-old at the time, was one of two deck hands. The other was called Earle Groves or "Early." Also aboard was "Captain Jeffery," a mate, and a young cook. The plan was for the *Managuan* to sail to the Miskito Cays; catch "scale fish"—mostly garopas and cut-eye snappers; put them in the well; and then sail back across the Caribbean to sell the catch in Jamaica.

The *Managuan* had scarcely arrived at the Miskito Cays when her helmsman carelessly ran her on a sandbank in broad daylight. It took almost twelve hours of laboriously unloading the ballast, laying out the anchors, and waiting for the highest moment of the tide before the crew could float her off. This mishap caused Captain Jeffery to change his plans, almost on a whim. He suddenly announced to his crew that instead of fishing the Miskito Cays, he would take the *Managuan* to the Serrana

Bank. He had heard there was excellent fishing near the bank. His spur-of-the-moment decision was to put his boat into the path of what would prove to be the worst hurricane to hit the region in living memory.

What came to be known as "The '32 Storm" began to develop northeast of Barbados on 31 October. Over the next eight days it strengthened into a full-fledged hurricane as it drifted east and then turned north, in a wide slow semicircle. The hurricane's track brought the eye a few miles northwest of Serrana before it looped up toward the Caymans. The eye passed south of Grand Cayman on 7 November with wind speeds of 150 miles per hour and then struck Cayman Brac, one of the two smaller Cayman islands to the northeast, almost dead center. By that time the winds at the eye of the storm were calculated to be over 200 miles per hour. After the hurricane finally left, one house near the shoreline on Grand Cayman was found to have been picked up and shifted inland a distance of 157 feet. At another exposed location on Grand Cayman called Spotts the storm surge—the extra height and reach of gale-driven waves coming ashore—was calculated at 29.9 feet.

South-West Cay on the Serrana Bank—"Big Cay" the Caymanians called it—has a maximum elevation of 32 feet. The threat to low-lying Serrana can be imagined. At that time two men were living on the Big Cay, "rangers" from Cayman Brac. "Ranger" was a local term for roving fishermen who were delivered by sailboat to remote, uninhabited islands, where they were dropped off with their nets and lines and small catboats to catch turtle and fish, including often nurse shark, valued for their fins. The rangers lived in isolation for weeks at a time until the mother ship came back to collect them. The two rangers on Big Cay, however, were not there to fish. They were collecting noddy eggs, packing them in boxes of five hundred and storing them in a shed, ready to be taken to Jamaica, where they would be hawked in the streets. As a sideline the two men were also filling sacks with phosphate-rich bird droppings to be sold as fertilizer.

Late on the afternoon of Thursday, 3 November, the two men on Big Cay, Bill Tibbetts and Will Ritch, saw the *Managuan*, which had arrived from the Miskito Cays and was hove to close in shore. The two rangers rowed out in the catboat to show Captain Jeffery the best place to anchor. Already they were worried by an ominous sign. A huge, slow swell was rolling in from the southeast. They did not yet know it was driven by the force of the approaching hurricane. The swell had washed up hundreds and hundreds of conch shells, tearing the shellfish from the sea floor and throwing them up on the reef. It was something that neither ranger had witnessed before.

When Tibbetts and Ritch woke up the next morning in the little hut that was their home on the cay, they were immediately aware that a major hurricane was on its way. The swell of the sea had increased, clouds were massing in the east, and the great mass of sea birds was strangely disturbed. Thousands upon thousands of noddies, boobies, and man-of-war birds were rising and circling above the island, rising and circling. The two islanders went again to the *Managuan* and advised Captain Jeffery to shift anchorage. Big Cay was too exposed. The little island was on the wrong side of the bank, the side facing the approaching storm. They suggested that the fishing boat go to the northern end of the Serrana Bank and creep her way into a patch of protected water between three small islets called Triangle Cay. There she should put down all her anchors and prepare to ride out the storm.

Tibbetts and Ritch then began making their own hurricane preparations. At that time Big Cay was just a raw expanse of sand and guano. The great juniper thicket had not yet been planted. The hordes of sea birds nested on the ground. There was only the hut and a larger shed for storing the fertilizer sacks. It was dreadfully exposed. They hauled their little catboat out of the water and dragged her as far up as they could on the highest ridge on the island. There the two rangers heaped sand around the boat and filled her with conch shells to try to stop her from being blown away. They buried big galvanized tins of food.

The sky was a monstrous portent. Recording his impressions nearly sixty years later, Andrew Powery still remembered how "it looked like heaven and earth was coming together. I never seen an element like that in my whole life before or since. . . . Clouds down here, clouds up here." The roiling clouds were "five, six, seven, yes ten storey" high. Bizarrely, they reminded him of popcorn.

The *Managuan* fled to shelter at Triangle Cay, and anchored. She was already leaky, and her hull had been further strained by the recent grounding on the Miskito Cays. The crew decided to get ready for the hurricane's onslaught by repairing the bilge pump, which was not working properly. They dismantled the pump but then with almost criminal negligence decided to leave completion of the job until the following day. They retired to their bunks to get some rest, leaving Andrew Powery on watch by himself.

Powery spent the first part of the night crouching in the forecastle, the little forward cabin. "She leaking like a basket," he recalled. The large fish well amidships blocked any water that leaked into the forward section of the boat from draining back where it could be removed easily. Shifting the ballast stones lying forward of the fish well to make a space where he could dip a bucket, he began throwing out the water. By ten o'clock he was so exhausted that he crawled into a bunk in the forward cubby hole and put his head down to get some rest.

He was woken up by shouts of panic. Bursting from the forecastle he found his fellow crewman, Early Groves, on deck. He was bailing frantically and yelling that the *Managua* was sinking. The seas were now running so high that they were breaking over the little fishing boat, threatening to bury her. Tons of water were arriving on deck so fast that it did not have time to drain overboard through the scuppers, the drain holes at the side of the deck. Pressed down by the additional weight of the water, the *Managuan* was rolling sluggishly and scarcely able to rise to each wave. Groves was working frantically to clear the surplus water with a bucket. Powery saw that the task was futile. There was no chance that Groves could keep pace with the onrush of water. The solution was to clear a wider path for the water to run overboard. By now the captain and mate had also emerged on deck, and the mate took an ax and began to hack at the scupper holes to make them larger. But it was slow work. The head of the ax kept getting stuck in the white pine. Powery found a handsaw and began to cut out a section of the "monkey rail," the low bulwark at the edge of the deck. When the monkey rail was nearly cut through he took up the ax. "I whopped! And that piece fell, that went out yonder, in the water. And the water went *r-r-rrrrrrsh. . .* and then the water start to run." He made a second cut in the monkey rail on the other side of the vessel, and, freed of the water flooding her deck, the *Managuan* was saved for the time being.

The wind was now increasing to full hurricane force, and after cutting down the mast to reduce the area exposed to the blast, the crew retreated to the cabin. There was little more that they could do. If they stayed on deck, they risked being swept overboard by the thundering waves. The *Managuan* heaved and pitched, tugging massively on her anchor chain. Every quarter of an hour Andrew Powery, as the strongest man aboard, was sent to crawl forward on deck with a flashlight. The wind and rain were so fierce that he had to clamp his hand across his face and peer between his fingers just to make his way along the deck. When he reached the hawsepipe where the anchor chain passed through the deck, he could only check the situation by touch. He reached down and felt the links of the anchor chain, bar taut. Looking forward into the sea he could see nothing in the black, howling murk punctuated by cresting waves which came roaring down on the *Managuan*. He felt desperately cold.

On Sunday morning the crew dumped as much as possible of the *Managuan's* deck gear into the sea. They hoped to lighten her still further, but it was a token gesture. Then someone on board suggested the technique of putting oil on a rough sea to reduce the breaking of the waves. But he did not realize that for this technique to be effective, the oil slick has to be started upwind of the boat so it can spread down toward the vessel. Andrew Powery was sent to the bows of the boat with an old blanket and a sugar sack soaked in oil with instructions to hold them overboard. Every time he did so, the waves threw the oil-soaked cloth back on the ship, and nearly washed Andrew Powery into the sea. He could see that his effort was useless and, angry with the crew sheltering in the cabin, he let go of the blanket and the sugar sack. In a moment they were swept away in the darkness. He went back below and resumed bailing.

While he was below, he suddenly felt the motion of the boat change. The *Managuan* was no longer heaving and snubbing—coming up with a heavy tug—on her anchor chain. She veered and swung, changing position. He jumped up on deck in time to hear the mate announce "Captain, she's gone!" For a moment Powery thought that the mate meant the anchor chain had snapped. Then Powery realized that he had deliberately slipped the anchor chain and let the boat go free. He was fearful that the *Managuan*, tethered to her chain, was about to founder under the press of weather. The mate judged that the boat stood a better chance of survival if she floated free.

The mate's action in slipping the anchor meant that the little fishing boat was now adrift, without mast or sails, and at the mercy of the sea. The captain and the mate stood at the wheel in an attempt to steer the ship. Andrew Powery, convinced that the mate had made a dreadful mistake, took a length of rope, wrapped it round a remaining section of monkey rail, and then looped the free ends over his shoulders and around his waist. He was determined he would not be washed overboard.

The *Managuan* was now surging downwind on the stormy sea. She seesawed as the waves rolled under her. On the front of each wave the bowsprit thrust down into the water. On the back of the wave the bows came up and the spar pointed to the sky. The fishing boat was out on control.

In the next instant there was a loud, scraping sound as the little boat slithered across the top of a reef. She had hit what the Caymanians called a pan shoal, a flat-topped table of coral and compacted sand. As the boat skidded and scraped on the pan shoal, the shock of the impact popped open the hatch of the fish well. As the water poured in through the shattered bottom of the hull, it flowed up and out of the hatchway. With the upwelling came the scale fish. Their catch, the garopas and others, swam back into the sea.

The *Managuan* was now doomed. Each time she thumped on the reef, her hull cracked open a little more. Soon entire sections of the planking were gone. It was time to abandon ship. Andrew Powery untied the rope that secured him to the hull, went down into the cabin to stuff his belongings into a flour sack, and found he was walking on the reef. Much of the lower hull had been stripped away by the coral and the floor of the cabin was now the top of the reef.

The crew gathered on deck and tried to estimate where the last mad headlong rush of their vessel had brought them. Peering through the driving spray they could make out a small cay. They thought they recognized it as a desolate cay called Anchor Cay. They had scarcely identified the cay when the gale, which had eased for a short time, came back with increased fury, and the speck of land disappeared in the spray and spume.

There was now a choice: Should they try to reach the cay in one of the sloop's two catboats which were lashed on deck, and risk the wrath of the sea; or should they stay with the crippled vessel hoping the *Managuan* would hold together long enough for the hurricane to ease enough for the crew to be able to clamber off onto the reef.

A heavier than usual wave washed along the *Managuan*, struck the cookhouse structure, and slammed it against the railing. She was gradually being pounded to pieces. Andrew Powery and Early Groves hauled their way to the uprooted cookhouse, grabbed it, and toppled it overboard. They then tied a safety rope to the bow of one of the catboats and led the rope back around the stump of the mast. That way, they hoped, the catboat would stay with the sloop even if her tie-downs gave way. Soon afterward a boarding wave did strike the catboat and washed it into the sea. The catboat flipped upside down, but the safety rope held. The boat floated there, off the stern of the *Managuan* and bottom up.

A moment later, the *Managuan* herself fell over. A wave picked her up, then dropped her heavily on the reef. She crashed over on her port side, her deck at a steep slope. Moments later the second catboat was collected by a large wave, ripped off her fastening, and swept away. The crew hung on. They clambered up the slant of the deck to where they could brace themselves, shoulders against the bulwarks and feet on the raised coaming of the hatchway. Someone found a small sail, the staysail jib, and hauled the wet cloth over them. It gave a little protection from the impact of the waves. But each time a wave hit the men, they were lifted up like a row of dolls. In a spirit of desperation the captain began singing, and the crew joined him.

Then the *Managuan* went under. She must have slipped off the reef or been washed into a gully. Andrew Powery was left on the surface, spluttering. The mate and Early Groves managed to grab the capsized catboat, which was still attached to its safety rope, and hung on, one on each side. Looking down into the water beneath his feet, Powery saw the glimmer of something pale. He realized it was the *Managua's* monkey rail. He swam across, hooked his foot under it, and pulled himself close. At all costs he had to prevent himself being washed clear of the wreck. If he was swept out to sea, he was lost. A moment later, with a gasp, the captain surfaced beside him and the two men hung on desperately to the rail.

The *Managuan* had settled with just enough of the superstructure showing to offer handholds for the crew flailing in the water. Early Groves and the mate let go of the catboat, floundered across, and also grabbed hold of the main vessel. Unfortunately they let slip the safety rope in the process, and the catboat floated away. Out of the confusion also appeared the young cook, and all five members of *Managuan's* crew found themselves united again on the battered remnants of their fishing boat.

Wave after wave washed over the heads of the men. They had no idea what was happening, where they were going. They felt the wreck shifting and shuddering under them. There was a heavy rasping sound. The swell picked up the *Managuan* and dropped her back on top of the reef and saved their lives. The wreck caught fast on the shoal with the bow sticking up far enough in the air for the survivors to crawl into the tiny forecastle. They sat there perched inside the bow of the boat, with the water sometimes swirling up to neck level, while "the '32 Storm" moved onward.

They spent Sunday night in this way.

"Monday morning," Andrew Powery remembered, "was pretty fair; the wind had gone down fine; the sea was gone down good." The men were so exhausted by the battering of the previous thirty-six hours that they spent most of the day on the wreck as it lay canted over on the reef. They could see a patch of dry land on a small sand cay not far away. But to reach it meant crossing a deep channel where the tide was running strongly. Eventually the captain asked Andrew Powery, who was the best swimmer in the group, if he would try to swim across, taking the end of a rope. If he succeeded, the rest of the crew would use the rope to transfer to the cay. But the current in the channel was too powerful. It nearly swept Powery out to sea. Only by pulling himself back on the rope did he manage to retreat to safety.

Pinned down to the wreck, the crew spent the rest of Monday and all of Tuesday in a state of increasing misery. They huddled in the forecastle cabin. It was soaking wet. The last time they had eaten was on Saturday and they had no food. Also there was no fresh water. To lessen their thirst, they occasionally got down from the wreck and on to the reef. They had only to step from the boat's rail and be on to the coral. They would pick up a whelk, prise out the gut of the shellfish, and hold it in their mouth hoping to extract some liquid. It brought little relief.

On Wednesday morning, according to his own account, Andrew decided that action had to be taken. He calculated that he would have a better chance to swim the channel and reach the sand bar if he did not have to carry a rope's end with him. On the previous attempt the drag of the rope had held him back. Of course if he tired this time, the current would sweep him out to sea, and he could not be hauled back to safety. He told the rest of the crew that he would make the attempt solo. If he succeeded in reaching the cay, then they would have to follow his example and get across on their own. Before wading into the water, he walked down to the end of the reef and "prayed to the good Master to take care of me and help me make it."

His faith in divine help, Andrew Powery was later to say, sustained him. "I was going with that determination that He would help me . . . so it wasn't long before I got across, made it to that little cay. . . . The current wasn't running bad at all that morning." The other four members of the crew watched his progress. Encouraged when he waded out on the far bank they too entered the water and, one by one, managed to struggle across to the tiny cay. At last they were on dry land above high tide level. It was the fifth day since their hurricane ordeal had begun.

They dug in the sand, searching for water. It was a slim hope but they made several holes. Each pit was dry. Their situation had improved by leaving the carcass of the *Managuan*, but not by much. The outside world had no idea that the *Managuan* was wrecked. Only when the fishing boat was long overdue would anyone go looking for her, and then the search would be in the wrong place, over on the Miskito Cays, her original fishing ground. Meanwhile the five castaways could die of thirst, stranded on their waterless sand cay. Their only thread of hope was to try to reach the Big Cay, where there was fresh water and—if they had survived—the two egg-collecting rangers.

But Big Cay was out of reach. The castaways had established their position only approximately. They knew they were standing on the Serrana Bank at a some point between Anchor Cay, where the *Managuan* had struck, and the nearest of the Triangle Cays, the original shelter anchorage. How far away they were from the Big Cay they did not know exactly. The Triangles lay between them and Big Cay, and they were "good high cays," Powery said. But looking to the south, the castaways could not see the Triangles. There was only the flat horizon of the Caribbean, and in the foreground the brown and gray shadows of the broad coral reef, washed over by the tide. Without a catboat, there was no choice except "to walk the reef."

Walking the reef is a punishing exercise. Weed makes the footing slippery and conceals the spines of sea urchins and the spikes of shells. Gullies and small channels force detour after detour. A person has to wade sometimes, to swim sometimes, and always to avoid turning an ankle, stepping into a hole, or shredding the shins on sharp rocks and jagged coral edges. The sea surge constantly threatens to push the reef walker off balance. On a rising tide he must identify a high spot on which to take refuge and, judging the moment, stay there until the ebb. "Walking the reef" requires careful judgment, and knowing when to call a halt.

The reef walk of the five *Managuan* castaways reached its impasse after less than five hours. They picked their way along the crest of the reef until they reached a broad deep channel. It was midday on Wednesday, and the channel was about three quarters of a mile wide. For most of the crew of the *Managuan* it was too far for them to swim. Once again, they turned to Andrew Powery. He agreed to attempt the crossing. If he succeeded, he would continue on along the reef by himself and try to get through to the Big Cay and fetch help. But no one was sure how far away he would have to travel, and in which direction precisely. The location of Big Cay was still vague.

Powery asked for someone to go with him. But there were no volunteers. So Powery began swimming on his own. Behind him the *Managuan's* survivors stood on the coral, holding up their arms as semaphores. Powery kept looking back. He was taking his directions from them as to which way he should swim. Ahead, his destination was invisible over the wave tops. Behind him the figures of his shipmates gradually grew smaller and smaller, until they too were lost from sight behind the waves. He kept swimming. He knew there was a current, and that it would set him off course. His best course was southwest but looking back he judged that he was traveling more to the south. So he altered his course.

"So I wheeled around," he recalled. " And I swim . . . and my legs felt like they were cramping up, they were string-drawing, you know. I swam out there till I was tired, looking for Mr. Tom"—a shark—"to come up there 'longside of me anytime."

The water around him "looked too blue out there for a lady to blue her linen." All he could see around him was "the dark horizon" and gradually he lost all sense of direction. He just "swum and swum," not knowing "whether I going east, west, north, or south." In the end, as the sun was dropping down, he came to the edge of the reef and clambered up onto the sand and rock. How long he had been swimming he had no idea. It might have been four or five hours. Nor did he know where he had come ashore or how far he had progressed. He looked around for landmarks. To the north there was nothing. Nor was there anything to be seen southward, the direction of Big Cay. If he was close, he knew he should see its light structure. Only to the west was there any land, a small cay which he guessed was one of the Triangles. He got up and started walking along the reef toward it, so tired that he was talking to himself. After some distance, he could make out some figures on the cay. Encouraged he headed toward them, expecting to reach help. As the gap narrowed, he recognized the figures. They were the crew of *Managua*. He had swum in a circle and come back to the cay that he had left.

A ndrew Powery was helped up the steps of his daughter's bungalow. He was still a big man with an impressive breadth across his shoulders, though his spine was now bent with age and his skin hung loose on the large frame. His pale skin was marked with the blotches of old age. His daughter Clarens gripped his arm to make sure he did not topple. He lived by himself. "Five years ago his wife died, and he sort of gave up," Clarens explained to me before she went to fetch him. Andrew lived close by, staying in his own little wooden house, surrounded by chickens and kittens. It was where he preferred, and he had his extended family all round to attend him. It was clear that Clarens and her family kept him in great affection.

Clarens had told her father that I wanted to know about his experience as a Serrana castaway, and she had dressed him very smartly for our meeting—checked shirt, light-gray cotton slacks, black slippers, and neat white socks, and a white hat on his head. Clean-shaven and with a head of tightly curled white hair, he looked trim and well cared for. He settled on the sofa next to me and gestured for one of his great-granddaughters to remove his black slippers so he could be more comfortable. Clarens leaned down and pulled up the gray trouser leg so I could see the shin. The leg was covered with a lattice of pale scars. They were the legacy of Andrew Powery's journey of survival.

"You should have seen my two legs, my two feet that night," said Andrew. "God knows what life is. Had hard punishment. He knows what I went through, He knows the pain that I felt." Andrew Powery had a marvelously rich deep voice. The delivery was long and slow and drawling, pulling out the vowels, then chopping off the final syllable abruptly. It had a West Country charm to it. "And you are waaalking in the night, and you are waaalking in the water, and it is so many things in the water that may take your life. . . . I look after shark that might eat me any time."

Andrew Powery had already slipped off into the memory of the twenty-two hours that followed his first attempt to fetch help for the survivors from the *Managua*. It was the defining event of his life and I had heard the story on a tape recording made by the Cayman Islands National Archive as part of its oral history program. But listening to him now, with his slow melodic voice, I began to appreciate the impact of that harrowing experience. The fragments that floated on the surface of his memory had a special importance.

He went back into the water for the second attempt at dawn the next day. He had barely slept all night but had lain in his wet clothes "shivering like a green leaf over fire." He had thought of the obstacles that faced him, the width of the channels, the difficulty of traversing the rough surface of the reef, the clawing of the waves that tried to suck him off the coral. At the first glimmer of dawn he got off the sand and left his companions on the cay with scarcely a word. "The sun was rising, she was just popping up out of the water when I start to swim off. . . . God help me, I carried a bee-line right down that morning, I always looked back and I seen myself going straight."

Swimming breast stroke, he crossed the first broad channel without difficulty and climbed up on the next cay and looked back. He could see the far shore, the place where he had come from. Already his companions were lost from view. He was on his own once more. Ahead of him lay the long, low curve of the Serrana Bank barely showing above water. He knew little about the reef, except that somewhere at its farthest end must be the Big Cay and, with luck, the huts of the two rangers.

He began to walk and scramble and flounder across the coral. He could take his general direction from the angle of the sun and the wind and waves, but his actual track had to follow the line of the reef crest. went first to the southeast, then curved back to the southwest. Often he was wading up to his waist with the sea washing over the reef and "the water boiling round my legs, catching me round my waist." He kept staring ahead, hoping to glimpse the lighthouse on Big Cay, but saw nothing. Seaweed, "gulf weed" he called it, came swirling past him, carried along by the current. It made him feel as if he was standing still and the sea was moving. It was also a warning that the current was dangerously strong.

Two waves met, combined, and before he could save himself, tripped him and suddenly washed him off the reef and into the sea. Off balance, he felt himself being swept into the deep water and then into the pull of the current. He swam desperately. There was no chance of scrambling back on the coral, the surge was too strong. The best he could do was keep swimming, keep his head above water, and keep watching the line of the breaking surf so that he did not lose his bearings. He did not know how long he was out of his depth, but he just kept swimming and praying. "All two legs and arms too, pretty well tired out. But anyway praying to the Lord to help me, was His will, I swum and I swum and I swum and I swum."

The water around him suddenly grew warmer. He knew it meant he was in the shallows. Cautiously he lowered his legs and his feet found bottom. He waded out on the reef again. He looked around and realized that the current had actually helped him. It had swept him down along the reef and he was nearer his destination.

He did not recognize the cay. It was a very small, long and narrow. It might have existed before the hurricane, or it might have been created by the storm surge. It was covered with hundreds and hundreds of conch shells, probably thrown there by the storm, and a few lengths of broken lumber which looked as if they were deck cargo swept off a ship.

Powery was exhausted. He was at the extreme limits of physical survival. He had not eaten nor had fresh water to drink for five days. He assembled some of the broken lumber to make a rough bed and lay down to get some rest.

When he awoke he had lost track of time and was not sure of his direction. He still could not see the lighthouse on the Big Cay but it seemed to him that he had nearly reached the angle in the reef where it turned to the southwest. He began walking the reef again.

He was now so tired and so light-headed from lack of food and water that he felt numb. He stumbled along the coral, sometimes splashing through the water, often scraping and slicing his legs. He did not feel the spikes of the sea urchins. If a shark had taken him, he later said, he would not even have felt the jaws close around him. He saw plenty of sharks, mostly small ones near the reef. After a storm he knew that the larger sharks also came to the reef, to feed. The worst fright was when his foot went into a hole and something—it was probably a small octopus—grabbed hold of him. He jerked his foot from the hole with a yell of fright so loud hat "I thought I waked them up on the cay."

There were more channels to swim across, mostly narrow ones, fortunately, and the sun was going down. By now Powery was reeling and staggering and tripping. He noticed that the tide, which had been ebbing, was exceptionally low. This gave him some hope. It was exposing more of the reef top than usual. He could not waste the chance. He forced himself into a weaving staggering run to try to cover as much ground as possible. He fell. He landed facedown in the shallows and grabbed at the coral as the sea threatened to suck him off the reef once again. His arms felt as if they were being pulled out of their sockets, but he didn't release his grip on the coral—he was once again on pan shoal—and he was able to pull himself back on the reef.

The sun set. Fortunately there was a bright moon and he could see well enough to keep moving. He blundered on, and at last began to distinguish the dark shape of his destination, Big Cay. Around him the surf breaking on the reefs glowed white.

Sometime around midnight he reached the last edge of the reef. Across the final channel lay Big Cay. From where he stood he still could not see the flash of the lighthouse. It was obscured by the central dunes of the cay. He paused, debating whether he should risk the crossing in the dark. He was very aware of the lurking sharks. "Well, it don't do for me to stop here," he said to himself, "I going to try it. God will help me."

He "pitched in" to the water and began to swim. Once again he lost track of time. He just kept swimming. Though he did not know it, there was one thing in his favor: the tide was slack. There was no current to sweep him off course. He kept his line and eventually, tired to death, he saw white water. At the same time he saw the flash of the lighthouse at last and could use it as his mark. He swam toward it, and kept swimming.

By now he had lost all sensation of where or how he was moving. He was in numb suspension. "So I didn't know anything till I felt my chest, my stomach brought upon it. Sand. On the beach. Well, I wouldn't even rise up right away. I just returned thanks to the Lord and laid myself there, and I caught a little wind." It was about four o'clock on Friday morning and Andrew Powery had survived as a castaway for six days without food or water and reached the Serrana Big Cay.

At that same moment the two rangers, Will Ritch and Bill Tibbetts, were lying in the remnant of the hut they had salvaged from destruction of "the '32 Storm." They had survived by taking shelter behind an empty thirty-gallon beef cask placed just below the crest of the highest dune on the lee side. For twelve hours they had sat there on the sand, arms clasped around their knees, while the hurricane blasted over them. The wind, the clouds, the rain, the sandstorm, the spume combined to darken the sky so that they did not know whether it was day or night. When the storm passed over, they emerged stiffly to find that the cay had been flailed bare. Hundreds of tons of guano that had covered parts of the island—the fertilizer they were there to collect—had simply been washed away. There was nothing left. The big shed where they stowed the guano sacks and the collected eggs had been flattened. There were no birds. The noddies, thousands upon thousands of them, had simply been blasted away by the gale like spindrift. Only a few boobies were left, and they had been buried alive. Here and there the beaks of boobies were sticking up from the sand, moving feebly. "We pulled all we could out of the sand" Ritch remembered, "and let them fly away, fly again, but most of them died there, buried alive."

Their little hut, their living accommodation, was wrecked. The roof had been torn off and lay half buried in a dune. Fortunately the two rangers had shovels left over from their guano work, and they used them to dig out the sand, burrowing under the fallen roof to make a small cave. They cleared enough room for a single cot and space for the second man to sleep on the floor. Food was not a problem. They located the big galvanized tins that contained their stores. They were intact. The storm surge had contaminated the freshwater well with salt water, but not permanently. The two rangers cleared the well of storm-blown sand, and extracted enough brackish water to boil up a fish stew for their first meal. Later, the rain would wash out the salt and filter into the well, restoring the fresh water supply. The two rangers settled down to wait until they were picked up by their mother ship, but wondered what had happened to the *Managuan*. They doubted that the vessel would have survived the storm.

Bill Tibbetts was stretched out on the cot and Will Ritch, as his junior, was lying on the ground inside the little shelter they had excavated. It was so cramped that Tibbetts's feet were almost sticking out of the low entrance, which served as their doorway. They were both awake in the small hours of that morning when Andrew Powery was washed up on the beach. "This night," recalled Ritch "we were talking about ghosts, of all things, and pirates, and all kinds of treasures, and all that stuff." The moonlight shining in through the doorway was suddenly blocked by a shadow. With his head full of ghost stories, Ritch was petrified. There was so little space in the shelter, he could not scramble clear. He lay there in fright. "Are you alive or are you dead?" he croaked. A voice replied, "Have you got any water?" "Are you alive or are you dead?" demanded Ritch again. "Well. I'm alive, but just about," came the answer. "Well who are you?" asked Ritch, and the voice said, "Andrew Powery."

"I've always known my father as a very strong man," said Clarens, proudly patting her father's shoulder. "He's called one of the iron men in Caymans. He's always so strong and could carry so many heavy loads. He would always pick up anything. Extra heavy loads . . . He is one of the bravest men you have ever known, a real good man."

I looked at the gaunt figure of Andrew Powery. He was a reminder of an era that was almost unimaginable in the context of the modern Cayman Islands with its cruise liners and more than five hundred offshore banks.

I asked Andrew what he thought had kept him alive during the ordeal on Serrana Cay. He did not reply immediately. He had slipped off into an old man's reverie. Clarens repeated the question, pitching her voice in a way that she knew would make her father respond. He had no hesitation in his reply.

"I know the Lord. He done nothing against me. He treated me fine. He kept the sharks from me. He kept me from drowning. He kept me life. Because it was just as easy to be drowned, just as easy for the sharks to eat me. . . . I went off the reef a couple of times, and I was down in the ocean and couldn't see a thing. Couldn't see nothing of shore at all. That's me out in the ocean. Ooooh yes. . . . God respect me. You can believe that."

His piety was worthy of god-fearing Robinson Crusoe. I reached over and took Andrew Powery's hand. It was half as large again as mine. The skin was mottled with age, the bones of the fingers showed clearly, but his grasp was steady. I gave his hand a squeeze of appreciation. I thought it was the best way to express my admiration and gratitude. My circuit of the Caribbean in *Ziska* had provided me with an island and a maroon, Salt Tortuga, and Henry Pitman, who were conspicuous candidates for the genesis of Robinson Crusoe. Andrew Powery had made me understand what it was like to be cast away.

After twenty-eight years on his island,
Crusoe returns to England to tell his story.

Chapter VI
CRUSOE FOUND

"The Sea Chest which belonged to Alexander Selkirk the prototype of Robinson Crusoe." These were the words on the museum label glued to the lid of the seaman's trunk in the stockroom of the Royal Museum of Scotland, the place where I had begun my journey of investigation. Now I had more than a suspicion that the label's long-accepted message fell short of the truth.

Also in this museum's collection is the little silver-banded coconut goblet that, it was said, Selkirk had used as his drinking cup during his lonely exile. Maybe he did so. But after visiting Juan Fernandez Island, where Selkirk spent his four years of self-exile, I now knew that coconuts do not grow on Juan Fernandez. If he had the little cup with him, then he brought it from somewhere else.

Alexander Selkirk, I was fairly sure, was not the prototype for Robinson Crusoe. He was the inspiration. The prototype was someone else.

Ultimately Crusoe springs from Defoe's own imagination. Like the novelists who followed him, Defoe got his raw material by observing, listening, reading. He certainly took material from the accounts of the two ship's officers aboard the *Duke* and the *Duchess* who were present when Selkirk was collected from Juan Fernandez, Woodes Rogers and Edward Cooke. The sensational story of Alexander Selkirk probably triggered the idea for Robinson Crusoe in the mind of Daniel Defoe. Selkirk was famous, and the salient details of his adventure—the goatskin cloths, the

menagerie of cats and goats, his nickname, "Governor" of the island—
are reflected in the story of Robinson Crusoe. Yet everything that Daniel
Defoe knew about Selkirk he had come by secondhand, and there was
not much: a few paragraphs in the voyage narratives of Woodes Rogers
and Cooke and a commentary by the essayist Steele, who may have met
and interviewed the truculent sailing master of the *Cinque Ports* galley.
Selkirk never wrote a book himself. Nor has any evidence come to light
that Defoe ever met Selkirk face to face and talked to him to glean the
extra details and the local color that embellish in *The Life and Strange
Surprizing Adventures of Robinson Crusoe.*

The surly Scots sailor remains a silent, flawed, and inadequate model
for Defoe's hero. Crusoe's resourcefulness, the central strand of his
character, is completely absent in Selkirk, who did little more than build
huts, capture goats, and wait for rescue. Making pottery, planting crops,
building a small boat, encountering cannibals, rescuing Man Friday—
there is so much in Crusoe's tale that has no equivalent in the history of
Alexander Selkirk. He was on a temperate island far off the coast of
South America whereas Crusoe is cast away within sight of the Spanish
Main in the Caribbean. My own travels to Juan Fernandez Island underscored how very far "Crusoe's island" is in both imagination and reality
from the place where Alexander Selkirk lived by himself for four years
and four months.

By contrast, Henry Pitman did write his little book, and it contains far
more about life as a maroon than Defoe could have extracted from secondhand reports of Alexander Selkirk's experiences. Also, Pitman's adventures took place in the Caribbean on an island within sight of the
mainland, as did Crusoe's exile; in Pitman's book there was a Man Friday
figure, a rescue engineered by the freeing of a prisoner, turtle catching,
pottery making, soap making from vegetable extracts, sewing with bone
needles, and so on. As I reviewed the contrasting claims for Pitman and
Selkirk as the more likely forerunner for Crusoe I realized that Pitman
was probably the same age as the inventor of Crusoe. Could Defoe and
Pitman have met?

There is one obvious overlap in their lives. At the time of the rebellion of the Duke of Monmouth in 1685, Defoe rode from London to the West Country to join the rebels. He could have met Pitman at that time. But their meeting would have taken place before Pitman was transported to the Caribbean islands as a "convict rebel" and before he had his adventures as a maroon. Only in May 1687 was it made public that Defoe had joined Monmouth's cause. In that year Defoe's name appeared in a list of royal pardons issued to those who had taken part in the insurgency. This was two years before Pitman published the account of his adventures as a "convict rebel," and Defoe was back in London. The best that can be said with confidence is that if Pitman and Defoe did meet sometime later, they certainly had much to talk about.

It was frustrating to know so little about Henry Pitman. There is only his little book, saved from obscurity and reissued by Professor Arber. It does not appear in the catalogue of Defoe's library. The rest of Pitman's life was a mystery. What happened to him when he came back to London from his adventures ? When or where did he live, this man with his extraordinary story of being a maroon among pirates?

Actually, there was a clue, but I had dismissed it prematurely.

Pitman finishes his book with an effusive paragraph thanking "the Eternal and True GOD, . . . who miraculously preserved me on the deep waters, and according to the multitude of His mercies delivered me when appointed to die etc etc." When I first read this paragraph in Arber's reprinted version I thought it was an overblown and meaningless formula. Then I heard Andrew Powery thank God for his salvation on Serrana Bank in similar terms, and I returned to Pitman's text to reread his last paragraph. This brought me to the final line of the book. There Pitman prints his name in capitals—HENRY PITMAN. To give added weight to the truth of his remarkable tale, Pitman also notes where and when he wrote his memoir: "from my lodging at the sign of the *Ship* in St. Paul's Churchyard, London. June the 10th, 1689."

"The sign of the *Ship*" seemed familiar. Then I remembered the picture of the lonely man in goatskins standing with his two muskets on the shore of the island. It faces a page on which appears the full title of the novel, *The Life and Strange Surprizing Adventures of Robinson Crusoe . . . etc. etc. Written by Himself.* At the bottom of the title page is the name of Daniel Defoe's publisher, William Taylor, to be found at the sign of "the Ship in Paternoster Row."

I turned back to Pitman's narrative, whose title page Professor Arber had reprinted. Pitman's publisher was a J. Taylor, and his bookshop was also located "at the Sign of the Ship"—only the address of J. Taylor's establishment was different: his shop was "in St. Paul's Churchyard," around the corner from Paternoster Row. Apparently he was using the same trade sign thirty years later. Was this pure coincidence? Taylor was a common name, and the bookseller-publishers of London at the time clustered around St. Paul's Cathedral. Fortunately, five years after William Taylor published the first volume of *Robinson Crusoe* he sold his business to an up-and-coming young publisher named Thomas Longman. The publishing firm Longman flourished. For the next two and a half centuries a member of the Longman family was at the helm, and the company has continued to use a sailing ship as its logo. A history of the Longman publishing house, now part of a larger publishing enterprise known internationally for educational books, revealed that Pitman's publisher was John Taylor and that he was the father of William Taylor, Defoe's publisher for *Robinson Crusoe*. It was a family enterprise. Father and son worked together, first at the sign of the Ship in St. Paul's Churchyard. Then in 1711 the son set up on his own, just around the corner in Paternoster Row, taking the trade sign with him. Until that time Paternoster Row had been a popular location for mercers, members of the cloth trade. And now I remembered that in 1689, the year Henry Pitman published his book, Daniel Defoe was a hosier, selling socks. The natural place for him to conduct his trade would have been among the mercers concentrated around Paternoster Row.

The coincidences were becoming more and more intriguing.

I returned to the British Library and asked to see an original copy of Pitman's book. Until then I had depended on Professor Edward Arber's reprint. When the original arrived, I compared it with Arber's text. They matched perfectly—the pages were the same, the title was the same. There was only one difference: Pitman's original book had an extra page. Professor Arber had not bothered to reprint it because the page was nothing more than a commercial advertisement. But this advertisement was a real surprise. It was from Henry Pitman himself, promoting his patent medicines. After telling the story of his adventures, he took the opportunity to tout his wares. At "1 shilling a bottle" he was selling "The Quintessence," which contained "the Powers of Scurvy Grass" and could be had in two versions "both plain and purging." He was also peddling two sorts of pills: Magisterium Anodium, "so called from its great and admirable faculty in easing all manner of pains," and Pillulae Catharticae for, among other complaints, "old and inveterate headaches." The fourth offering in his pharmacopeia was Spiritus Catholicus, which was good for "Cholick, Stone, Gout, Scurvy, Hypochondrial Melancholly, Kings-Evil, Rickets, Fevers and Agues." Pills or potions, the price was the same—one shilling per box or bottle.

Apparently Pitman's preparation of these medicaments drew on his experience as a surgeon to pirates and mariners. Clearly Henry Pitman, after returning from his Crusoe-esque adventures as a white slave, a runaway, and a maroon among pirates, set himself up in London as a surgeon-pharmacist. While writing his book, he was also finding time to prepare and sell medications.

But that was not all. I had supposed that the address Henry Pitman gave as the address where he also lodged, at "the Sign of the Ship," was some sort of accommodation address—a formality. But his medical advertisement ended with an exhortation to his customers to come to buy his preparations at the place where "these medicines are prepared and sold (with printed directions giving a more full account of their virtues etc) by Henry Pitman." The address was "the Sign of the Ship in St. Paul's Churchyard."

I had stumbled on the final link: When Henry Pitman, the former maroon, came back from the Caribbean he rented rooms at the premises of the publisher of his adventures. He wrote his book there, presumably while living over the shop; he was grinding and mixing his medicines there; and he was selling his pills and potions over the counter to customers who came through the door. In sum, he was a family fixture in the publishing house that was later to publish the story of Robinson Crusoe. The chances were thus very high that Daniel Defoe, if he visited the mercers of nearby Paternoster Row on business, met Henry Pitman at the Sign of the Ship in St. Paul's Churchyard. Much more important, Pitman must have known William Taylor, the son of the family, and surely talked to him about his adventures. Even if Henry Pitman had gone elsewhere or died by the time the Taylors moved to Paternoster Row and Daniel Defoe came to William Taylor with the draft of *Robinson Crusoe,* it is inconceivable that his publisher did not tell Defoe about the ex-maroon who had shared their shop. If the Taylors had a left-over copy of *A Relation of the great sufferings and strange adventures of Henry Pitman, Chirurgeon,* surely they would have drawn Defoe's attention to it before William Taylor agreed to publish *The Strange Surprizing Adventures of Robinson Crusoe.*

So there was a real-life maroon whose adventures on an island in the Caribbean were known to Daniel Defoe, either in print or in person or both: The man whose true story provided details for the creation of Robinson Crusoe was the "Chirurgeon to the late Duke of Monmouth"—Henry Pitman.

Mutineers setting their captives ashore on
Crusoe's island.

A NOTE ON SOURCES, AND ACKNOWLEDGMENTS

The patient perceptive work of an American scholar, Arthur Wellesley Secord, provided the baseline for my survey of how Daniel Defoe might have created the character Robinson Crusoe. In 1924 Secord published *Studies in the Narrative Method of Defoe* in the University of Illinois Studies in Language and Literature. Summarizing Defoe's sources for the "island story," Secord drew a neat little table with three columns headed "Sources Certain," "Sources Probable," and "Sources Possible." He placed Peter Serrano in the "Possible" column, along with two earlier novels about island life, one in German, the other in Dutch. In the "Probable" category he put the manuscript notes of an English sailor, Robert Knox, who lived for nineteen years in Sri Lanka. Secord believed that Knox had the strongest influence on Defoe and that the two men very probably met. So Knox's published book *Ceylon,* which was in the library sold after Defoe's death, heads the "Sources Certain" column. The other items in that column are the published accounts of Selkirk's adventures; William Dampier's recollections; the writings, probably fictitious, of a French traveler, François Leguat; and Henry Pitman's *A Relation.* Secord was apparently unaware of the possibility of a direct link between Defoe and Pitman, though it was Secord's mention of the surgeon Pitman that eventually led me to Salt Tortuga.

My working copy of *The Strange Surprizing Adventures* was the Norton Critical edition prepared by Michael Shinagel (1994). Professor Pat Rogers's urbane *Robinson Crusoe* (George Allen, 1979) provided a wide-ranging field guide to further reading. Defoe's mysterious and incredibly productive life continues to fascinate biographers, and I am grateful to J. R. Moore, *Daniel Defoe: Citizen of the Modern World* (University of Chicago, 1958); Paula R. Backscheider, *Daniel Defoe, His Life* (Johns Hopkins University Press, 1989); Richard West, *The Life and Strange Surprising Adventures of Daniel Defoe* (HarperCollins, 1997); and Maximillian Novak, *Daniel Defoe, Master of Fictions* (Oxford University Press, 2001).

Of the writings of four sea captains that provided essential source material, two works—Captain George Shelvocke's *A Voyage round the World*, with notes by W. G. Perrin, and Captain Nathaniel Uring's *Voyage and Travels,* with notes by Captain Alfred Dewar—were rescued from oblivion when they were reissued by the Cassell's Seafarers' Library. Both editions appeared in 1928, as did the third and better-known captain's narrative when G. E. Mainwaring provided a new edition of Captain Woodes Rogers's *A Cruising Voyage Round the World.* The fourth work by a captain is the one by William Dampier; I have used extracts from the sixth edition of his classic *New Voyage Round the World* as they appear in *Dampier's Voyages,* edited by John Masefield (E. Grant Richards, 1906). Of the two surgeons who wrote about their experience as maroons, Lionel Wafer's *A New Voyage and Description of the Isthmus of America* was meticulously prepared by L. E. Elliott Joyce for the Hakluyt Society (1934). Henry Pitman's *A Relation of the great suffering and strange adventures of Henry Pitman, Chirurgeon* has not received a modern edition since Edward Arber's quaintly named *English Garner* (1903). (When quoting from seventeenth- and eighteenth-century sources I updated spelling and punctuation where necessary for the convenience of the modern reader.)

In the South Sea my main guides were R. L. Megroz, *The Real Robinson Crusoe* (Cresset Press, 1939); Ralph Lee Woodward, *Robinson Crusoe's Island* (University of North Carolina Press, 1969); and Professor Glyndwr Williams, *The Great South Sea* (Yale University Press, 1997). Both Woodward and Williams have outstanding bibliographies. I would also like to thank Tod Stuessy of the Herbarium, Vienna University, for help with the identification of the flora of Juan Fernandez Island; William Lopez Forment for similar expertise about the plants Henry Pitman found on Salt Tortuga; and Hector Maldini of Santiago, Chile, for his dogged persistence in pursuing the question of miniature coconuts.

In the Caribbean I was generously given access to the transcripts of interviews with Andrew Powery created and held by the Cayman National Archive. This section of my book, including Andrew Powery's quotes, draws heavily on the account of Andrew Powery's experiences as recounted in *The '32 Storm,* compiled and edited by Heather R. McLaughlin and published by the National Archive in 1994.

DHL Worldwide Express were so kind as to provide me, once again, with logistical support on the maritime sector of my travels, and special mention is due to Bernardo and Gabby Meyer for assistance with revictualing *Ziska* on Margarita island. Professor Glyndwr Williams and Dr. James Kelly, both expert in seventeenth- and eighteenth-century Caribbean and Pacific history, generously took time to read through my text and, with Nick Blake, my desk editor, pointed out lurking errors that required a course correction. But if my text has still hit rocks of historical inaccuracy, this is my responsibility, not the pilots'.

My colleagues on different sectors of my search for Robinson Crusoe have already been met—the crew of *Ziska*, Kendra McSweeney, Murdo Macdonald, and Trondur Patursson. Their excellent company made my journeying very enjoyable as well as instructive.